WHEN WILL YE BE WISE?
THE STATE OF THE CHURCH OF ENGLAND

Also edited by Anthony Kilmister
THE GOOD CHURCH GUIDE

WHEN WILL YE
BE WISE?
THE STATE OF THE CHURCH OF ENGLAND

General Editor Anthony Kilmister

Blond & Briggs

First published in Great Britain in 1983 by

Blond and Briggs, Dataday House, Alexandra Road,
Wimbledon, London SW19

Copyright © 1983 Blond and Briggs

British Library Cataloguing in Publication Data

When will ye be wise?: The state of the Church
  of England.
  1. Church of England
  I. Kilmister, C. A. Anthony
  283'.42   BX5131.2

ISBN 0–85634–146–0

Printed in Great Britain by Billing & Sons Ltd., Worcester

CONTENTS

For
RICHARD NEVILL HETHERINGTON
who has been for my wife and me
not just a much loved priest and friend
but the custodian of the eternal verities.

The title of this book
WHEN WILL YE BE WISE?
is derived from Psalm 94 verse 8
in the Authorised Version i.e.
The King James Bible

PREFACE

WHEN WILL YE be wise? My query directed to Bishops and Synodsmen alike is born of anxiety, even anguish, and not of mere, idle curiosity.

For some years now I have been viewing with increasing concern the state of the Church of England, the Church of the land, the national Church. I had seen the Professor of Moral and Social Theology at King's College London, Canon G. R. Dunstan, pose the question '*And what have the righteous done?*' in a most challenging article and had shared his mood of sharp, critical discontent with the Church itself as well as sharing a questioning judgement of some of the very things the Church most liked to boast about. Professor Canon Dunstan wrote that the character of Anglican Christianity was being radically changed by ecclesiastical manipulation and that the Eucharist had become, at best a children's service, at worst a psycho-social manipulation, a pale paradigm of the cocktail party, in which we work up warm feelings for one another, shake hands, wave and say Hi!

His exposition made chilling reading and then I came across this passage: 'The spirit of the cocktail party is not the God whom the saints adore in awe and wonder. The very notion of the sacred is being exorcized from our churches. In place of the sacred silence we are incited to chatter, and worse.'

The whole attitude of the Church seemed topsy-turvy and it was of some comfort to read in a splendid letter to *The Times* (12 October 1982) by Keith Arnold, Bishop of Warwick, that he clearly recognised the drift when he wrote: 'What I hear the Church's critics saying is that it is going the world's way in concentrating on material poverty – and hence by implication on economic salvation – rather than on spiritual poverty. Yesterday's Church took it for granted that the purpose of life was spiritual development and mental and physical development were subsidiary goals. To find or fight one's way to Heaven was every person's first duty, and safety, comfort, peace and security were not ends in themselves, but only the reward for honest spiritual endeavour. Material prosperity was the unworthy dream of the few. Today these priorities have been reversed and the Church allows itself to be heard echoing materialist (and incidentally, Marxist) assumptions when it pleads for economic justice. Meanwhile, today's Lazarus, in Europe anyway, is not likely to be nursing an empty belly so much as an empty soul; dying that is for want of anything worth living for – unaware of his value because no one wants his labour and no one has told him he is loved. We seem to have lost the ability to recognise spiritual starvation when we see it.'

I had a strong desire to speak out about the direction the Church has been taking on a number of issues and the encouragement to do just that, which I have received from the publishers of this book, was what I needed. It seemed best to assemble a symposium of essays on various symptoms and some treatments for our Anglican disease, although clearly it would not be possible to deal with them all.

I am deeply grateful to those who have written the essays which follow and ask for their tolerance of my own contribution later in the book. All my fellow contributors have had complete freedom to write whatever they wish about the topic I have suggested. Many have written more in sorrow than in anger but all are responsible for their own essay and that alone. None of the essayists has seen the full range of this book so none of them could possibly be held to account for what has been written by someone else. Far from there being any collective responsibility for all the views expressed some contributors may very well disagree about the subjects covered or the content of another's essay. All, however, will share my concern for our national church.

A goodly proportion of my contributors are 'men of the cloth'. They will note the complimentary remarks made at varying points about the clergy and also the criticism – some of it sharp. I hope they, like me, would smile at the remark made about a century ago

2

by Dr Jowett, the Master of Balliol. 'My dear child,' he told Margot Asquith, 'you must believe in God in spite of what the clergy tell you.'

I hope this book will prove a lively and useful contribution to debate in the Church. I am grateful to one of the contributors to this book in particular, Ian Thompson, for the help and encouragement he has given me, but no thanks of mine can be greater than those due to my wife, Sheila. Not only do I thank her for pounding her typewriter but also in this, our Silver Wedding year, for twenty-five blissfully happy years of marriage. I look forward to many, many more during which I hope that we shall see our national church returning more clearly to its historic mission.

C. A. A. KILMISTER

ONE

THE CHURCH OF ENGLAND: HAS IT A FUTURE?

BISHOP STEPHEN NEILL

NOW THAT I am retired, I am less often in the pulpit than I used to be, and have more opportunity to attend services as an ordinary worshipper. All too often I come away from such services with the feeling that the only thing to be done is to join either the Roman Catholics or the Salvation Army.

But there are difficulties in the way. The Roman brethren expect me to believe a good many things which I do not believe. So on the whole I had better opt, not for the certainty of a first-class ticket to the infernal regions for pretending to believe what I do not believe, but for the faint chance of sneaking into paradise unobserved on the ground of invincible ignorance. But the brethren of the Salvation Army want me not to believe a number of things that I do believe. Being of a rather charitable disposition, I think that these friends may be saved, even though they have not been baptised. But I do believe that baptism is 'generally necessary to salvation' in the correct understanding of those words. I have read General Booth's defence of the abandonment of baptism by the Salvation Army; it seems to me a marvellous piece of special pleading, and entirely unconvincing.

So perhaps I had really better stay where I am.

In the strange ecumenical ministry which the Lord seems to have given me in my old age, I have occasion to fraternise with a great many other churches, from the Orthodox to the Seventh Day Adventists (but not with the Moonies). The Church of England is undoubtedly awful; but I find these other churches, as I study them, to be so much more awful that in the end I return with relief to the place from which I came. And after all, if the Church of England could only be true to itself, I would have very little to quarrel with in its ways and in its life.

If the Church of England as it is today is really awful, it might be profitable to enquire why it is so awful.

Our friends of the Partnership in Mission programme tell us that it is due, in part, to being an established church. I thought that it was rather impertinent on their part to judge that they know better than we how we ought to conduct our affairs. And I think that they are just wrong. More people saw the Royal Wedding in 1981 than have ever before seen any spectacle in the history of the world. What impressed those who saw it, especially in the United States of America, was that this was not just a royal pageant (this it certainly was, and we do these things better than any other nation upon earth) but it was a simple Christian service, in which the two chief actors quite clearly accepted and sincerely believed all that they said. The whole world saw that the British people, in some strange way, still wish to be regarded as a Christian people, something that perhaps cannot be said of any other nation in the world. If the Church of England was no longer a national church but only one of a number of competing denominations, such things could not happen. Quite rightly, representatives of other churches were invited to take part; but such things could not happen unless one church was charged with giving expression to the Christian faith by which the nation has lived, and still to some extent lives. If the establishment came to an end, I would not shed a single tear; the loss to the Church would be minimal (in Ireland we know that very well). But the loss to the nation and to the world would be very great; and I would be sorry to see that happen.

Perhaps what is basically wrong with the Church is that it has never taken quite seriously the fact of urbanisation and the problems that it has brought with it.

For a thousand years the Church of England had been a village church. The vast majority of its people lived in villages many of which were quite small. The aim, never perfectly fulfilled, was to provide an educated clergyman in every parish, however small. Even in the twentieth century an elderly cousin of mine was squire and parson of a village which I think never had more than a hundred inhabitants. The Church of England was slow to change. It cannot be said that it was wholly unaware of what was happening.

More than a century ago Bishop C. J. Blomfield of London was fired with the desire, to use his own words, 'to expatiate over the metropolis', and there came into existence under his inspiration many large gaunt neo-Gothic churches, which were never filled, because they did not seem to meet the needs of those for whom they were built. I think that the Nonconformists perhaps did better with their small chapels and extensive use of a lay ministry. Years ago I heard a splendid sermon by that great ecumenical figure Nathaniel Micklem, in which he told us of those small and ugly buildings – perhaps intentionally ugly so that they should not be confused with the stately edifices of the established church – to which they gave strange Hebraic names: Peniel, because there they saw the face of God and lived; Bethesda because there they had felt the angel descend from heaven to stir the waters; Bethel, because to them that was the house of God. There they could feel at home; so much at home that, when Methodist union took place in 1932, it proved impossible to persuade people to leave the place in which they had always worshipped even to join up with other Methodists of another persuasion, and so it is in some places to this day.

In some cities we have had Anglican house churches. This is not quite as new as some people imagine. In the old days we used to call them 'cottage prayer-meetings'; these served much the same purpose of providing a local centre, and worship of a much simpler kind than that which was available in the parish church. But it was never imagined that such meetings could take the place of the central place of worship, to which it was assumed that those who frequented the simpler meetings would remain attached. The house church can be a useful supplement; I do *not* believe that it can ever take the place of the parish church.

The main cause of failure, however, I believe lies in the failure of those who control the destinies of the church to realise the extent and the gravity of the losses that have taken place. My memories go back a good long way beyond 1914, the year of the outbreak of the First World War, which I believe was a dividing point in history and in church history more than is usually realised, and I can remember rather well how things were in those now distant days. What have we lost in the years between?

We have lost almost all of our great working class parishes. In the early years of the century, J. E. Watts-Ditchfield, who became Bishop of Chelmsford in 1914, regularly had three hundred men in his Sunday-afternoon Bible class at St James-the-less, Bethnal

Green. At the same time, at Liskeard in Cornwall, my father had an attendance of about two hundred, almost all of them belonging to what was then called the working class, for a men's service on Sunday afternoon. In those days when hours of work were long and holidays few, working men as a rule sensibly stayed in bed on Sunday mornings, but were ready later to come to church for something which seemed geared to their interests and their needs. I wonder how many parishes of that kind exist today.

We have lost the village people. When I have the privilege of taking services in country churches, I always have a congregation, but it is made up almost entirely of commuters and retired people who have bought a country cottage as a home for old age. I have often seen in vestries photographs of flourishing choirs of men and boys in earlier days. In many years I have never encountered one of the kind. Of course in many areas, village populations are much less than they used to be – the mechanisation of farming has seen to that. But it seems to me that something that was of great value has just disappeared.

The parishes seem to me in those days to have depended to a very large extent on the services of lay people. When my father was vicar of St Mark's Church, Cheltenham, he had the help of sixteen 'district visitors', ladies of a certain age and a certain measure of economic independence, also with a fair amount of leisure – those were the days when domestic servants were still available – each of whom had an area of the parish from which she would bring to the notice of the vicar matters which required his attention. Needless to say these women neither expected nor received any remuneration for these services. To these must be added the vast army of Sunday-school teachers, all volunteers. Many of these were untrained and the teaching which they gave was amateurish; but almost all were deeply devoted, and had a sense of personal responsibility for the well-being of the church and parish. Lay responsibility is no new thing, though it has taken on new forms with the changed social and economic conditions of today.

Perhaps the worst of all our losses is the disappearance of Even-song. When I was a boy, Anglican Evensong was reputed to be the most popular service in the Christian world. In poorer parishes and in the countryside Evensong was a little different. On Sunday morning father stayed in bed, and mother was fully occupied with the preparation of that great sacrament of English family life, Sunday dinner, the only occasion in the week on which the whole family was together. There was very little to do in the evenings. The movies had not yet appeared (I remember the opening of the first 'electric theatre' at Cheltenham in 1909). So women and young people filled the churches in the evening. For that reason my father always had Communion after Evensong on one Sunday in the month. He said, 'Say what you like, that is the only time at which a working mother with children can get to Holy Communion.' Evening Communion was not, as has been often supposed, an evangelical eccentricity; it had in fact been introduced by the High Church Dean Hook, when Vicar of Leeds, for exactly the reason adduced by my father. But in those days it was regarded by Anglo-Catholics as the abomination of desolation. Now that the Pope says we can do it, of course we all do it; when I am unemployed, I go down to Christ Church Cathedral in this city for the beautiful sung Eucharist which they provide for us at 6.00 p.m. on Thursdays.

I have never been quite sure of the causes of the disappearance of Evensong. The difficulty of lighting churches at night during the Second World War may have had something to do with it. But I suspect that the reason should be rather sought in the availability of cheap cars and motorcycles, and the almost universal introduction of television. When people have settled down comfortably to watch TV, it is not too easy to stir them out of their comfort to attend an evening service. I am not one to deny the immense value of services and religious programmes on the air. I wonder how many people listen to the famous service of lessons and carols from King's College Chapel on Christmas Eve. The success of the series *Priestland's Progress*, with the beginnings of which I had the privilege to be associated, indicates the wide extent of interest in religion, and the accessibility of large numbers of people to a religious programme that makes sense to them. But of course nothing takes the place of actually being present in the fellowship of the faithful in church. I understand that the authorities in Rome have laid it down that you cannot receive absolution by telephone; nor can you receive the Holy Communion, nor for that matter can you effectively take part in a meeting of the Society of Friends without being physically and actually there.

When at length I came back to reside in England, in 1975/76, after many years abroad, I was startled by the changes that had taken place. It seemed to me that the Church of England had become simply the ghetto of the upper-middle class. We are in a missionary situation. A great deal is talked about evangelism, but not much of it seems to be taking place. What passes under the name might in a number of cases be better called church extension; it is often a praiseworthy attempt to win back those who at one time or another have been Christians, and have for one reason or another drifted away; or those who have had some kind of connection with Christian teaching and practice, but have never come to the point of making any kind of Christian commitment. But few of us seem to have discovered the way to break out of the Christian ghetto into the vast area where the Gospel is never heard and perhaps never has been heard.

In such a missionary situation, the attitude must be 'All hands to the pump'. One of the discoveries of recent years, though it is in reality obvious, is that evangelistic work is far better performed by the laity than by the clergy. They are there all the time in places where members of the ordained ministry are not – in most comprehensive schools, in factories and offices, on the institutions of local self-government, in trade unions and social organisations of many types. They are the ones to whom the work of bearing witness has been committed. But it is no use sending lay people out to bear witness, if when they encounter the unbeliever they have nothing to say. The lay person who is prepared to accept the apostolic commission must be committed, competent and courageous. And how is this most desirable object to be obtained?

I have been alarmed by the spiritual impoverishment which seems to have taken place among those who are members of churches and regular church-goers.

In the earlier days of which I have been writing, the Anglican church-goer was familiar with Morning and Evening Prayer, with the Litany and the Communion service according to the Prayer Book, and had a pretty good idea of what happened at baptisms and confirmations. Now I find that many of my younger friends, especially those who are new believers, have never sung the *Te Deum* or the *Nunc Dimittis*, have never joined in the General Thanksgiving, have never once heard the Litany. We seem almost to have come down to the liturgical level of the Roman Catholic Church in preconciliar days.

At the same time there seems to me to have been a general diminution of the Christian knowledge possessed by the ordinary good church-goer. The Communion services, Rite A and Rite B, in the Alternative Service Book (ASB) are already rather long services, if carried out in full; the result is that in a number of churches the sermon does not last more than seven minutes, and this is the only piece of Christian instruction which many worshippers receive in the week.

I wonder whether some parishes could try an experiment which has been carried out with great success in some places in the United States. Last year I was asked to visit a rather prosperous parish in Connecticut, where there are two services every Sunday morning. The first is a rather short popular service at 9.15 a.m. The second is a more elaborate service at 11 a.m. But those who come to the earlier service are asked to stay for the Forum, which lasts the best part of an hour, from 10 a.m. till nearly 11 a.m. and those who come for the later service are asked to arrive in time for the Forum. I was asked to give a series of four Forum lectures on the non-Christian religions. On each Sunday there was a good crowd, and on one of them I had certainly not less than two hundred, all eagerly attentive to what I had to say. Clearly such a plan holds out immense possibilities of planned Christian education. I do not know whether it would work in England or whether it already exists anywhere here.

A good many people would be surprised today if they knew what went on in the way of Christian instruction in the days of their grandparents. Sermons of course were longer in those days, often indeed too long; but they usually contained solid biblical instruction, in many cases rather conventional but stressing the details of the biblical texts and their application. In addition every self-respecting parish had a number of study groups, on the Bible or missionary matters. And people really did study. Every year the combined missionary societies used to publish a study book, a solid work of 200 pages or more; these were written by experts and some of them became classics – *The Outcastes' Hope* by G. E. Phillips, *The Reproach of Islam* by the great Arabist, Temple Gairdner, and others. Indeed, I once produced one of these books myself, *Builders of the Indian Church* (1934), which in a very short time sold 11,000 copies, and surprisingly became an accepted text for Indian church history in a number of theological seminaries in India.

In almost every home which made any pretension to being Christian family prayers were regularly held. These could be too long and tedious, but at least they brought home to the children the fact that their parents regarded prayer as a serious business. Now, when children never see their parents pray, and perhaps do not even know whether their parents pray or not, it is much more difficult to persuade them that prayer really matters.

About fifty years ago, when I was staying with a distinguished civilian in India, who must have been born sometime in the 1860s, he told me that the great change in his lifetime had been the much greater frequency of the celebration of the Holy Communion. In the old days, he said, 'if you were going to Holy Communion, it meant a real spring cleaning' – I remember this rather picturesque phrase. The Eucharist is celebrated more frequently now than in the days of which he was speaking. But I wonder whether it is taken so seriously. The little book which I was given at my Confirmation laid it down that preparation for Communion should begin on Friday evening, and half an hour was regarded as the minimum. One manual produced in the nineteenth century provided preparatory prayers for a week before receiving Communion, and prayers of thanksgiving for a week after having received the Sacrament. Perhaps this was carrying it a little too far. But I do miss the immense solemnity of the Eucharists of my early days as a believer. There was nothing in the least gloomy about them; there was a solemn joy, but equal stress needs to be laid on the adjective as on the noun.

All this leads up to the central point – that we have to consider carefully what it is that we are trying to do in the Church. 'Our people have been sacramentally trained. The trouble is that many of them have never made a personal commitment to Jesus Christ.' Who is this speaking? It is not some died-in-the-wool evangelical or follower of Billy Graham. The writer is Basil Hume, Cardinal Archbishop of Westminster. When such a man speaks in such terms as these, we ought to give heed. I sometimes wonder how much of the time of Anglican priests is spent turning unconverted people into good churchmen. There is a tendency at the present time to underplay Confirmation, possibly even to drop it completely as a separate ceremony. This is exactly the opposite of my point of view. The only excuse for baptising infants is that we make it a thoroughly congregational act, the congregation accepting full responsibility for creating the atmosphere in which the child of God can grow up as a child of God, and every possible step being taken to ensure that the human response, in the form of a public declaration before the congregation of acceptance of the gift of God conveyed in the divine initiative in baptism, is adequate to the splendour of the divine gift.

Theoretically, of course, the child once baptised should grow steadily in grace and Christian obedience, and so develop into full Christian maturity. All evidence shows that, in our largely de-Christianised society, this rarely takes place. Of the theological students I have had to deal with in the last five years, well over a hundred in number, only one reports that he cannot remember a time when he was not a believing Christian. He came from an exceptionally devout Christian home. Of the remainder the great majority can record a definite time at which, in their rather improper phrase, 'I became a Christian', or 'I was converted', or 'I made a definite commitment to Christ'. All without exception can speak of a time of rebellion, sometimes against tepid Anglicanism at home, or the boredom of rather bad religious teaching at school, almost all of a deliberate and conscious rejection of the standards of Christian belief and conduct; all, I think, of an intimate experience of the existence of the rebel will which is not subject to the will of God neither indeed can be. My experience may not be typical. But it does suggest to me that we have to take far more seriously than we often do the idea of 'conversion' (or by whatever name we choose to call it, if the word conversion has too many suggestions of Billy Graham and all that). But the students with whom I deal have by no means all come from an evangelical background, and not all are committed to an evangelical position in their allegiance to the Church.

The Church of England, as I have experienced it, has a tendency to spend a great deal of time on what can only be regarded as secondary things. Just after the Second World War a great deal of time was spent on the revision of the Canon Law of the Church of England; I suppose a necessary task, but perhaps one that did not need desperately to be taken in hand while all the foundations of Church and world had been shaken by those disastrous six years. There was a strong case for revising the liturgy and this was both inevitable and to be welcomed. In point of fact, liturgy, whatever the authorities may say, is always changing; the number of churches in England in which the Athanasian Creed is said thirteen times a year must be rather small. (The Church of Ireland, always more prudent, prints the Athanasian Creed as a historic witness to the faith, but does not require the use of it in public worship.) Need the process of revision have taken so long? And need it, in the end, have produced so unsatisfying a result? The committee under the chairmanship of Cyril Bowles, Bishop of Derby, charged with the final revision, struggled valiantly with their task. Fortunately, despite the shortness of time available, the Chairman was able to achieve some measure of success. A number of the less happy features of the embryo A.S.B. as left by the Liturgical Commission were removed and a wider variety of alternatives was brought in. But if the revision was intended to unify the Church then it has most singularly failed in its objective.

Where I live, we enjoy an almost undiluted diet of ASB. I have tried very hard to like the new services. But exposed as I regularly am to the blatant mis-translations in the canticles, to the vacuity of many of the modern collects, to the apparently fixed intention of the revisers to reduce the poetry of the Psalms to banal and undistinguished prose, not to mention the generally vague theology which seems to underlie the new book, I find that I have to pray very earnestly before each service not to be so much distressed by what follows as to lose the capacity for worship. Naturally, therefore, I hope that a great deal more work will be done, before 1990, by which date we may hope that a generally acceptable book may be in the hands of Church people everywhere. But the first need is that we should do a great deal of hard theological thinking as to what it is that we want liturgically to express. We learnt in 1927/28 that the idea that you can change liturgy without changing theology is an illusion. The theological task must come first. I find it highly disturbing that the American revision has completely omitted the great words in the baptismal service, 'in token that hereafter he/she shall not be ashamed to confess the faith of Christ crucified, and manfully (in these days of women's lib, better read 'valiantly') to fight under his banner against sin, the world, and the devil, and to continue Christ's faithful soldier and servant unto his/her life's end'. If we omit such words, do we not entirely change the character of the service of infant baptism?

We live in a missionary situation. It seems to me that we have to think very hard about what we are doing in the training of those who are to be called to the ordained ministry. Are we training apostles and evangelists, or are we preparing domestic chaplains for the Christian ghetto, which for the most part includes the members of the affluent society? I must confess to a feeling that we have not yet begun to ask the right questions.

Less than half of what we teach in our theological schools will be of any use to those whom we send out into the active ministry. We have them only for three years, sometimes less; this means that the selection of subjects to be taught demands the most careful

13

consideration. When I asked a class of fifteen or sixteen how many of them had read the Communist manifesto, only three of them admitted to having seen it. But in almost any parish they will meet among teachers and factory workers many men and women who have been profoundly influenced by the Marxist understanding of society and of religion. In some parishes today the majority of the inhabitants belong to one or other of the ethnic minorities and to the religions that have come in from Asia or other parts of the world. In most theological schools the non-Christian religions are a peripheral or optional subject. Can Christian theology be taught today otherwise than it was in the early church, in ceaseless dialogue with the non-Christian world which surrounds us? Of course it is important that the coming generation of clerics should understand the difference between Monophysitism and Monotheletism. But perhaps distinctions such as this could be dealt with in a paragraph. And many things that are at present included in the curriculum could better be learnt on the job – if the bishops could agree that the first four years after ordination are to be regarded as a time of intensive theological training.

This is only the beginning of my anxieties. Students tend to be so hard pressed for time that they have little or no time to acquaint themselves with the great traditions of Anglican theology, from Hooker through Bishop Butler and Maurice and Moberly and Temple up to the present day. Still less have they time to acquire that broad general culture, in literature and art and music, which was characteristic of the Anglican clergy in past days. It is recorded that in a seminary in the United States a professor once prayed in chapel, 'Lord, don't let any man be ordained from this seminary, without having read *The Scarlet Letter*.' Nathaniel Hawthorne's *Scarlet Letter* is a rather moving work, though not in my opinion a great one. But how sad that any one should be ordained to the Anglican ministry without having read *Alice in Wonderland*, *The Pilgrim's Progress*, *Barchester Towers* and *The Brothers Karamazov*.

And sadder still that man or woman should leave theological college or seminary imagining that he/she knows enough to enter on the sacred ministry. We hear that in these days the clergy have no time to read. If this is so, it means that they have got their priorities wrong. Cyril Garbett, later Archbishop of York, left it on record that when he was vicar of Portsea, the largest parish in England, he read for two hours every day and visited for four. He was never anything approaching a scholar, but he was a remarkably well-read man. Once when I was staying with him at Wolvesey, I made a reference to the letters of John Keats; the next morning the book was on the breakfast table, and Garbett was able to show me conclusively that I was wrong.

Perhaps this is the point at which we fall most seriously short of what we ought to be doing. If any man or woman leaves our hands without an inexhaustible desire to know, not only theology but something of all the wonderful fields of human knowledge, we have indeed failed in our task. I wish we were doing a better job; but with all the pressures brought to bear on us from those on high, perhaps it is surprising that we do even as well as we do.

I hope that no one reading these pages will think that I see any reason to be downhearted. It is my good fortune in old age to live among the young. When I look at the theological students who come to us, I thank God who is sending us such good material. They are different from the theological students of fifty years ago. They come from a far greater variety of backgrounds than their predecessors. Many of them have been out in the world, earning their own living in a variety of ways, and bring in their experiences as part of their contribution to the common life. I admire their zest in living and the vitality of their faith. Many of them, as I have mentioned, are what we nowadays call new believers. They have surprisingly limited knowledge of the Bible. Not long ago when the Book of Esther was read aloud at Morning Prayer, I got the impression that some of the hearers were totally unfamiliar with the book. A number of them have had very little experience of the liturgical life of the church, and find it hard to adapt to the regular and rather formal worship which belongs to the Anglican tradition. Like many other Christians, they have never read the rubrics in the Prayer Book, and are surprised to learn that the rule of the Church of England is baptism by immersion. Those who have specialised in scientific subjects might have difficulty in assigning an exact date to the Crusades. But they are eager to learn, impatient of trivialities, alert to the social implications of the Gospel, anxious to get down to the hard and sometimes unrewarding work of preaching the Gospel in the modern world. Their patience with an aged friend gives a promising indication of what they may be like in the pastoral ministry of the Church.

I cannot imagine anyone living in Oxford and being discouraged. Four churches in the city and one in the nearby countryside are packed to the doors every Sunday, with a good sprinkling in each of students. We are getting so many adult conversions that a colleague and I are thinking of finding a quiet place in the Thames with a sandy bottom where baptisms can be carried out in proper Anglican fashion – but, in Oxford, I think only in summer. Those who present themselves for Confirmation are thoughtful and evidently sincere. It is clear that where the Gospel of redemption is preached clearly and with an appeal to reason as well as to emotion, there will be a response.

Having lived for many years abroad, I am impressed with the sheer niceness of people in England. There is something to be said for living in a Christian country, even in one that has become so secularised and post-Christian as England. I mean quite ordinary people, like the clerks who make out my ticket when I travel by air, the delightful young electrician and the kind plumber who come in when anything needs to be attended to, the skilled craftsman who has mended my rather valuable screen when with the clumsiness of age I knocked it over, and also as a bonus got my rather precious clock a-going. Like any minister of religion I know the dark side of English life – the increase in crime, the lawlessness of unhappy young people who have never had a job and see very little hope of ever getting one, and all the rest of it. But surely there is something pleasing to the Lord of all good life in this kindness and generosity and good humour? Where does it come from but from Him?

I believe that there is much more diffused Christianity in the country than we sometimes allow for. It does not mean very much that so many children are brought for baptism (and I hope are not refused by over-conscientious priests), and that so many come to be married in church. It may not mean very much, but it does I think mean something. I know only one scientific study of diffused or residual Christianity – that was carried out in the city of Hamburg by the son of my predecessor in the University there, Dr Justus Freytag, sociologist and theologian. This was translated into English under the unfortunate title *Nominal Christianity*. Nominal Christianity is something quite different; the name always suggests something not quite sincere, a measure of play-acting. Residual Christianity is spontaneous and almost unconscious; it speaks of deep memories, of half forgotten truths. But how is that which is unconscious to be brought into consciousness, and related to that which the church alone can offer?

But my heart goes out especially to those who seem to have no thought at all of these things – these fine young people that I meet

16

walking about the streets. I am sure that they have their cares, concealed with that courage which is typical of the English people. But the idea of God is very far from their thoughts, and it rarely if ever occurs to them that the church could be interested in them, or that the church might have something to offer in which they could possibly be interested.

How do we reach them? How do we break out of the Christian ghetto in which most of us have become immured? None of us seems to know. We are upper-middle class, and upper-middle class it seems that we are destined to remain. And if ever we do manage to draw in anyone from a different social milieu, we very soon succeed in working him/her over in our own image, so that they join the gang and become indistinguishable from it.

At 82 there is not very much that one can do about it – except pray, and that perhaps is the most important thing of all. In the old days people used to pray. My mother once told me that, in four years as a medical student at Edinburgh, she never once missed her hour of prayer and Bible study in the morning. They were giants in those days. Today we are not giants but just very ordinary people. But it does at times seem to me that the Church is dying on its feet through a famine and a drought of prayer. Even the clergy, devout and diligent as so many of them are, seem to find it difficult to set aside regular time for prayer; and many among the church-going lay-people seem to feel that they have done quite well, if they have managed a rather hasty repetition of the Lord's Prayer just before getting into bed. In the old days every self-respecting parish had a prayer meeting, not attended by the clergy, on Saturday evening to pray for the services of the following day. Frequently to be heard was the rather old-fashioned prayer, 'Lord, give him souls for his hire' – the intercessor probably did not know that this was a quotation from a Victorian poem not much remembered today, F. W. H. Myers' St Paul, 'Souls for my hire, and Pentecost today.'

Once I was to preach at a large Presbyterian Church in Berkeley, California. After settling the details of the service, the minister said to me, 'My laymen will be just finishing their prayer meeting; perhaps we could go in for a minute or two.' We went in and found between twenty and thirty quite ordinary laymen engaged in earnest prayer for the service that was just about to follow. If the lay-folk would really uphold us in this way, they might get fewer bad sermons than they do. And perhaps the reverend clergy would be stimulated to follow the advice which I always give to young friends about to be admitted to the sacred ministry – 'Live on your knees, and develop a sense of humour.'

TWO

DOCTRINE: HOW WOULD HOOKER VIEW ANGLICANISM TODAY?

THE REVEREND CANON JOHN JACQUES

THERE CAN BE no doubt that the Church of England is suffering from a crisis of identity. Before we can answer questions about the future of the Church of England we need to know what the Church of England is; what she believes and teaches and what position she expects to occupy in society. Beneath the multitude of faces she appears to present, is there anything permanent, solid, essential?

Who is there who can give us an answer to these questions? For the Church of England possesses no master theologian like Calvin, Luther or Thomas Aquinas, to whose teaching appeal can be made in the search for authenticity. The Book of Common Prayer – her crowning glory – is fast falling into disuse and her Thirty-nine Articles have recently been described as having an historical rather than a normative significance. (*Reasonable Belief, A Survey of Christian Faith* by Anthony and Richard Hanson; O.U.P. 1980, p. xi.)

However I believe that there is one man who can claim to be a trustworthy guide to what might be called the spirit of Anglicanism; who might even claim to be the chief and most brilliant of the founding fathers of that spirit, although he would have been puzzled by the word 'Anglican' for he never used it and had never heard it. He was content simply to be a Church-of-England man. He was the Elizabethan theologian, Richard Hooker (1553–1600). His great work *Of the Laws of Ecclesiastical Polity* is directed against the Puritans of his day and as such is a work of controversy closely related to the spirit of his age. However, he is so determined to take every issue back to first principles that his writings are a very full account of theology, although not an actual *summa theologica*, and for generations, indeed for centuries, he was regarded as the paradigm theologian of the Church of England appealed to by High and Low Churchmen alike. Certainly if there is one theologian who represents the mind of the Church of England it is Richard Hooker, and to read him is to be forced to think deeply about the nature of the Church of England, her doctrine and her place in society.

Hooker is a philosopher, theologian and political thinker as well as a church historian, at home both with Scripture and the early Fathers. He draws on Luther, Calvin and Aquinas with equal authority. In his immense erudition he is one of those who made the parochial clergy of the Church of England at one time the *stupor mundi* (wonder of the world) for their learning. If he is little read today, this is partly because his magnificent style, which has procured for him a place in all the histories of English literature, is hardly suited to our journalese-drenched minds, and his wide-ranging theological scholarship and vision seem too vast for our concern with the immediate issues of the day, which derive their importance from our obsession with the ephemeral ever-changing spirit of the age.

Hooker was an Elizabethan and he shared the ambition of his Queen, and indeed all the statesmen of his age, that the people of England should be included in one ecclesiastical body, the national established church. All of them, including Hooker, would have been amazed at the very idea that a pluralist society such as our own could survive as a united community. But somehow we do, even if a little uncertainly. Clearly the situation of the Church of England today must be very different from that of the church in Hooker's day. Then both the government and the whole national community were possessed of some loyalty to the Christian religion. Today we are a multi-racial, multi-religious society with a government which is mainly neutralist in religion except on official occasions. Even the Christian element in the population is fragmented into a number of different denominations and sects.

The result is that the role of the official established church is clouded in ambiguity. Yet it need not be. Perhaps the truth is that a fragmented pluralist society such as our own has a greater need for an established church than a society more united in its community life and allegiance to the Christian religion. For the Church of England still remains one of those institutions which play a part in expressing and continuing the tradition which constitutes the basis of our national identity. The existence of the Church of England bears vital testimony to the fact that we are a people rooted in a Western civilization which had its origins in a Christian society. In an age in which technology and materialism have such a predominant influence, it is important that this witness to the spiritual part of our cultural roots should be kept vigorously alive, and it is a remarkable gift of grace that the Church of England which has been an integral part of those cultural roots is still alive at all to give her testimony.

Since this Anglican version of the Christian religion is a strand and an important one in the tradition we have inherited, it is not surprising that people return to it in moments of crisis, at times when they feel the need for a supernatural link in their lives; in bereavement, at marriage and when children are born. Committed church-people often feel unhappy about this seemingly uncommitted fringe of half-believers who haunt the periphery of church life and seem to be simply using the church. It is easy to dismiss their behaviour as empty convention but it is not to be despised for all that. Convention is one of the things which hold society together and we are a society desperately in need of being held together at the moment. This may perhaps seem to be too much of a pragmatic and political defence of external religious behaviour. Hooker would have argued that a church which did not concern itself with even the minimal needs of the community in which it existed was evading its responsibilities.

All this may seem a long way from Hooker's defence of the established church composed of one community represented by the state on its secular side and the church on its spiritual side. Nevertheless Hooker does show how important it is for the church to accept her responsibility for the life of the whole community. His controversy with the Puritans made it clear to him how easy it would be for the church to become an inward-looking group concerned only with the doings of those who were convinced that they had achieved salvation. Hooker knew that a national church needed to be broad based and possessed of considerable tolerance. He would have warned us of the danger of trying to compensate for the reduced numbers and influence of the church in the modern world by organizing congregations as exclusive groups of totally committed members. This would perhaps be the easiest way out of the church's present difficulties but it would be the most dangerous.

It would transform the church into a sect. A sect results from the confusion between the visible and invisible church and this was a distinction that was important to Hooker. He argued that not everyone in the visible church on earth would be numbered among God's elect who would constitute the membership of the invisible church. The visible church is inevitably a mixed body and we must be content to have it so. We do not know who is saved and who is not. This was why Hooker was so bitterly opposed to any attempt to confine baptism to the children of a restricted band of God's elect. He writes: 'A wrong concern that none may receive the sacrament of baptism but they whose parents, or at least one of them, are by the soundness of their virtuous demeanour known to be men of God, hath caused some to repel children (from baptism) . . . Thus, whereas God hath appointed them ministers of holy things, they make themselves inquisitors of men's persons a great deal more than need is.' (Bk. V, lxiv, 5.)

Hooker's readiness to be tolerant of the weaknesses of the visible church and its members does not proceed from any lack of theological conviction on his part; quite the contrary. He is far too devout and earnest a Christian to treat the church simply as a political convenience with little concern for the faith which that church taught and the spiritual purpose for which the church existed. Both as a philosopher and a theologian, Hooker is vigorously positive in all he says in defence of the Church of England. It is this foundation in positive principle which makes it possible for him to take the charitable view he does.

To begin with, Hooker's method is thoroughly metaphysical, and to most English philosophers and to some theologians, metaphysics has been a dirty word for over a generation. For metaphysics claims to deal with a world beyond the familiar world of sight, sound and touch, of science and everyday life; a supra-sensible world beyond space and time, the source of ultimate reality, the dwelling place of God, of immortal souls and perhaps of angels; for Hooker certainly, of angels. Metaphysics is the name for the attempt to study what lies beyond the natural, perceived order. Consequently if you do not believe that there is anything behind the perceived, natural order you do not see the need for metaphysics. This has been the fashionable view of many philosophers in the twentieth century and it has been widely influential not only in philosophy but in theology as well. If there is nothing behind or beyond the world of space and time then metaphysics becomes redundant. Certainly, it has to

22

be admitted that people do worry about what might lie behind
space and time but this is irrational. So philosophy has taken on a
new role; not to teach metaphysics but to deliver people from
metaphysical anxiety.

Hooker, on the other hand, was certain that in addition to this
world of space and time there was another world of eternity in
which dwelt the divine creator of heaven and earth. No one can
read the First Book of *Of the Laws of Ecclesiastical Polity* without
being deeply moved by Hooker's account of God as the source of
all law both in time and eternity. Law begins in the very being of
God himself and Hooker's wide-ranging account of law extends
from the law which controls the angelic order, through the laws of
nature, to the laws which govern morality and salvation. Law keeps
order in the universe and in society and the basis of law is reason.
Reason offers man the means to understand the work of God in
creation and to control his own behaviour in society. Hooker believed that by his power of reason man was linked to that eternal
world in which all law had its origin and only fulfilled himself
completely when he allowed himself to be drawn into relationship
with that eternal order.

This is not the place to defend Hooker's view of God and reason.
It was not original. It was part of that perennial philosophy which
had come down from Plato and Aristotle and had been kept alive
in the church by such thinkers as Augustine and Aquinas. It had
been despised by Luther and frowned upon by Calvin but Hooker
cherished it and used it as a link between Renaissance humanism
and Christian faith.

If something like Mr H. G. Wells' *Time Machine* could transport
Hooker into the twentieth century and set him to work on contemporary theology, I believe he would begin by being critical of our
dislike, even fear, of the appeal to reason. Theology has become
infected with the modern philosophers' suspicion of reason. The
only certainties are those of sensible perception and beyond them
the mind must flounder. All our thinking is socially conditioned
and in a secular society eternal truth becomes unthinkable. The
eternal dimension, the metaphysical background, must be sifted out
of theology. If religion has any meaning at all it is only on the
level of psycho-analysis to cure human beings of their metaphysical
anxieties or to help them to deal with the fears hidden in the depth
of their being. Those to whom this does not appeal, seek to bring
Christianity up to date by making it the adjunct of welfare-econ-

omics or Third World internationalism. Doctrines which derive their relevance from their reference to eternal truth are disregarded. So at the moment it would appear to be possible to remain as an active minister in the Church of England and deny the existence of God, regard the Incarnation as a myth, and refuse to give real personal meaning to the idea of life after death.

Faced with the momentous problem of restoring the faith of the Church of England, Hooker would not appeal to the Pentecostal enthusiasm of the charismatic movement, nor to psycho-analysis, social theory, nor existential anxiety. He would stand firmly on the claim of reason to be the essential link between the divine and the human.

This appeal to reason has one element, at least, in it which is of importance to us. That is the high estimate it makes of human dignity and destiny. Hooker would see that we have not only lost our faith in God. We have lost faith in ourselves as well. Hooker's vigorous assertion of the classical view of man's dignity and destiny as a rational and eternal soul acts as a refreshing counterweight to modern theories which present us to ourselves as naked apes or as repressed and defeated egotists; as victims of social circumstances or as the terminals of elaborate cerebral computers. Hooker would pertinently ask how, if any of these bizarre theories were the whole truth about us, we could ever have discovered them. Only, surely, because we possess a divinely bestowed power of reason which we can abuse and misuse, to produce such strange theories about ourselves.

Hooker's firm grasp of human dignity and the power of human reason does not make him a secular humanist or rationalist. For he does not believe that man possesses the means to achieve his own destiny without the help of God. He is all too aware of the Fall and the power of sin. Man is frustrated by his own sinfulness in any attempt to achieve eternal life. Only with divine help can man reach out to the destiny God has intended for him and the royal path to this salvation is mapped out in Scripture. To the Puritans, Hooker's defence of reason seemed to limit the authority of Scripture and Hooker certainly did teach that in certain areas of life man had to rely on reason rather than Scripture. He resisted strongly the Puritan attempt to bring the whole of national life, including all morality and politics, under the mantle of Bible teaching. In these spheres he believed that reason could be as much a God-given guide as Scripture was in matters of salvation. But in its own sphere,

Scripture was supreme. It was to Scripture and Scripture alone that men must turn for their salvation. In this Hooker was as Protestant as Luther and Calvin. He repudiated entirely the finding of the first Council of Trent that over and above what was contained in Scripture, there was an additional body of essential, saving truth contained in church tradition. Nothing should be asked of faith except what Scripture taught men. There alone was saving truth to be found.

In his enthusiasm for reason Hooker was both a man of the Renaissance and also a firm upholder of the *philosophia perennis* which had supported Christian theology at least since the time of Origen and Clement of Alexandria. In his loyalty to the conviction that the path of salvation was mapped out in Scripture and nowhere else Hooker was a Protestant; but he was a Protestant with a difference. For he found the key to the interpretation of Scripture in the life and tradition of the church and not in the direct individual inspiration of the Holy Spirit granted to each believer. His interpretation of Scripture involved a great scheme of participation which reached from man the sinner unable to realise his divine destiny because of his sins, to the very throne of God in his eternal glory.

Hooker believed that God reached down from heaven to deliver man from the helpless misery of sin; but God did not snatch man to salvation. Hooker would have been sceptical of the modern idea that there was some one kind of religious experience by means of which people could be jumped out of their sins into the full glory of eternal life without any process of growth or development. He would have endorsed the call in II Peter 3, 18, to 'grow in grace'. If the Church of England has been suspicious of enthusiasm and fanaticism, it is this conviction rather than apathy that has been the reason for it.

Hooker taught that there is a progression in grace; God coming down to man's rescue and man ascending to God by means of the appointed stepping stones of grace. The central figure in the whole process is Jesus Christ. For Hooker rests his defence of the Church of England on his doctrine of the Incarnation as he expounds it in Book V of his great work and here we see him interpreting Scripture in terms of traditional doctrine. Accepting the orthodox teaching about the Person of Christ from the Councils of Nicea and Constantinople, he proclaims Christ as the great receiver. Christ is the Son of God and as the Second Person of the Trinity receives his deity from God. Christ, as the earthly Jesus, receives his humanity from the Virgin Mary and his divinity from the Son upon whom it had been bestowed by God. In Jesus Christ, the deity received from God by the Son and the humanity received from Mary are united in one person.

For Hooker the foundations of his theology are the great doctrines of the Trinity and the Incarnation. He begins with them and not with the human Jesus of the Gospels. The humanity of Jesus is an essential link in the chain of Hooker's argument but it does not stand alone as it so often does in modern theology. Hooker would have been critical of what he would have regarded as our over-emphasis on the humanity of Jesus, because by isolating it we never get beyond it. It is not for nothing that the three creeds have appeared so prominently in the worship of the Church of England. The creeds put the account of the human life of Jesus within the metaphysical background of the Trinity and Incarnation, and so give that life the meaning it must have if it is to be seen as the means of man's salvation.

For Hooker the important thing was that the two natures, human and divine, are so united that they form the perfect link between man and God. This is no mere piece of academic speculation, for this downward process of participation from God to man creates the means by which fallen man can ascend to God.

By this means Hooker defends the sacramental church life of the Book of Common Prayer and the Church of England. This sacramental emphasis came under much criticism from the Puritans and is now regarded by many as an optional additional extra to whatever they regard as the real heart of Christianity. But for Hooker the two sacraments of Baptism and Holy Communion are essential. By them we are made partakers of the Body of Christ and so begin to share in his divine life which is the reason for the Incarnation. By Baptism we are made members of the church which St Paul taught us to regard as the body of Christ. By Holy communion we partake of the Body of Christ in regular feeding. So through these sacraments the essential link with the divine life of the Trinity was formed for us through our share in the humanity of Christ provided by the church and her sacraments. Hooker was firmly convinced that the sacramental life of the Church of England provided her members with a direct ladder of participation from earth to heaven. It is this which makes Book V of *Of the Laws of Ecclesiastical Polity* the greatest defence of the Church of England that has ever been written.

What is so evident is the masterly linking of doctrine and devotion, of theology and life. Hooker was not afraid of theology as we appear to be. He would have been critical of the life of the Church of England today for thinking that theology was unnecessary or that Christian faith could be sustained with an attenuated doctrine watered down to suit the taste of our secularised anti-metaphysical age. There is no suggestion in Hooker that theology has to take a back seat behind moralism or social concern or a vague spirituality. He believed that the destiny of man was to become a partaker of the divine nature (II Peter, 1, 4), and the possibility of this could only be realised by a high and supernatural doctrine of the person of Christ and the full Trinitarian view of the deity. He believed that these were built into the life of the Church of England and were expressed in her sacraments and worship.

The importance of Hooker as a theologian for all time lies in the masterly way in which he unites in one synthesis, the Reformation appeal to Scripture, the classical and mediaeval view of reason, and the traditional emphasis on the importance of the sacraments and the corporate life of the church. Hooker is a theologian who is equally at home in the Protestant and Catholic traditions. Of course in his day it would have been almost as much as his life was worth to have defended anything on the ground that it was Roman Catholic or popish. But again and again he defends his church and her Prayer Book and services by appealing to tradition, to the wisdom of the past, to the general consensus of the church and to reason.

Hooker was the first theologian to see that a church could be both Protestant and traditional; that Reformation did not mean that everything which had come down from the past had to be jettisoned, as many of the Puritans seemed to think, and a completely fresh start made in the life of the church. In this he was among the first to point the way to a Protestant Catholicism and a Catholic Protestantism. It would be Biblical and reformed and yet traditional and sacramental. He found the basis of such a faith in the Church of England and he did his best to make that Church proud of such an achievement. I think it is a mistake to regard the theology he produced as a compromise or even a *via media*. It is a genuine creative synthesis and the ability to hold these different traditions together in one common faith and life is the chief glory of the Church of England.

At the moment we are living in the aftermath of the failure of

27

the General Synod of the Church of England to endorse with a sufficient majority the scheme for reunion called Covenanting for Unity. The Church of England must share a great deal of the blame for the failure of these various modern attempts to achieve unity and indeed for encouraging them to get under way at all. The vocation of the Church of England is not to distribute episcopacy far and wide as if that were the panacea for divided Christendom. The Church of England has a better gift to offer; the pattern of a church both Catholic and Reformed in which those who value the Protestant emphasis and those who are moved by the Catholic tradition can learn how to live and worship together in harmony.

In recent years we have been asked to believe not in our own particular church but in what has been called 'the coming great church.' Unfortunately that coming great church has failed to emerge and the ecumenical movement is in considerable disarray. I believe that the time has come to look again at what the Church of England stands for in herself as a living community in which the Catholic/Protestant dichotomy which has divided the church since the Reformation finds resolution. By this I do not mean the brute fact that people of Catholic and Protestant sympathies have found it possible to survive in a state of feud or indifference in one common organisation. It is not the conflicting existence of two or more parties in the Church of England that makes her a bridge church. Behind the differences there must be some consensus which holds the Church together and prevents the parties from tearing it apart. It is possible that the most important task for the Church of England at the moment is to recover awareness of that consensus, to appreciate it and build upon it.

This idea of bringing together in one consensus the best of Catholic tradition and Protestant reform was built into the Book of Common Prayer by the liturgical genius of Thomas Cranmer, but it was Hooker who first saw what this meant in clear theological terms. It is this which makes the study of Hooker so worth while at the present time.

No doubt it would be of historical interest to speculate on what Queen Elizabeth I or Lord Burleigh would have to say about modern government; to speculate on Drake's possible views on the Navy or Walsingham's criticism of our secret service. The appeal to Hooker has more than such historical interest. Religion has a way of reviving itself by turning back to its roots and origins. Protestants have harked back to the Reformation leaders; the Tractarians to the Fathers, Catholics to Thomas Aquinas. The road forward often begins with a look backward in search of the inspiration of the past. Hooker merits consideration as one who set the Church of England on the road she followed for almost four centuries. He was a theologian of broad views and wide sympathy and yet with an intense loyalty to the Church to which he belonged. These are much needed virtues which we can learn from him and perhaps with some humility offer as the Anglican contribution to the life of the church at large.

THREE

WHITHER ANGLICAN THEOLOGY?

THE REVEREND DOCTOR ERIC MASCALL

I – Theologians all awry

WHEN I WAS ORDAINED in the early 1930s it had been common for some years for those in authority to explain that there were in the Church of England three 'schools of thought' – the term 'parties' was eschewed as too divisive – the 'catholic', the 'evangelical' and the 'liberal', and it was frequently proclaimed that it was the glory of the Church of England that this was so. Both the history of the Church throughout the previous century and the behaviour of the more militant members of the three 'schools' suggested that the proclamation manifested the anxiety to make a virtue of necessity rather than the conviction of a coherent and constructive theological position, let alone a canonical commitment. This fact was skilfully concealed by the policy which, with almost complete success, Archbishop Randall Davidson imposed as a matter of loyalty and discipline throughout his long primacy, that, whatever their private views might be, the bishops must always show a united front in public. The maintenance of the three-school myth was felt to depend on each of the schools being kept within reasonable limits; at all costs the boat must not be rocked. The evangelicals on the whole caused little difficulty. Their admirable fervour had little tendency to come into conflict with authority, except when their desire for open communion hit the headlines, as it did in the Kikuyu controversy of 1913–15.[1] The liberals, in spite of their vagueness about the virginal conception and the bodily resurrection of the Saviour, usually confined their unorthodoxy to academic circles or explained it soothingly away,[2] until Bishop E. W. Barnes of

Birmingham drew upon himself the rare phenomenon of a public rebuke from the Archbishop of Canterbury.[3] The Anglo-Catholics presented a much more serious practical problem. Not only had their particular beliefs much more direct and visible effects upon the public worship of the Church, but apprehension could be relied on to arise spontaneously in the English mind at the threat of anything that could be colourably presented as in any way 'Romanising'. Half a century later it is almost ludicrous to read about the intense but unformulated terror which the bishops felt at the disaster which they were convinced would fall on the Church if the laity were allowed to pray before the reserved Sacrament or even to know where it was reserved.[4] Whatever (one finds oneself wondering) was the calamity which they thought this would provoke? And what would they have said if they had known that some of their successors would carry the Host in procession and give benediction with it?

The fundamental incoherence of the three-school theory can be seen from the obvious fact that the existence of each one of the schools can be justified only on the assumption that its characteristic theological assertions are true. But in that case the characteristic theological assertions of all the three schools must be mutually compatible. And in that case there is no reason why we should not accept them all and a great many reasons why we should. But then what will have happened to the three schools? It is quite ridiculous to envisage the Church as a tricorporate society, each of whose parts is committed to holding one third of the truth. Regrettable as this no doubt is, it is because each school has *not* been convinced that everything that the others were holding was part of the truth that the schools have remained recognisably distinct. I am sure that much good can come from patient and charitable dialogue between those of different background and outlook and I shall say more about that later. But that is a very different thing from the ecclesiology which appears to hold that the existence of the three schools is of divine institution and is of the *esse* of the Church.

Supporters of the three-school theory have sometimes appealed to Friedrich von Hügel's famous classification of the three elements of religion as the institutional, the intellectual and the mystical and have associated them with the catholic, the liberal and the evangelical school respectively.[5] This identification needs considerable qualification. It is true that, in the second chapter of the celebrated work in which he introduced the Three Elements of Religion,[6] the Baron associated them respectively with the High Church, the

Latitudinarian and the Evangelical school in historic Anglicanism.
But he also tried to make a similar association with the Jesuit,
Dominican and Franciscan orders in the Roman communion and
then found it difficult to locate the Benedictines and the Oratorians.
He had furthermore to admit that some of the most outstanding
Jesuits, Dominicans and Franciscans fitted very uncomfortably into
the niches assigned to them; and he expressed his own judgement
that, 'The most largely varied influence will necessarily proceed
from characters which combine not only two of the types, as in our
time Frederick Faber combined the external and the experimental;
but which hold them all three, as with John Henry Newman in
England or Antonio Rosmini in Italy.'[7] It should also be remembered that Evangelicalism in its purest forms, so far from welcoming
the mystical and experiential, has rejected it as contaminating the
objectivity of faith and denying human creatureliness.[8] What we
can say is that all three elements may be expected to exist in a
healthy balance in any sincere Christian, though their proportions
and mutual relations will vary enormously from one to another. But
this extremely important truth of ascetic theology ought not to be
degraded to the level of ecclesiastical politics.

Closely associated with the three-school theory is the notion of
Anglican comprehensiveness, and indeed it is difficult to see how
the former could exist without the latter. There hangs about it the
same aroma of a virtue made out of necessity. It has received a
very careful and detailed analysis and critique from Professor
Stephen Sykes in his book *The Integrity of Anglicanism*[9] and it will be
well worth while to devote some space to his remorseless investigation of it.

In order to be as relevant as possible Sykes starts from the
statement on comprehensiveness in the Report of the Lambeth
Conference of 1968 and he discerns in it three components of very
different types and provenance. The first is a distinction between
fundamentals, on which agreement is necessary (and is assumed to
exist), and non-fundamentals, on which disagreement is legitimate.
Sykes remarks that this distinction has a continuous history from
the time of Hooker, though the boundary between the two areas
would not be drawn by anyone today exactly where it was drawn
by Hooker or even by Newman. The second component is the
existence in Anglicanism of both catholic and protestant elements,
which are at present unreconciled but whose reconciliation is hopefully awaited, as both are necessary to the whole truth though

they appear contradictory. The third component is that there is a development in apprehension of the truth which necessitates a willingness to allow liberty of interpretation. Sykes points out that these last two components – the principle of complementarity and the doctrine of new truth – are logically quite distinct though the Report weaves them together in a confusing way with what he describes as happy and characteristic modern Anglican euphoria. Perhaps the most original – and it will certainly be to many the most shocking – feature of Sykes' critique is the baleful character which he attributes to the influence of F. D. Maurice and which he traces to Maurice's commitment to a romantic idealist view of national character and destiny, combined with a dislike of ecclesiastical parties which made him ready to accept the notions of complementarity and compromise. Those who, inspired by the justly respected figures of Michael Ramsey and Maurice Reckitt, have come to admire F. D. Maurice as the *fons et origo* of Christian social thinking in Anglicanism, will no doubt bridle at the suggestion that there were deep-seated *theological* ambiguities in his thought, but I believe that Sykes is correct in holding this view. I will give two examples from my own admittedly sketchy study of Maurice. It seems quite impossible to determine – and enquiries from the accepted Maurician authorities have thrown no light on the matter – whether Maurice believed that grace actually brings about a change in human nature or merely reveals what human nature already is. Secondly – and this is all the more surprising in view of the fact that the Social Movement in the Church of England has consistently recognised him as its founder[10] – his romantic nationalism led him to support the existing relation of Church and State on the ground that it enabled the Church to bring its influence to bear on social and political issues, in spite of the notorious subservience of the English bishops to the parties to which they owed their appointment.[11] I think that Sykes may perhaps be judged to have blamed Maurice too narrowly for a situation whose causation should be located over a wider area, but he is, I believe, entirely right in his assessment of the results of Maurice's doctrine of comprehensiveness:

Coined at a time when internal party strife was at its most acute, it apparently offered a non-partisan refuge for that large body of central Anglicans who properly speaking belonged to no party, neither evangelical, nor high church, nor yet in any committed sense to the more radical of the liberals. Theologically speaking, however, the effect of the proposal has been disastrous. It must be said bluntly that it has served as an open invitation to intellectual laziness and self-deception. Maurice's opposition to system-building has proved a marvellous excuse to those who believe they can afford to be condescending about the outstanding theological contribution of theologians from other communions and smugly tolerant of second-rate theological competence in our own; and the failure to be frank about the issues between the parties in the Church of England has led to an ultimately illusory self-projection as a Church without any specific doctrinal or confessional position.[12]

And again:

Lots of contradictory things may be said to be complementary by those with a vested interest in refusing to think straight. . . . And there is a great difference between saying that a body like a church has found it practically possible to contain people who hold opposed and contradictory views, and saying that that church believes that all of the contradictory views are true and in some hitherto undiscovered way reconcilable. . . . And it is greatly to be feared that generations of Anglicans, learning their theories from Maurice and his disciples, have substituted for the form of catholicism or protestantism which any convinced believer of these respective forms of Christian discipleship would recognise a tame and Anglicanised *tertium quid*.[13]

As a final historical observation Sykes refers to the transition from tractarianism to liberal catholicism in the nineteenth century, with Charles Gore as its obvious representative. Gore was in the happy situation of believing not merely that credal orthodoxy and critical scholarship would prove to be ultimately reconcilable but also that, properly understood, they were reconciled already; for him, therefore, the question of priority as between faith and reason was a purely hypothetical one. 'Gore's viewpoint', writes Sykes, 'on this issue was that criticism would not question the credal substance of the faith, and that the Church of England was secure in maintaining that it did not. On both counts he was wrong; on what grounds, therefore, is his "liberality" held up as a model of the Anglican method of theology in operation? . . . The fact is that, far from adopting a uniquely Anglican stance, Gore was defending a position which a German Lutheran pastor, Melchior Goetze, had adopted over a hundred years earlier in a controversy with Lessing. He was trying to use historical argument to support a position which had never been adopted for historical reasons, and in doing so he was necessarily making it vulnerable.'[14] And a later generation of liberal catholics, such as A. E. J. Rawlinson, Wilfrid Knox and E. G. Selwyn, felt obliged, in various degrees to yield the point. Unready as they were to admit that that there was in fact any inconsistency between what were described as 'the assured results of modern criticism' and their rather minimised versions of the essentials of the catholic faith, it was inherent to their position that *if* (which might God avert!) there should be a head-on collision between faith and reason, it would be faith that would have to give way. Hardly ever was it admitted that perhaps the assured results of modern criticism might turn out not to be so assured after all, or that a deeper study of the matters at issue might show that the problem had been wrongly formulated at the start. And hardly ever was it admitted that reconciliation of faith and reason might depend on data not yet accessible to scholars and therefore was not to be achieved at present. All the answers were now available, at least in their main outlines, to the methods of modern scholarship, so they confidently held.

I shall not follow Professor Sykes' argument further at this point, merely remarking on the disgraceful way in which it has been virtually ignored by those directly concerned who might most have profited from it. Complacency has shown its stock reaction of looking its challenger firmly in the face and then stepping smartly to one side. I will however underline his complaint about the almost complete lack of serious attention in our universities and theological colleges to the teaching and study of systematic theology. 'For 70 years at least', he writes, speaking of Oxford and Cambridge, 'no systematic or dogmatic theology has been taught. . . . But the neglect of systematic theology in the universities also partly accounts for its neglect in the seminary training of Anglican ordinands. For the teachers themselves, never having been taught the discipline, found neither the impetus nor the time to devote themselves to the proper cultivation of systematics outside the university. . . . The result is as we see it today. Not merely is there no tradition of systematic theology in the Church of England, there is no recognition of the part it could play in fostering a critical self-understanding without which no church is truly alive.'[15]

I have given my own account of this situation in the first chapter of my book *Theology and the Gospel of Christ*;[16] it agrees in its main points with Professor Sykes'. And it receives vigorous support from a lecture given to the Theological Society of King's College, London, in November 1978 by the present Bishop of Salisbury.[17] Canon John Austin Baker, as he then was, drastically condemned most contemporary theology, so called, for the basic defect of simply not being *thought about God*, and he blamed this very largely on the teaching in our universities and colleges. How many theological students, he asked, expect on their course to learn about God, as opposed to learning what other people say about God?

> All theological syllabuses start at the wrong end. We ought to start students off with questions like, 'Is there a God?' or 'Why do people suffer?' – or rather, if they do not wish to ask such questions, transfer them to English Literature or Civil Engineering, for if they do not want to find answers to such questions they have no business reading Theology. . . .
>
> Though God may often be mentioned, his role is described in terms which make him wholly superfluous. To be quite blunt about it, he does absolutely nothing – or rather, the things he is said to do are No-things. . . .
>
> Grace is felt more and more to be something that is given through our own attitudes and behaviour to one another. . . . Where does God come into it? Is he, so to say, just the moral *primum mobile*? If so, could not a better case be made for Jesus as this *primum mobile*? And is that not precisely what for many theologians Jesus is anyway, the One who by words and actions no longer significantly recoverable set in train an enterprise which has developed far beyond his vision, and now has its own constantly maturing character and momentum?

And the first point, says the Bishop, about those Christians today 'who seem to be talking about God as real but are not', is the highly significant one that 'they will not accept, as in any sense an objective reality, that event without which there would have been no Christian faith at all: the Resurrection of Jesus'. And that, he insists, is to eviscerate the Cross of all meaning:

> By all moral, human standards of judgement the Cross was a disaster and a defeat. It may have been a victory on Jesus' part to accept such defeat rather than bend or desert his convic-

36

tions – but how do we know that that has anything to do with God? To talk about Jesus as revealing God's love on the Cross is mere self-delusion. There was no way, no way at all in which anyone could at the time have seen in the Crucified Jesus anything approaching a revelation of God. . . . It is a matter of simple historical fact that we have learned to see him as such only because of the primitive Church's belief in the Resurrection. That is what connects Jesus with God, that and that alone.

And the Bishop presses his conclusion home remorselessly:

If we accept this resurrection faith then we are, I believe, accepting that bogey of all right minded philosophically trained theologians, an interventionist God. . . . God can and will act within history, not totally submerged in ordinary realities, but between these realities, in unique and discontinuous ways. And what sort of a God is that? How are we to think of him? Theology *is* about God. Christian Theology ought to be about the God implied by the foundation beliefs of the Christian community.

And finally:

I am convinced . . . that to jettison faith in that act [sc. the Resurrection] as superfluous is to do one's damnedest for the victory of evil against God. If our doctrine of God does not allow for the Resurrection of Jesus then Theology's first task must be to find a doctrine of God that does allow for it, for that alone will be the truth. And if there is anything more important than finding for our lost and bewildered race the truth about God I do not know what it may be.

Professor Sykes and the Bishop of Salisbury have approached their problem from very different angles but they are at least agreed that Anglican theology has badly lost its way. The Bishop appeals for a solution but does not offer one, at least in the lecture from which I have quoted, and his audience appears from all reports to have reacted to his appeal with a response of polite incomprehension. Professor Sykes confesses truthfully that his work has been mainly critical and destructive[18] and I must regretfully say that his final chapters – which I heartily commend to readers – do not seem to me to provide the answer for which he is looking. But now for reasons of space I must turn to another aspect of the question.

II – Believing and belief

Three times in this century Commissions of the Church of England have produced reports on the Church's doctrine. The first, which was published in 1938, was the work of an *ad hoc* body appointed as long before as 1922 by the two English primates 'to consider the nature and grounds of Christian doctrine with a view to demonstrating the extent of existing agreement within the Church of England and with a view to investigating how far it is possible to remove or diminish existing differences'. Although it repudiated any claim to be an Anglican *Summa* it covered systematically the whole range of Christian doctrine. Without explicitly accepting the three-school theory, it elegantly asserted that

> The Anglican Churches . . . are the heirs of the Reformation as well as of Catholic tradition; and they hold together in a single fellowship of worship and witness those whose chief attachment is to each of these, and also those whose attitude to the distinctively Christian tradition is most deeply affected by the tradition of a free and liberal culture which is historically the bequest of the Greek spirit and was recovered for Western Europe at the Renaissance.[19]

Of the vast number of comments which the Report provoked, one of the most valuable was the Memorandum prepared by Fr A. G. Hebert, SSM, for the Theological Committee of the Church Union. His conclusion was that the Commission had failed in its task of removing or diminishing existing differences because it did not set itself to go to their root:

> The Report [he wrote] marks a 'retreat from Modernism'; it is at the same time a concession to Modernism, in that it erects an excellent superstructure of soteriology on an inadequate doctrine of Revelation; and it has the air of belonging to the last generation rather than to this.[20]

But one of the most discerning, and indeed prophetic, judgements was made by an anonymous writer in an obscure publication, the *Quarterly Review* of the parish of St Mary, Graham Street, London. At a time when Evangelicals and liberals were often to be found in a pragmatic but conscientious alliance against Anglo-Catholicism he made the claim whose full force would appear only forty years later: 'There does exist today, as perhaps never before, a basis upon which Catholicism and Protestantism might find a point of departure for agreement, namely a profound belief in revelation and the supernatural; and this the Report hardly ever even considers.'[21] But at least the Commission focused its attention on the objective content of Christian belief and did not, like the later Commissions, deliberately direct its gaze inwards upon the subjective activity of believing. The very titles of their Reports are significant of this reorientation, *Christian Believing* (1976) and *Believing in the Church* (1981). The former of these manifested its failure in constructive achievement by simply attaching to a brief joint statement two signed appendices and no less than eight individual and unco ordinated essays, of varied type and quality, none of which bears any indication of its particular topic. The later document, which undertook the task of examining the corporate nature of faith, simply consists of a set of essays and attempts even less to make a synthesis or to draw any conclusions; and it must be noted that the words 'in the Church' are taken as indicating the Church as the *locus* and not, as in the creeds, as an *object* of Christian belief. It is difficult to avoid the impression that both the Commissions (and it must be remembered that the personnel of the Doctrine Commission was entirely renewed in 1977) had lost either hope or interest in achieving agreement on the content of the faith. Not *what* to believe but *how* to believe was their concern, not the *fides quae* but the *fides qua*. But, as Dr Alec Vidler has remarked in reviewing the recent reprint of the 1938 Report, 'the ordinary Christian or enquirer is normally (rightly or wrongly) more interested in what than in how to believe, and to that extent at least the 1938 Report still speaks to his condition'.[22] (There may be matter for reflection in the fact that the person chosen to write the Preface for the reprint[23] had recently denied the doctrines of the Trinity and the Incarnation with an explicitness that would have startled the liberals of 1938.[24]) I think it is not unfair to describe the Commissions of 1976 and 1981 as having, corporately if not individually, succumbed to a loss of theological nerve, and the judgement of Dr Vidler which I have just quoted is confirmed by the lukewarm reception which their Reports have received from the Church as a whole. In spite of their impressive academic weight they have clearly not addressed themselves to the concrete pastoral and evangelistic situation in which the Church finds itself today. And that is the situation whose imminence the Graham Street writer discerned in 1938; its concern is with the significance, and indeed the very existence, of revelation and the supernatural order. It extends far beyond the boundaries of the Anglican Communion and is the overriding theological issue in the currently turbulent forum of Roman Catholicism, though there it has tended to be obscured by the essentially different matters of the ecclesial character of the Papacy and of the Roman curia. Stated as simply as possible the question is simply this: Is the Christian religion something revealed by God to man in Christ having an unconditional claim on our obedience, or is it something to be constructed by us for ourselves in response to our own desires and the pressures and assumptions of contemporary culture? It is in accepting the former of these alternatives that traditional Catholicism and evangelical Protestantism stand side by side against the liberal modernist relativism and naturalism. And there are welcome signs today that this new understanding between Catholics and Evangelicals is more than a pipe-dream. The volume *Growing into Union: Proposals for forming a united Church in England*,[25] produced at the time of the proposals for Anglican-Methodist union, was one public expression of this, but much more has taken place on a private and informal plane. And quite recently a most striking phenomenon has appeared in the United States, where the erosion of the historic Christian communities by liberalism and relativism has gone to an extreme and has eaten deeply into the Roman Catholic Church itself, and where the only Protestant reaction has seemed to be that of an obscurantist fundamentalism, often committed to the political right. However, in October 1980 there met in Ann Arbor, Michigan, a widely representative group of eight evangelical Protestant and Roman Catholic scholars and pastoral leaders to consider the challenge to Christian life and thought made by modern changes in technology, social structure and ideology. The Anglican participation seems to have been thin, but it included the Evangelical James Packer and the English layman Harry Blamires. The papers read, and the set comments on them, were published in book form under the title *Christianity Confronts Modernity*;[26] it is thoroughly to be commended, and not only to Americans. As the editors stress, the meeting did not attempt to seek avenues to reunion:

Rather the purpose of the colloquy was to achieve a better understanding of the situation of all Christians vis-à-vis contemporary secular society. It was assumed that evangelical Protestants and Roman Catholics hold enough in common to make such an endeavour possible. The colloquy, then, was an exercise in collaborative rather than dialogic ecumenism.[27]

Space will not permit of anything like a detailed comment on these very impressive papers; I will only suggest, in connection with Dr Stephen B. Clark's appeal 'for orthodox scripture scholars to band together across the old divisions of Catholic and Evangelical so that they can support one another',[28] that this synchronic alliance needs to be extended by a diachronic inclusion of the insights of the great Christian figures who, while they belong to the past chronologically, are our contemporaries in Christ. This will occur naturally and necessarily if we are witnessing indeed 'a movement signalling a historic realignment among Christians, bringing together evangelical Protestants, Roman Catholics, and, potentially, Orthodox around a set of pressing pastoral and theological concerns'.[29] And one consequence of the recognition that we are involved together in this common task will be our deliverance from the unhealthy and untheological pressure for formal unity which comes from the assumption that the devising of unity schemes is the only task which it is worth while for Christians to work at together or the only one that is possible. And it may well be that the obstacles to unity may in the long run be more effectively dissipated by sharing in a common task than by direct *ad hoc* negotiations. As the Ann Arbor editors wrote:

> Learning to work side by side in the cause of Christ plays a practical part in the larger process of overcoming the divisions in the Christian people because it fulfils what Cardinal Ratzinger termed 'the task of responsible Christians', which is 'to create a spiritual climate for the theological possibility of unity'. To serve one another by helping each other respond successfully to the challenge of modernity is to promote such a spiritual climate.[30]

And they add, with optimism and frank realism:

> An evangelical-Catholic alliance must be hopeful and confident even as it is sober in the face of serious challenges. We are at a moment in history when more men and women fill the earth

than at any time in the past, and when the opportunities for bringing the gospel to the whole world are greatly multiplied. At this moment Christianity faces one of its most serious challenges. It is locked in a struggle to maintain its true identity and way of life in the midst of modernisation's shattering social and intellectual changes. The struggle is the present phase of a much older battle between God's kingdom and the dominion of his enemy.[31]

This I believe to be entirely true, and, as an Anglican, I am encouraged that the Ann Arbor editors in their concluding summary quote this passage from Mr Harry Blamires:

Surveyal of contemporary movements in religious thought leads one to the conclusion that, in the near future, the dominating controversy within Christendom will be between those who give full weight to the supernatural reality at the heart of all Christian dogma, practice, and thought, and those who try to convert Christianity into a naturalistic religion by whittling away the reality and comprehensiveness of its supernatural basis. This conflict is already upon us and is pushing into the background the controversies which caused deep and bitter strife in previous ages. The old controversies over grace and free will, faith and works, authority and individualism, are of course still with us; but they no longer in themselves represent the gravest disunity within Christendom.[32]

The editors add:

The message of the colloquy is that Blamires's 'near future' is now. In Donald Bloesch's words, 'The time is ripe for a new evangelical alliance, one that will embrace Bible-believing Christians in all branches of Christendom.'[33]

I would add my own comment that the colloquy also indicates that, as Protestants and Catholics engage on this common task, it is urgent that they also get down to the hard work of synthesising theologically the two aspects of revelation which they have respectively tended to stress, namely the written word of Scripture and the living tradition of the Church; it may be relevant to recall that St Thomas Aquinas uses *Sacra Scriptura* as a synonym for Christian doctrine and that Trent itself declared it is 'the Gospel of Christ' that is the source, the *fons*, of both saving truth and right behaviour.[34]

III – Recovery and renewal

What, we must now enquire, is the task of the theologian, and in particular of the Anglican theologian, in such a situation as this? Fundamentally, I believe, it is the same as that of any theologian in any situation, namely to deepen his and his fellow-Christians' understanding of the Gospel which has been revealed in Jesus Christ and to communicate that understanding persuasively to his contemporaries. In doing this he will have to utilise the language, thought-forms and cultural expressions of his time and place, while exercising the greatest care to ensure that he is using them as media for communicating the Gospel and not subtly adjusting the Gospel to fit in with them. If it is suggested, as it sometimes is, that such a task of discrimination is either impossible or undesirable, it must be replied that it has been done with success more than once in the Church's history, as when in the fifth century the conceptual scheme of contemporary ontology was radically refashioned in the service of Chalcedonian Christology. As Lewis Carroll's Humpty Dumpty remarked, it is simply a question of who is to be master. As Lionel Thornton argued at length, in his much neglected work *Revelation and the Modern World*,[35] Revelation is neither simply transcendent to the environment nor is it the product of the environment, but it *masters* the environment, because God identifies himself with human history in order to transform it. Now the Christian theologian, if he is a baptised and practising Christian and not merely an interested external observer, is himself living within the revelation which it is his business as a theologian to interpret; he has therefore access to resources to which the mere observer has not; and his access to them will depend on the closeness of his union with Christ in the Spirit by grace. His understanding of divine realities will be radically that 'knowledge by connaturality', which he will share with Pascal's 'charcoal-burner' and the pious old woman of the manuals; but because it is his special vocation as a theologian to serve God by his intellect, that knowledge by connaturality will englobe a whole structure of systematic and discursive theologising, which it will support and invigorate to do its own job, as grace does not destroy or ignore or manipulate nature, but establishes and perfects it. (It will be clear that by 'theology' here I am referring to that systematic study of 'God, and other things in relation to God' whose virtual disappearance from our universities Professor Sykes has deplored, and not the mass of respectable ancillary disciplines which have appropriated the title. It is fascinating to discuss the date of the Exodus or the ambitions of Cardinal Wolsey, but that is not, strictly speaking, to be doing *theology*.) Essential as it is, however, for the theologian to maintain his personal union with Christ, it is not his function to get messages down the hot line from the Lord; that would make him a prophet, not a theologian. The revelation which he is to study and interpret is not a private revelation given to himself; it is the revelation given in Christ to the Church and handed down by and in the Church through the ages. But then his religion itself, if he is a Catholic Christian, is not a merely self-enclosed cultus from which any participation by others is carefully excluded, nor what A. N. Whitehead described in one of his least happy phrases as 'what a man does with his solitariness'. It is the outflowing of the sacramental life which he shares with the whole of Christ's body as one of its members; and theology, to which he may hope in faith and humility to make some tiny contribution, is that life's progressive and always imperfect articulation. God, declares the Epistle to the Ephesians, 'raised [Christ] from the dead and made him to sit at his right hand in the heavenly places, . . . and he gave him to be head over all things to the Church, which is his body.'[36] 'In him dwells all the fullness of the Godhead bodily' is the Apostle's word to the Colossians.[37] The mind of the ascended and glorified Christ is the one human mind which, in one total contemplative act, possesses God's truth in its fullness, and it is that truth which he communicates to his Body the Church according to the various needs of time and place and its capacity to receive it. *Quidquid recipitur recipitur ad modum recipientis* runs the tag, and the Church's understanding of the truth is limited by the stupidity, imperceptiveness and even downright sinfulness of its members. Nevertheless, the Church *is* Christ's Body and is indwelt by the Holy Spirit; truth can make itself heard even under the most unpromising circumstances and can be seen on certain paradigmatic occasions to have not only surmounted but even to have utilised the limitations of contemporary thought and culture.[38] And not only professional theologians but pastors and, above all, saints will provide the theologian with the material for his own contribution to the Church's understanding of the revelation which she has received and in which she exists.

44

If all this is true, then I very much doubt whether there is any real justification or need for the view that there should be a specifically Anglican theology any more than that there should be a specifically Anglican 'position'. I have remarked already on the artificiality of the 'three-school' theory which was popular in administrative circles in the nineteen-twenties and -thirties. It is startling to see it reappearing today with a fourth recruit in a set of essays from the United States with the ominous title *The Spirit of Anglicanism*.[39] The authors define Anglicanism as 'a way of being Christian that involves *a pastorally and liturgically orientated dialogue between four partners: catholics, evangelicals and advocates of reason and of experience.*'[40] They accept enthusiastically the notion of comprehensiveness, and applaud the Lambeth Conference of 1978 for 'the proper use of this great principle in the decision of Anglicans to live together with varying conceptions of episcopacy and divergent views on the Virgin Birth', while considering it to have used the principle 'improperly' in tolerating opposition to the ordination of women to the priesthood and episcopate.[41] Clearly, heads I win – ! What is entirely lacking is any sense of Christianity as a divine revelation that places us under obedience and with it any sense of the Church as transcending our present lifetimes. And with this goes naturally the assumption that, not only as regards their legal force but also as regards their theological competence, synodical assemblies elected and operating on the model of democratic political institutions possess, if not infallible, at least irreformable authority for their decisions. If there is no need for a specifically Anglican theology there is, I would submit, both need and scope for Anglican theologians.

Had I unlimited space this would be the place to discuss the relation between the theologian and the bishop, for, reluctant as bishops often are to accept this responsibility, it is to the bishop, and not to the theologian that, according to Catholic understanding of the Church, the duty of both preserving and preaching the Gospel is committed. And if, as I have maintained, the task of the theologian is to deepen his and his fellow-Christians' understanding of the Gospel and to communicate that understanding persuasively to his contemporaries, the task of the bishop and that of the theologian, while clearly distinct from each other, are closely linked and, so far from being either isolated from or in competition with each other, should be mutually supportive. Both, in their essence, are *ecclesial*, and this is confirmed by the fact that, while this is necessarily exceptional, some of the Church's greatest theologians have in fact been bishops.

But to return to the theologian and to theology. If it is true that the theologian, as such, is an ecclesial person and that theology is an ecclesial function, we can only view with alarm the tendency to abandon theology, on economic grounds, simply to our secularised universities. 'Religious studies' – and the novelty of the term is significant – is a legitimate and valuable academic discipline, but it must not be confused with theology or made a substitute for it. And an academic training is not sufficient to make a Christian theologian; however useful that may be, it is in his prayer and at the altar that the heart of his theological formation will take place. There is really nothing new about this – *pectus facit theologum* is an old enough maxim – but it is certainly not taken very seriously today. But it has been seen plainly by a man whom many think to be the greatest Christian thinker of our time and I will leave the reader with the lesson as he has put it before us.

Fr Bernard Lonergan, SJ, in his *magnum opus Method in Theology*,[42] has provided what his main commentator, Fr Frederick E. Crowe, SJ, has described as the much needed Organon – the method and instrument – for the understanding and handling of the spiritual and material issues of our time.[43] I cannot attempt to summarise Lonergan's method in its elaborate structure and detail; it invites both study and criticism. But I will draw attention to two features which Fr Crowe emphasises, as they make a very effective support for the position which I have been arguing. First, Fr Crowe points to Lonergan's insistence that the insight to which he invites us is not to be achieved by taking an impartial glance from a detached standpoint but needs a moral and religious conversion, which is costing and irrevocable:

> Do I allow questions of ultimate concern to invade my consciousness, or do I brush them aside because they force me to take a stand on God? With such questions we are being forced to the roots of our own living, challenged to discover, declare, and, if need be, abandon our horizon in favour of a new one in which our knowing is transformed and our values are transvalued. We are also abandoning the neutral position of an observer, and entering another phase of study altogether.[44]

And secondly, the needed renewal of theology and philosophy cannot come about through our existing academic institutions:

Can you even imagine, much less contemplate as a serious proposal, inviting your university colleagues to a discussion and informing them casually that the spirit of the meeting would be a prayerful one, and that a good part of the input would be the self-revelations of your interior spiritual life and theirs? . . . Still negatively, the average theological congress will not be the vehicle for this theology – for the same reason that applies to the university, and for the additional reason that the average congress is described, with a degree of exaggeration but with a grain of truth too, as a dialogue of deaf persons. One goes there to get off one's chest the ideas that no one back home will listen to; no one at the congress listens either, but the speaker is not so acutely aware of it.[45]

Prayerful retreat, the charismatic movement, street-preaching, interdisciplinary discussions – all these Fr Crowe suggests are needed if theology is to mediate between religion and the cultural matrix. But, perhaps of necessity, he is both revolutionary and vague about details: 'Doctrines of one kind or another we are bound to have, but in my view even the best of them will be *ad hoc* constructions till we really face the upheaval of our times and begin that total reconstruction of theology the situation calls for. Meanwhile, we are muddling through.'[46]

'Communications' is the final phase or 'specialty' of Fr Lonergan's Method, and communication is the field in which theologians today are most obviously and turbulently involved. But I suspect that it is to the sixth specialty – that of Doctrines – that, at any rate in the Anglican Communion, theological attention most needs to be directed today; for, as the example of the Doctrine Commissions shows, we have found it easier to discuss the process of communication than what we have to communicate by the process. The needs of the Church for theology, in the proper sense of the word, are, I believe, immense; but so also are our resources. And I would conclude with some words from one who, more than any other Anglican writer whom I know, has shown the organic unity between theology, prayer and social concern:

The gulf between 'academic' theology and the exercise of pastoral care and spiritual guidance has been disastrous for all concerned. . . . The study of theology, or at least of Christian theology, cannot survive in a healthy state apart from the life of prayer and the search for holiness. The theologian is essentially a man of prayer. As Evagrius expressed it, 'A theologian is one whose prayer is true. If you truly pray, you are a theologian.' Or St John Climacus, 'The climax of purity is the beginning of theology.' . . . Theology is an encounter with the living God, not an uncommitted academic exercise. This encounter cannot survive if its only *locus* is the lecture theatre or the library. It needs the nourishment of sacramental worship, of solitude, of pastoral care and the cure of souls. Theology must arise out of and be constantly related to a living situation.[47]

'Theology is an encounter with the living God' – if Anglicans were really convinced of that, it would be the renewal of Anglican theology.

References

1 G. K. A. Bell, *Randall Davidson* (OUP 1935), ch. xlii.
2 E.g. Hensley Henson and the Hereford bishopric, Bell, op. cit., ch. liii.
3 Bell, ch. lxxxi.
4 Cf Bell, ch. 1. Also the astonishing provision in the 1928 Prayer Book that, wherever Reservation is, it must not be 'immediately behind or above a Holy Table'!
5 The three 'systems' are in fact listed by F. D. Maurice in the 1830s, though, in line with his rejection of the notion of systems, it is only to repudiate them. (*The Kingdom of Christ*, Part III, ch. ii.)
6 *The Mystical Element of Religion* (London, Dent, 1927).
7 ibid., I, 65. Cf also J. P. Whelan, *The Spirituality of Friedrich von Hügel* (London, Collins, 1971), ch. iv.
8 Cf my *He Who Is*[2] (London, Darton, 1966), 147ff; *Christ, the Christian and the Church*[2] (London, Longmans, 1955), ch. xii.
9 London, Mowbrays, 1978, ch. i, 'The Crisis of Anglican Comprehensiveness'.
10 Cf Maurice B. Reckitt, *Maurice to Temple* (London, Faber, 1947).
11 The impression produced by Maurice on an outside observer is well illustrated by the following passage:
    'While he teaches on the one hand that the entire human race is created and has its essential nature in Christ, as its ideal Head, he seems to maintain on the other hand that it is only in the Church of England that the Kingdom of Christ has attained actual existence. This is a contradiction that a German intellect finds it hard to comprehend, or can only explain by supposing that the strong national feeling of the Englishman has got the better of the intellect of the theologian.' (Otto Pfleiderer, *Development of Theology* (1890), cit. A. R. Vidler, *The Theology of F. D. Maurice* (London 1948), 213.)
12 *The Integrity* . . . , 19.
13 ibid., 19f.

14 ibid., 22.
15 *The Integrity* . . . , 80ff.
16 London, SPCK, 1977.
17 ' "Theology is about God" Discuss', *King's Theological Review*, II (1979), 49ff.
18 op. cit., 87.
19 *Doctrine in the Church of England* (London, SPCK, 1938), 25.
20 *Memorandum on the Report of the Archbishops' Commission on Christian Doctrine* (London, SPCK, 1939), 45.
21 Spring 1938, 41.
22 *Theology*, LXXXV (1982), 451.
23 *The 1938 Report with a new introduction by G. W. H. Lampe* (London, SPCK, 1982).
24 Cf my *Whatever Happened to the Human Mind?* (London, SPCK, 1980), ch. iv.
25 By C. O. Buchanan, G. D. Leonard, E. L. Mascall and J. I. Packer (SPCK, 1970).
26 Edited by Peter Williamson and Kevin Perrotta (Ann Arbor, Mich., Servant Books, 1981).
27 op. cit., 4.
28 ibid., 185.
29 ibid., 239.
30 ibid., 242.
31 ibid., 243.
32 ibid., 239f.
33 ibid., 240.
34 *Conc. Trid.*, sessio iv.
35 London, Dacre Press, 1950, 1ff et passim.
36 Eph. i. 20, 22, 23.
37 Col. ii. 9.
38 The Council of Chalcedon is an example of this; cf. my *Whatever Happened* . . . , ch. ii.
39 William J. Wolf (editor), John E. Booty, Owen C. Thomas (Edinburgh, T. & T. Clark, 1982).
40 op. cit., 165.
41 ibid., 180f.
42 London, Darton, 1972.
43 *The Lonergan Enterprise* (Cambridge, Mass., Cowley Publications, 1980).
44 Crowe, 57.
45 ibid., 94f.
46 ibid., 97.
47 Kenneth Leech, *Soul Friend: A Study of Spirituality* (London, Sheldon Press, 1977), 35f.

FOUR

AUTHORITY IN THE CHURCH

THE REVEREND FRANCIS D. MOSS

Historical sketch

BY 'AUTHORITY' here is meant competence to determine the authentic Christian Faith, to affirm the criteria or tests of orthodoxy. 'The Church hath . . . authority in controversies of Faith . . .' reads Article 20 of the Church of England, and in possessing authority she must have some means of exercising it, of defending her teaching from misinterpretation, dilution or unwarranted additions.

By the end of the second century, at any rate, Bishops had emerged as the accepted leaders of the Christian Church and as the guardians of her doctrine. Yet no one has supposed that omniscience and inerrancy are among the gifts conferred at consecration, so that individual bishops are themselves manifestly capable of misleading their people. A partial solution to this dilemma was found in the development of the Synod, enabling bishops to consult together and to reach agreed decisions. Eventually the local Synod inspired the idea of a 'General' or 'Ecumenical' Council which could claim to speak for the whole Church of Christ.

But which of the many assemblies convened were ultimately accepted as General Councils and, even then, should inerrancy be credited to them? The human element cannot be eliminated, even at a Council. The conduct of the bishops, even at Councils which have received general recognition, was far from impeccable.

If discrimination between assemblies on the basis of outward appearances was difficult, if not impossible, Orthodox and Anglicans found a partial solution by associating the authenticity of a

General Council with the *subsequent* acceptance of its decisions *by the whole Church*. Rome, it is true, has taught the infallibility of the Bishops in General Council in much more juridical terms, stipulating, for example, that a true General Council must be convened by the Pope. The position for Anglicans vis-à-vis the powers of assemblies is greatly affected by the words italicised above. The Church of England, unlike Rome and the Orthodox, could not claim to be in itself the whole Church of Christ in which alone maximum authority or indefectibility could be located. Equally, the Church of England could not accept the claim of Rome or of the Orthodox to be in isolation the one, true, Catholic Church.[1] Hence, for Anglicans, the full teaching authority of the Church could not be exercised after the eleventh century schism between East and West, and no Council summoned after that time could be deemed a Council of the whole Church and therefore Ecumenical and authoritative. Why should the Church of England, seemingly arbitrarily, draw the line at four General Councils when *seven* (generally) accepted Ecumenical Councils met before the eleventh century Great Schism? Perhaps the Church of England was asserting its right to subject even the Acts of General Councils to *its own* verdict of compatibility with Holy Scripture, finding elements in the pronouncements of the later Councils 'unscriptural'. In fact, 'the Elizabethan Act of Uniformity accepted as its definition of heresy that which "heretofore have been determined, ordered, or judged to be heresy by the authority of the canonical Scriptures, or by the first four General Councils, or any of them, or by another General Council wherein the same was declared heresy by the express and plain words of the said canonical Scriptures" '.[2]

As a matter of history, the Tudor ideal of a National Church coterminous with the nation was not to be realised. Fairly 'Comprehensive' and relatively tolerant the Church of England might be, but perhaps for that very reason it could not comprehend those who yearned for a Church more united internally and disciplined under a 'living voice' or 'Confessional' authority.

Finally, the effects of eighteenth and nineteenth century philosophy and scientific development upon Christian teaching and Western culture greatly strengthened the liberal element in the Church of England. There has been a tremendous shift in the presuppositions regarding truth, knowledge, and the possibility of 'absolutes' over the whole field of our culture with the result that the Bible Christian, the traditional Christian, often finds himself

51

unable to communicate even with fellow members of the same denomination.[3]

Notably the classical logic – if a thing is true the opposite is not true – has been abandoned in favour of the Hegelian methodology of synthesis. The late Professor Joad summarised the Hegelian system thus: 'Let us suppose that somebody entertains a particular idea or doctrine. It can be shown by careful examination to be self-contradictory, since in the course of our examination of the doctrine we shall be led to envisage the opposed doctrine which denies and refutes it. But this opposed doctrine can be shown to be no less faulty than the original doctrine. Where, then, does truth lie? In a third doctrine which unites the essential features of the original doctrine and its opposite. This third doctrine will, however, on analysis itself be shown to be inadequate, and the "dialectical process" continues.'[4] Thus all is relative, all is changing, and must continue to change; there are no fixed positions.

The pressure from elements so affected upon a loosely-knit or dispersed type of Church authority could prove irresistible, in practice at least pointing inexorably to an 'Open Church' defensive only of what must clearly threaten its continued existence. When the new General Synod of the Church of England appropriated from Crown and Parliament in 1974 a very large measure of freedom in the interpretation of doctrine, this meant a potential shift in stress from the constraints of the past to the drive of contemporary policy. This policy may be summed up under the heads of Ecumenism, Liturgical Revision and Accommodation of the new Radicalism in theology. Each and all suggest a Church even more comprehensive than the Church of England of the past, if not a fully 'Open Church', and the question that must be asked is whether such further inclusiveness must prove intolerable, with consequent disruption and re-grouping.

The dilemma restated

The problem is nicely introduced by Paul Elmer More in his introductory essay to *Anglicanism* by More & Cross, published in the mid-thirties. More takes up Chillingworth's admission that the Bible, though infallible in fundamentals, is not an infallible *guide* in fundamentals. Would he, and those for whom he spoke, at a later date and in the face of the evidence of critical examination, have been prepared to acknowledge inconsistencies and contradictions in the

Bible itself? Upon an affirmative answer to this question, according to More, depends the identity of the Anglican spirit as manifested in that day and in ours. 'Thus much is at stake, namely whether the Church can be said to have moved in a straight direction, whether, in a word, it is proper to speak of any such thing as Anglicanism.'

Later More takes Newman to task for pleading for an infallible organ of authority, compounded of 'Scripture, Antiquity, and Catholicity', of which the Church of England is the sacred custodian: 'It is a disputable thesis, but one for which a good case might be made, that Newman, deep down in his heart, was never in full sympathy with the liberal spirit of the 17th century, and that the Oxford Movement, so far as it was swayed by his genius, has not been without danger of leading the Church away from the line of its normal development.'

Many Anglicans, perhaps a majority today, would agree that More was here witnessing to the authentic spirit of Anglicanism. But More himself still clung to the idea of 'fundamentals' as is evidenced by his comment on '*Lux Mundi*': 'That book . . . in its frank extension of fallibility to the Bible, while insisting on the Personality of Christ and on the Incarnation as the fundamental dogma *on which the whole fabric of Christianity rests*, once breathes again that air of larger freedom which frightened Newman into the prison-house of absolutism.' Indeed, one wonders how More would have reacted to such further results of unfettered criticism as when, quite recently – I quote Professor R. P. C. Hanson – 'both the Regius Professors of Divinity in the Universities of Oxford and Cambridge declared publicly in print that they could not believe in any form of the doctrine of the Incarnation, and one of them had expressed doubts as to whether any practical norm of Christian doctrine was attainable'.[5]

To put it another way, if in living memory it was possible for Anglicans to stress agreement in fundamentals, diversity in non-essentials, with built-in safeguards in practice (such as the invariable (re)ordination of Free Church Pastors wishing to minister in the Church of England) as the formula of internal agreement, that is scarcely so today. There has been a noticeable lurch towards greater comprehensiveness and greater liberalism since the Report on Doctrine in the Church of England published in 1938. Then the Commission resolved, inter alia, that although assent to formularies and the use of liturgical language in public worship should be understood as indicating general acceptance *without implying detailed assent to every phrase or proposition*, the Church had a right to satisfy itself that those who taught in its name adequately represented and expressed its mind (cf. the stance of the two Regius Professors mentioned above, and the storm of protest from a considerable number of prominent Anglicans when the Vatican withdrew Professor Küng's licence to teach *as a Catholic theologian!*).

A more recent Report on Doctrine, *Christian Believing* (1976) referred to 'different conceptions of the nature of religious truth', divergences of a fundamental kind . . . generating conflict . . . but the tension must be endured! Clearly the agreement in essentials (see above) no longer applies, nor does the possibility and general acceptance of a common authority in doctrine. In ecumenical discussion, notably in the narrowly unsuccessful Covenanting Proposals, the 'invariable practice' of (re)ordination for Free Church Ministers, already cited, was put on the line without regard for the sensibilities of the 'Catholic' minority. But, more seriously for this outdated and unofficial formula, Biblical studies have put in question any hard-line distinction between Bible and Church, or between Biblical and Church teaching, so that doctrines once regarded as peripheral, like that of the nature of the Church itself, can no longer be so categorized. Thus the ordinand of today in his Biblical studies learns that the New Testament texts themselves reveal a progression or development in the faith of early Christian communities. In which case the Church's faith and the Scriptural texts cannot be separated, isolated and contrasted in the manner once beloved of Protestant controversialists.

Speaking in General Synod on 25th February 1981 the Right Revd. Graham Leonard, Bishop of London (when Bishop of Truro) said:

> For some of us you cannot separate sacraments, ministry, from our understanding of the whole faith. You experience the Holy Trinity in worship, in Baptism, in Holy Communion, in Absolution. You know the atonement; you experience it in those ways. That is why they cannot be regarded as a second order, as it were.[6]

Now consider the formularies specified in Canon A.5 (incorporated in the Church of England (Worship & Doctrine) Measure, 1974):

The doctrine of the Church of England is grounded in the Holy Scriptures, and in such teaching of the ancient Fathers and Councils of the Church as are agreeable to the said Scriptures. In particular such doctrine is to be found in the Thirty-nine Articles of Religion, the Book of Common Prayer and the Ordinal.

The insistence upon the Supremacy of Scripture is presently qualified by the methodology of critical schools, some of which assert 'a gospel within a gospel', others superimposition in many places of early Christian belief (either way the Church is not subordinated to the Scriptures but rather to the pretensions of modern scholarship). Similarly, the teachings of Fathers and Councils are time-conditioned glosses, or even distortions, according to some radical scholars.

The Book of Common Prayer is in a category of its own, in the sense that some leading churchmen claim that liturgy is the highest enshrinement of doctrine. We have already seen that the Doctrine Report published in 1938 did not require ex animo subscription to the detail of liturgical texts. The appropriate sub-committee of the 1958 Lambeth Conference reported:

Now it seems clear that no Prayer Book, not even that of 1662, can be kept unchanged for ever, as a safeguard of established doctrine', and went on to ask 'What elements in the Book of Common Prayer are due to the 16th and 17th century misunderstanding of what is primitive in public worship, and what elements need to be substituted or added in order to make Prayer Book services truer to the ideal towards which Cranmer was feeling his way?

In the ecumenical context there has been talk of 'getting behind' the Reformation controversies to find in primitive liturgy a common ground. Whatever may, or may not, be said for this, what is proposed is a by-passing of Anglican theology during its formative period. The appeal to the 'primitive' is also highly selective and reflects a certain Anglican tendency to wander in the garden of history picking fruits at will.

The vulnerability of the Ordinal, or at least of the Preface thereto, has already received mention. The new ordinal doubtfully reflects the teaching of the old, as its greater acceptability to many Free Churchmen suggests. Against the pattern of ecumenical dialogue, vacillation, or just plain politics, may be seen in the invitation to Free Churchmen to adopt episcopacy without restriction to any theory of episcopacy; to accept episcopal ordination without commitment to any theory of priesthood. Latterly the essential distinction between priest and layman has been blurred by scholars such as Dr R. P. C. Hanson.

What of the Thirty-nine Articles? Ever since Newman, to some minds tendentiously, argued that the Articles were capable of a Catholic interpretation, verbal warfare has raged over the exact terms of assent. *The Oxford Dictionary of the Christian Church* observes: 'Much variety of interpretation has been put upon many of them without improperly straining the text, and probably this licence was deliberately intended by the framers. Since 1865 the clergy have not been required to give ex animo subscription to them, and in 1975 a new form of assent was authorised. Though by no means all would agree with him, the Van Mildert Professor of Divinity in the University of Durham has written: "One effect of this new declaration is to dispense the clergy of the Church of England from the need to examine themselves closely as regards their assent to the Thirty-nine Articles" '.[7] Indeed, why change the wording if something of the kind were not intended?

No consensus on authority

However scholarly or ingenious one's theory of authority in the Church of England, it is unlikely that many fellow Anglicans will accept it! These are the days of Situation Theology, Situation Ethics and theological subjectivity. Very inadequately, these pages try to show how loosely the reins of an already-dispersed authority rest upon the Church of England today. It could be argued that all is negotiable, all is dispensable, nothing is actually definitive or binding at least in the sense of being enforceable. All is fluid in the interests of current policy, ecumenical goals, and the commitment – above all – to comprehensiveness. It is unthinkable that officially anyone should be charged with heresy in the contemporary Church of England when it is a tenet of an accepted school of thought that there are no fixed criteria for the determination of theological truth and error.[8] Further confusion arises from the varying fruits of ecumenical discussion, the comparative 'weight' of the ARCIC 'Agreed Statements', for instance, with the content of the proposals for Covenant. In 1978, the Faith & Order Advisory Group issued

Guidelines for the General Synod (GS Misc 76) which, while advising against new doctrinal statements, urged that 'no enquiries should be pressed that would make the assessment of sufficient doctrine more specific and more restricted than that *presently enjoyed* within our own Church'.

A Church's attitude to authority in doctrine is crucial to its understanding of the nature of the Church, of the meaning of Catholicity, and of the ecumenical goal. Whereas the Church of Rome and the Orthodox Churches see unity (and catholicity) in terms primarily of faith and order, and as a present possession, the Church of England clearly sees the ecumenical goal chiefly in terms of an organization tolerant of a wide range of beliefs and customs with unity as the end of a negotiating process. Rome and Orthodoxy thus conceive of catholicity in quite a different way from High Church Anglicans, unless the latter are failing to relate to their Church and to its dominant trends. Encouraged these may be by some considerable revolt against papal authority within the Church of Rome, where again pressures could lead to disruption and regrouping, some elements aligning with the 'Anglo-Catholics'.

If I write so critically it is because so few Anglicans, and perhaps especially clergymen, seem at all concerned for the continuance – or recovery – of a distinctive Anglican ethos. Seemingly they cannot wait to sacrifice what remains of an Anglican identity. Can they not see that the ecumenical movement is unlikely to make real progress from now on unless it can reach agreement on the *kind* of Church God wills, the *kind* of unity, and the *kind* of authority necessary thereto.

Yet more importantly, the whole character of Christianity as revealed religion, as personal religion, the express Image of God being given in Christ, is threatened to the extent that man permits himself radically to 'demythologise' the Saviour Himself, 're-mythologising' Him in his own image and likeness, divinising the authority of the creature rather than submitting to that of the Creator.

References

1 Bicknell, 'A Theological Introduction to the 39 Articles'.
2 *The Crisis of the Reformation*, Norman Sykes.
3 *The God who is There*, Francis Schaeffer, H & S.
4 *Guide to Philosophy*, C. E. M. Joad, Gollancz.
5 *The Times*, 2.8.80.
6 General Synod Report of Proceedings, Vol. 12, No. 1, p. 203.

7 *The Integrity of Anglicanism*, S. W. Sykes, Mowbray, 1978.
8 Article in '*Theology*', Prof. M. Wiles, Jan. 1974.

FIVE

THE CHURCH IN POLITICS

T. E. UTLEY

1 Church, State and Christian Society

MUCH OF THE confusion and animosity generated by the current debate in Britain about the role of the Church in politics springs from two simple and connected causes. The first is the wide variety of senses in which the word 'Church' is now used in ordinary discourse. To some people – probably including the great majority of newspaper readers – it means simply the clergy plus those lay attachments (the laymen who belong, for example, to the General Synod) who are not easily distinguishable from clergymen. So it has come about that when the Synod utters on the legitimacy of nuclear warfare or a bishop denounces the institution of property, it is assumed that these opinions have been given some sort of ecclesiastical authority and even that their acceptance has been announced as a necessary condition of personal salvation. No matter how often church leaders may repudiate such pretensions (and they are not always quick to do so), the impression will inevitably remain that 'the Church' has taken a stand and that those who refuse to follow it are, if not quite excommunicate, then, at least, under some grave ecclesiastical censure.

The second cause of error and uncharity in this matter is the total though gradual and largely undefined change which has taken place in the relations of Church and State since the beginning of the century. The Church of England came into being as a national church. The premise on which the Elizabethan Church Settlement was based was that all Englishmen, not actually traitors to the Crown, belonged to it and that all its members were English.

Church and State, therefore, were but two aspects, the spiritual and the temporal, of a single entity, the Christian nation. Accordingly, there was nothing odd about laymen bearing office in the Church (provided that they did not usurp the functions expressly reserved by Scripture to the clergy) or about the clergy holding political office or discharging political duties.

Paradoxically, these arrangements made it easier rather than harder to draw a distinction, at least in theory, between the respective functions of the spiritual and temporal swords. The assumption that the Church is coterminous with the nation prevented it for many centuries from developing a social or political philosophy of any great dimensions. Its Articles of Faith contain only two clauses which can properly be called political: the first declares that 'it is lawful for Christian men at the commandment of the magistrate to wear weapons and serve in the wars', a proposition which falls far short of declaring that it shall be obligatory to serve in all wars commanded by 'the magistrate'. The second declares that 'the riches and goods of Christians are not common, as touching the right, title, and possession of the same as certain anabaptists do falsely boast. Notwithstanding, every man ought, of such things as he possesses, liberally to give alms to the poor, according to his ability'. That proposition falls far short of making the institution of property in any specific form one of the essential marks of a Christian society. The chief Elizabethan apologist of the Anglican Reformation, Richard Hooker, took his stand on the view that forms of church government were to be determined not by direct appeal to revealed truth but by reference to expediency and historical circumstance. If so with church government, how much more with the temporal arrangements made from time to time for the administration of civil society. Certainly, there is a strong historical relationship between the Tory Party and the Church of England, arising from the fact that, throughout some part of English history, the maintenance of the Church's own institutions, and particularly of episcopacy, was the central issue in English politics. Yet, the Church of England was at least equally famous for its adaptability (in the manner of the Vicar of Bray) to successive political changes. As Dr Edward Norman has taught us, the Anglican clergy has been conspicuous throughout the ages for reflecting the prevailing intellectual prejudices of the educated class to which until recently it belonged.

Here then is the picture of a pliant institution, devoted indeed to the maintenance of social order but refraining from sanctifying forever any particular form of social order, willing to make political alliances for the preservation of the fundamentals of its own form of internal government but conceiving itself as an integral part of the nation and, as such, reflecting changes in the nation's philosophical fashions, but always refraining from claiming divine, absolute authority for any opinion which could not be directly derived from Scripture.

What, then, has happened to this institution in the present century? It has, in effect though not formally, dissolved its connection with the nation. It believes itself (possibly with exaggeration) to be living in a hostile environment, in a country which has largely repudiated Christianity. It has very largely also dissolved its relationship with the State. It has largely liberated itself from the control of Parliament; it has acquired a substantial though not complete control of its own appointments; it has been given its own legislative institution. That all this should have tempted it to think of itself not as the spiritual aspect of Christian society but rather as a society within society cannot cause much surprise.

All this has been accompanied by other developments. To an ever-accelerating extent, throughout the twentieth century, the State has appropriated many of the material tasks which used to be performed under ecclesiastical patronage. The care and moral regeneration of the poor and of 'fallen women' have, for example, become the concern of the bureaucracy. The notion has accordingly grown that a Christian's duties in such matters are to be discharged via politics rather than personal service. Faithful to its inherent tendency as an established church to go along with fashion, the Church of England has fallen in with these trends. A crucial though little remembered event in this process happened as long ago as 1923, when the Church Assembly decided to set up a social and industrial committee. Archbishop Randall Davidson almost resigned over the issue. He foresaw that it would plunge the Church into contentious politics. Today, that prophecy has been amply fulfilled. When the General Synod affirms that one-sided nuclear disarmament is not right but that the first use of nuclear weapons is wrong, it is, no doubt, not adding a fortieth Article to the Anglican faith; but it is proceeding on the assumption that it is natural and proper that Christians should agree with each other on a highly debatable proposition to which the very least objection (in the present context) is its strategic absurdity. The multiplication of such issues on which 'the Church' seeks a common mind is rapidly reducing it to the status of a political party, and this with much damage to its unity, the fundamental purposes for which it exists and the mutual charity of its members.

What is called 'the liberation of the Church from the State' – the process by which the Church of England has ceased to regard itself as representing the spiritual aspect of a Christian nation and come to regard itself as a separate society within the nation – would not have been attended by these consequences but for the spiritual and intellectual climate of the age. Churchmen might well have reacted in a quite different way – withdrawing from the world, concentrating solely on personal salvation and patiently awaiting the day of judgement. Such a reaction was impossible for the Anglican church in this century because of its inheritance as an established church, the legend that it was still there to sanctify the whole of national life and its consequent tendency to swim with the tide of articulate public opinion rather than to oppose it. In a sense therefore, the Church of England, in its relationship to British politics, today displays all the worst features of an established church and of an independent sect. It is conformable to secular fashions of thought, but not in a relatively quiet and quiescent way; rather it converts those fashions into dogmas claiming personal and universal validity. The only reason why the more vociferous of its spokesmen have succeeded in acquiring a reputation for independence of mind is the relative slowness with which they have adapted themselves to certain remarkably rapid changes in public opinion which have happened in the last two or three years. They have not got used to the fact that there are now respectable intellectuals willing to defend capitalism and defensive war on moral grounds. Indeed, the awful prospect which awaits us is that when this change has become apparent to a conformable clergy, we shall be confronted with a new kind of offence to religion – not the identification of the Christian gospel with liberal-rationalism and one of its derivatives, socialism, but the identification of Christianity with another wing of the liberal-rationalist movement, that which exalts liberty as the supreme good and supports crusading wars for its extension. In the meantime, Anglican opinion about social and political matters is in a mess. A variety of traditions is competing for its control, many of them mutually incompatible and simultaneously represented by the same oracles. In this there is nothing especially reprehensible; what is so is the stridence and arrogance with which these oracles utter.

Throughout the ages, the clergy has never been wholly free from such vices; but, in the Church of England, these vices have generally been tempered by a sense of the civility which members of the same nation owe to each other and a wholesome reluctance to claim as permanent what is transient and as revealed truth what is private speculation.

2 Christian political radicalism

I do not propose to describe and document here the many varieties of Christian political radicalism which are currently being proposed to us. I merely want to distinguish some trends, to suggest their pedigrees and to indicate the objections to which they are open.

In the matter of pacifism, there is clearly an authentic Christian tradition. There have for long been Christian men who believe that it is their duty to withdraw from a sinful world, to take no part in its conflicts, to await patiently the judgement of God and the establishment of His Kingdom by the exercise of His own power.

In the Christian pacifist movement today, however, it is hard to see any evidence of such views. It rests not on a philosophy of withdrawal but on the belief that there are certain actions which might be taken by governments which would in fact secure both peace and justice – to wit, that the abandonment of nuclear weapons by the Western powers would elicit such a sympathetic reaction from the Soviet Union as to ensure total and lasting reconciliation. Plainly, there is nothing intrinsically unchristian about this view: my own belief is that the view that the Soviet Union is inexorably committed to extending its empire throughout the world for ideological purposes is much exaggerated. It would be still more absurd to suggest, however, that there is any biblical authority or any authority in the Church's tradition for the view that contemporary Russia has only limited political objectives. The Bible and the Church throughout the ages did not envisage the Soviet Union. Political judgements about Russia's possible reactions to different forms of behaviour by the West are not religious matters. They are questions about which conscientious Christians may legitimately disagree.

What is more, there is certainly no biblical support for the view that actions of self-abnegation invariably disarm potential assailants. We may be told that it is our duty to turn the other cheek, but we are not in any way guaranteed that it will not be smitten. The view that there are certain actions which will automatically produce world peace belongs to the tradition of secular humanism not to that of Christianity. That does not mean, of course, that Christians are in theological error when they accept it; it merely means that they have not the least right to enjoin it upon their brethren as an opinion which has the explicit sanction of their Creator.

Moral evasion is a very unpleasant thing, and one which Christians should be particularly careful to avoid. The largest moral evasion in respect of this particular matter is represented by a platitude to which very highly placed Christians are now specially devoted. It is the proposition that 'war is not acceptable as a means of settling international disputes.' The implication of that remark, insofar as it has any meaning at all, is that nation-states are in the habit of getting together and deciding that they will settle their disagreements by the ancient method of trial by combat, accepting the result as an intimation of divine judgement. This, of course, is not what happens. The question to which the Christian conscience must address itself is what should happen when one nation decides to advance its interests at the expense of others by an armed attack.

Those who have attended to this question at all have returned, somewhat late in the debate, to the medieval doctrine of the 'just war'. That doctrine has two principal elements: the first, the principle of proportionality, is sheer commonsense. It lays down that wars should not be undertaken without thought to the consequences – to the possibility of winning them, to the damage which would be done in the course of winning them and to the relativity between that damage and the harm which would follow from not fighting them. The second element relates to discrimination between combatants and noncombatants. The intentional destruction of noncombatants as a means to victory is condemned; their accidental destruction as an inevitable by-product of the legitimate use of force is not so condemned. How far the distinction between combatants and noncombatants can be said to be morally valid, whether in relation to medieval or modern times, may be questioned. On the face of it, it seems to postulate the doubtful view that those who fight in armies consent (or ever have invariably consented) to do so, and thereby accept a measure of moral responsibility for what they are doing. It is nevertheless clear that the prospect of destroying thousands of civilians, unintentionally but foreseeably, in the process of attacking a legitimate military target presents the Christian conscience with a dilemma. It is a dilemma, however, which can only be settled by reference back to the principle of proportionality – by comparison between the consequences of surrender and those of fighting. It is that uncontentious principle, therefore, in which the only residual value of the doctrine of the 'just war' consists. The appalling moral arithmetic which it involves is no excuse for shirking the issue or for pretending that there is any clear biblical or ecclesiastical authority which can settle it simply; nor is it an excuse for supposing that Christians, facing this issue in good faith, will necessarily reach the same conclusions.

It should certainly not be the pretext for a particularly irritating kind of moral evasion in which many who take part in this controversy now indulge. This is the argument that it is perfectly right to keep nuclear weapons provided that it is publicly and strongly declared that they will never be used. If their sole legitimate value is their deterrent effect, that effect will certainly be destroyed by such public declarations. If the weapons are kept and the declarations cease, there must at least be a possibility that the deterrent will in fact be used. Here again there is a dilemma for the Christian conscience, and one which cannot be avoided.

In its attempts to avoid it, the General Synod of the Church of England seems to have made the worst of both worlds. It has pronounced against one-sided nuclear disarmament, but it has also pronounced against the 'first use' of nuclear weapons. The essential purpose of the nuclear deterrent in its various forms is to redress the balance between the Soviet Union's conventional forces in Europe and those of the West. Forswear the 'first use' of nuclear weapons, and there will assuredly be no reason to use them at all, since Russia will be able with comparative ease to conquer Western Europe. Whereas it is possible to conceive circumstances in which it would be morally necessary to use nuclear weapons to stem that attack, it is far harder to conceive of circumstances in which it would be legitimate to deliver a nuclear attack against the Soviet Union simply in reprisal for a devastating nuclear assault already delivered by the Russians against us. The notion that this curious moral compromise represents any sort of Christian leadership to a bemused and conscience-stricken country is strange indeed. The truth of the matter is that the whole Christian debate on this subject has been marked by moral evasiveness, intellectual incompetence and political stupidity. It bears the marks of an attempt by an organisation which has largely abandoned the tasks for which it is qualified to undertake tasks for which it is peculiarly disqualified.

What is said by Christian leaders on this subject owes little to specifically Christian inspiration. Possibly, there is very little of such inspiration available for a moral and political calculation of immense and terrifying complexity. A few broad and rather uncontentious principles, mostly comprised in the principle of proportionality, may be stated; but for the rest, the Christian qua citizen must make his own mind up in the light of his own interpretation of historical experience. What he must not be asked to accept as divine revelation is the optimistic, humanist assumption that there is some readily available panacea for perpetual peace. The Bible clearly indicates to him that there is not.

The other great preoccupation of Christian political radicalism today is the condemnation of capitalism. Here again there is a long tradition of Christian thought to be called on. From the Peasants' Revolt down to Sir Richard Acland's Common Wealth Party, formed during the last war, there have been intermittently, in English and British politics, extreme egalitarian movements, the inspiration of which was indisputably Christian. Such movements have taken the Apostolic concept of communal living as a model for the economic and social organization of society as a whole. They have started from the premise that God created the world for the common use of mankind, and they have inferred from this that anything, like the institution of private property, which appears to interfere with that purpose, is wrong.

These same ideas no doubt have a part in the Liberationist theology which plays so important and malign a part today in the affairs of Central and South America, though in this theology simple, Christian egalitarianism has been overlaid by Marxism. The Church has traditionally rejected these various brands of revolutionary egalitarianism, partly on the ground that they are revolutionary and thereby imply a lack of regard for the intrinsic merits of social order, and partly on the ground that they ignore the fact that the virtue ascribed in Scripture and in the practice of the early Church to common ownership depended on its voluntary character, on the fact, that is to say, that those who shared their goods did not do so under compulsion. The point which is being made here is simply that there are those in every generation who have read the Bible as indicating a form of social and economic organization of an egalitarian kind which should be the blueprint for all Christian polity. However misguided this interpretation may be (and the traditional wisdom of the Church is that it is wholly misguided), it may at least be described as Christian in the sense that it derives from a misunderstanding of the teaching of Christ.

There is another sort of economic and social radicalism which also deserves the epithet Christian. It is that body of social doctrine deriving from the economic precepts of the Canon Law and reinforced by several papal encyclicals in the last century, which was preoccupied with the wickedness of usury and with the principle of the 'just price' and the just reward for labour. This view of economic morality tends to support a corporatist organization of the economy – corporatist, that is to say, in the correct meaning of the word and not in the slovenly sense (as synonymous with 'collectivist') in which it is now generally used by politicians and journalists. This particular kind of Christian radicalism does not oppose property but conceives it to be a trust held on specific conditions of social service, to be enforced by the moral and legal authority of professions and guilds or other associations of producers united by a common purpose of service and the maintenance of standards. This kind of Christian guild socialism had much intellectual influence in Britain between the wars. It is vulnerable to the serious objection that it tries to apply to the conditions of a modern economy based on freedom of contract, and to those of contemporary society based on contract rather than status, moral ideas which were only applicable to a stable, agrarian community. However, again, whatever may be thought of this particular branch of Christian social teaching, it is manifestly Christian in its sources.

What is most remarkable about the kind of social teaching proferred by the more articulate sections of the clergy in Britain today is that it has no distinctively Christian characteristics at all. Few bishops now use the sort of language which Archbishop Temple used to use in advancing Christian criticisms of the capitalist system. Few, it must be gratefully acknowledged, use the language of liberationist theology or simply base their exhortations on the sort of premises which the Diggers used in the seventeenth century. The clergy do, it is true, appeal to the Bible in support of their right to speak about politics at all; for this purpose they commonly turn to the Old Testament, which makes no distinction between spiritual and temporal authority, though they seem conspicuously less inclined to accept the authority of the Old Testament over matters such as the legitimacy of war and the importance of the nation. When it comes to comment on contemporary political and social affairs, however, it is not to the teaching of the Bible or the Church that they turn, but rather to what was until yesterday the accepted wisdom of most politicians and secular thinkers. Contemporary Christian social thinking in Britain, therefore, has lost all distinctiveness.

In denouncing unemployment as cruel and a fearful waste of human potential, in deploring the neglect of inner cities and in demanding governmental aid for under-developed countries, Christian pastors are not offering anything which can be properly described as 'Christian insights'; they are simply registering the sentiments of ordinary decent people and proposing the sort of remedy generally favoured by the political establishment until recently.

The essential assumption of that proposed remedy is that once specific social evils have been identified, they can be corrected by the simple fiat of the State. Consider, for a moment, what form a theology of unemployment might take. The premise of Christian thinking about economic activity is, surely, that, when it is legitimate, it is undertaken for purposes outside itself. The classic formulation of the Christian doctrine of work is that it is done for the glory of God and the improvement of man's estate. Christians who are concerned about unemployment should, one might suppose, be interested not merely in the statistics of those out of work but in the extent to which those in work are engaged in socially useful activity. All this, one would have supposed, would dispose the clergy to Mrs Thatcher's distinction between 'real' and simulated jobs. The notion that a man's 'dignity' can be fostered merely by giving him employment in the formal sense regardless of whether he is creating anything of intrinsic value or making any effective contribution to the satisfaction of the needs of others is an example of humanist philanthropy rather than Christian thinking.

It is not my intention to suggest that there is anything in itself unchristian in the various demands for State intervention and the adoption of broadly 'progressive' social policies which so often emanate from the clergy today. These demands reflect political judgements of a perfectly legitimate though highly debatable kind. What is objectionable is the implication that they derive directly and necessarily from Scripture or the Church's traditional teaching. Occasionally, it is true, the clergy in their pronouncements about politics do seem to draw on positively unchristian sources of inspiration. This is so, for instance, in the case of the 'liberationist' theologians who have accepted more than it is seemly for them to accept of the philosophy of Karl Marx. One may also discern in the comments of some of the clergy on that broad category of subjects now usually comprised under the heading 'the permissive society' a similarly alien influence. True it certainly is that Christian acceptance of heterosexual monogamy as a divine institution does not commit Christians to the view that this standard of behaviour can or ought to be imposed by the laws of the State or, indeed, that the widespread breakdown of Christian marriage should not be reflected in those laws. What is not open to a Christian is to accept personal liberty as an end in itself and to approach these matters from the standpoint of John Stuart Mill's distinction between 'self-regarding' and 'other-regarding' actions. Some Christian advocates of 'permissiveness' seem to fall into this error. It is also true that the confidence with which many of the clergy now espouse proposals for the reform of society through the exercise of political power sometimes has an unchristian flavour about it and suggests that they are attributing to politics a capacity for promoting moral regeneration which Christians claim for the Church rather than the State. They forget Archbishop Temple's warning: 'No form of organisation can save man from sin; and sinful men will pervert any form of organisation.'

My contention is that in all these respects reformist thinking in the Church about politics owes far more than its practitioners commonly recognise to non-Christian influences and in particular to the general influence of the liberal, progressive and rationalist tradition, and that these influences have not been incorporated into a coherently theological view of the meaning of Christian social order. It will be objected, however, that there are many passages in the New Testament which lend at least apparent support to the causes which Christian social and political reformers now tend to espouse. Is not the Sermon on the Mount, it will be said, an authoritative statement of the principle of Christian pacifism and for that matter also, in its exhortation to share material goods, a blueprint for a Christian socialist commonwealth?

The Sermon on the Mount is, indeed, the source of a central dilemma in the lives of most Christians. Considered as a blueprint for perfect Christian polity, it would seem to propose not a socialist state (for such a state depends uniquely on the use and the threat of public force) but a kind of Christian anarchism which would seek to remove force and the threat of force from any part in the running of social relationships. Virtually no one actually so interprets it;

those who cite it as a condemnation of war in the defence of national interest do not generally see it as a condemnation of all compulsion in human affairs and many of them find it perfectly compatible with the advocacy of violence as a means to the attainment of social justice. If it is to be seen as having a political message at all, that message must be construed as a summons to Christians to withdraw from secular society and form their own independent society based entirely on the rule of love. Early Christians who lived in hourly expectation of the day of judgement often so interpreted their duty; but this is not an interpretation which is easily to be found today, and it is, of course, one which completely rules out preoccupation with political action in the cause of social reform. It also renders incomprehensible Christ's affirmation (also contained in the Sermon on the Mount) that he came not to destroy but to fulfil the law not a single jot of which would pass away.

A familiar reaction to this dilemma is to say that the Sermon on the Mount is a counsel of perfection, that it portrays some utopian society towards which we are required to move at whatever pace the sinfulness of man permits. This also is wholly unsatisfactory. Christ commanded his disciples to be perfect, not just to pursue perfection as an ideal. So Christians have been driven to another attempt to circumscribe the application of these impossible precepts. They are to be found contending that the absolute non-violence and complete selflessness which Christ's words seem to enjoin are recommendations about personal not public morality, that they belong to the sphere of private not public affairs.

Even this, however, is grotesquely unsatisfactory. How many people can seriously and honestly maintain that if they are struck in a hostile and indefensible manner they will feel it their duty, not merely to refrain from retaliating, but to invite a further assault? How many people will honestly maintain that if their overcoats are stolen from them, they will respond by offering their jackets as well? The complaint against such injunctions is not practical but moral: it is not that such a degree of self-abnegation, without thought to the social consequences, is beyond the frail capacities of human nature; it is rather that such behaviour is repellent to the consciences of ordinary decent people. To treat the Sermon on the Mount as a series of moral precepts is, therefore, as absurd as to treat it as a political programme. Viewed as either, it is morally insupportable.

It must, therefore, either have no meaning at all or some other meaning than that which is often attributed to it. In reality, it has a profound meaning and one which is fundamental to the whole of Christian living. It is a piece of poetry designed to describe that absolute submission to the divine will, that absolute subjection of the self to the divine order which is the basis of holy living. Its aim is to dispose men's hearts and minds to total service to God and total submission to His order. Men are different because they hear these words continually recited to them. Having observed their meaning and the submission which they enjoin, they go back into the sinful world fortified and ready to grapple with the moral and political dilemmas which it presents. Not only is the New Testament not a book about politics; it is not a book about morality either; it is a book about religion. The conversion of its teaching to a political or even a moral purpose is misconceived and even impious. The attempt to make that conversion is the particular fault of Christian political and social radicalism.

It is not part of the intention of this essay to deny that an honest Christian, seeking to interpret his duty in the contemporary world, may be drawn to radical conclusions in politics. In the process of reaching those conclusions, however, he will have to make a number of contentious judgements for which he cannot properly claim the authority of Scripture or the Church's teaching. It is this distinction which a number of the clergy now seem constantly to overlook. There is a sense in which the role of the Church (whether it be established or not) in relation to the nation is analogous to that of a family chaplain. A chaplain does not (if he is prudent) aspire to a detailed control of the affairs of those he is serving; he does not try to arbitrate between husband and wife, to prescribe precisely how they should treat their children or dispose of the family income. He addresses their minds to the criteria by which these decisions should be reached; he offers comfort and blessing to them in their attempts to arrive at the right conclusions. The reticence he observes is intended not to circumscribe but to enhance his influence by concentrating it on those fundamentals which are his proper business. Those who urge that the Church should display a similar reticence in relation to politics are not seeking to reduce the effect which it has on secular life but rather to increase it by directing it properly.

On many complex political matters, Christians now find themselves deeply divided, and the argument between them is not to be settled by a simple appeal to divine revelation. For example, it is arguable that the principle of apartheid is directly contrary to the teaching of Scripture. To leap from that premise to the conclusion that it is a Christian duty to boycott investment in South Africa or to refrain from playing games with South Africans is, nevertheless, to make a whole series of debatable assumptions about the possible effects of these actions. To affirm that a particular kind of social order is unjust is a different matter from asserting that it should be destroyed regardless of the consequences of doing so.

In relation to war, Christians are also deeply divided. In modern times the habit has grown of supposing that wars can only be justified when they are fought for high moral and crusading purposes such as the liberation of mankind from tyranny or the establishment of perpetual peace. In proportion as those waging wars have arrogated to themselves these lofty purposes, they have become more ruthless in the methods by which they wage them. There is another tradition of Christian thought on this subject, however, which has fallen into neglect. It is the view that just wars are in their nature limited and defensive in their objectives. This is closely associated with the view of our ancestors that war was an evil arising from original sin, that in a fallen world nations came into conflict with each other without there necessarily being a monopoly of good or evil on either side. On this view, it is the duty of a Christian statesman to seek with diligence and subtlety to reconcile those inevitable conflicts of national interest from which wars spring. If he fails, it is his duty to wage war in as humane a manner as possible and to seek the earliest moment for bringing it to an end on tolerable terms. Throughout, his mind will properly be fixed, not on the ultimate interests of mankind which are incalculable, but primarily on the particular interests of that part of mankind for which he is responsible and whose welfare is his sacred trust.

It is this earlier view of the character of war which is reflected in the Anglican liturgy. The prayer of Thanksgiving For Peace and Deliverance from our Enemies reads thus: 'O Almighty God, who art a strong tower of defence unto thy Servants against the face of their enemies; We yield thee praise and thanksgiving for our deliverance from those great and apparent dangers wherewith we were compassed: We acknowledge it thy goodness that we were not delivered over as a prey unto them; beseeching thee still to continue such thy mercies towards us, that all the world may know that thou art our Saviour and mighty Deliverer; through Jesus Christ our Lord. Amen.' Where is the note of national self-glorification in that prayer? Its emphasis is rather on the mercy of God, which is assumed to be unmerited. Much nonsensical controversy about the Falklands Thanksgiving Service could have been avoided if the true nature of traditional Anglican thinking about the theology of war had not been forgotten. As it was, the arguments seemed largely to be conducted between those who believed that God automatically underwrites the objects of British foreign policy and, on occasions of victory, must be congratulated for His good sense in that matter, and those who believed that He has equipped us with some simple panacea for peace and justice which we decline to employ because of invincible national arrogance and bloodlust.

The perennial debates between Christians about social policy are befogged by an equal confusion. Unemployment, bad housing, poverty, inferior provision for health and education are all, beyond doubt, contrary to the will of God. We are not warranted, however, to jump from this premise to the conclusion that they can all be instantly removed by the fiat of the State exercised in a particular way. Those who believe (as the present Prime Minister does) that the natural affections on which the family rests and the wider spontaneous benevolence which they generate are at least as important to the task of overcoming these evils as the action of government, and that government has, indeed, by usurping the role of the family, done much to hinder social improvement have, at the very least, an arguable case and one, to put it mildly, which cannot be ruled out of court by any simple appeal to Christian teaching. They may be wrong politically, but that is a proposition which has to be proved by political not theological argument. Insofar as Christian political radicalism now rests on the assumption that once an evil is identified it can be abolished by a simple exercise of public force, it rests on a heresy.

Yet, there remains in the minds of most Christians a lingering doubt best summed up in the proposition that Christian morality stands for harmony and cooperation whereas much secular political thinking, normally described as Right-wing, elevates the principle of competition. It would indeed be true that an economic doctrine or a philosophy of society which laid it down that individuals should or must inevitably pursue their own material interests without the least regard to the welfare of their fellows could properly be condemned as unchristian. But where is such a doctrine to be found? Reduced to its simplest expression, the view of traditional liberal economists is that the result of the working of competition, within the limits of general rules of law, will produce a harmony of interest. This may or may not be true and is probably only in part true; but it is not a conception which can be stigmatised as unchristian, the more so because the motives which lead men to pursue their own interests cannot be comprehensively described as merely 'selfish'. What is there in Christian teaching which denies the legitimacy of particular obligations such as those of a man to his family? What is there which forbids him to enter an honourable competitive process the results of which he genuinely believes will promote the common good? It is a naive puritanism, owing more to the doctrines of the Enlightenment than to any Christian authority, which postulates that to be virtuous an action must involve painful self denial and rest on a specific calculation of what the interests of humanity at large are in any given case.

In the same way, the Christian conscience, when it addresses itself to the legitimacy of war, is principally afflicted by one text: 'Those who live by the sword shall die by the sword': so indeed it is. The object of war is to defend material and perishable institutions, yet institutions which exist under the divine sanction and are therefore meet to be defended. There are things too high to be fought for. One does not fight for the spiritual regeneration of mankind or the creation of heaven on earth. Those ends are to be promoted by the use of the spiritual and not the temporal sword, a fact that does not exclude the legitimacy of using the temporal sword for the purposes for which it is intended. The ultimate objection to Christian political radicalism of the extreme kind is not that it is a nuisance to the State but that it is a blasphemy in that it politicises religion and thereby reduces it to a relatively menial role. It is the Church not the State which should be chiefly on guard against the tide of opinion which has been described in this essay.

SIX

ECUMENISM RUN RIOT

THE REVEREND CANON GEORGE AUSTIN

As the successor to St Augustine greeted the successor to Pope Gregory in Canterbury Cathedral on Pentecost Eve, 1982, the barriers of centuries began to crumble in the face of the warmth and determination of two good men. It was a sign that the power of God was at work through His Holy Spirit, thrusting the Church forward in a manner and with an urgency which no prophet dare have foretold even thirty years ago. How completely God has turned upside down the world of the English Roman Catholic is evident when it is recalled that in those days a priest was forbidden to recite the Lord's Prayer with other Christians or a lay Catholic to worship in non-Roman churches. It is a mark of their openness to change that the new attitudes have been accepted with such ready warmth.

Another commentator would have begun on a gloomier note than the historic meeting between Pope and Archbishop. In July 1982, the proposals for a Covenant for Unity between the Church of England and some of the English Free Churches failed to achieve the necessary two-thirds majority in the Anglican General Synod. He might have suggested that the culmination of sixty years of sincere effort to heal the broken Body of Christ had been frustrated by the intransigence of reactionary and unrepresentative members of the Synod's House of Clergy, who once again had rejected the guidance of the Holy Spirit. How long, he would have asked, can Anglican clergy be allowed to continue to oppose the will of God? Why do they lack such openness to change that the old attitudes are grasped with this limpet tenacity? Yet at the fourth meeting of the Anglican Consultative Council in 1979, the Secretary General in his Review Address pointed out that the last major unions which bridged the 'episcopal/non-episcopal ravine' were those in North India and Pakistan as long ago as 1970. Since then, union schemes in which Anglicans were involved in England, New Zealand, USA and elsewhere 'have declined and are unlikely to succeed now'. While it is natural that those who have invested long hours of discussion and prayer in the formulation of schemes to promote the unity of the Church should feel hurt, rejected and sometimes angry when their efforts appear to have come to nought, it is sad that, faced with the fairly consistent pattern of failure in such schemes, there is so little readiness to ask if God is not telling the Church that His plans point in another direction. Is it a lack of openness to change that the old attitudes have been grasped with such limpet tenacity? Does not the failure of the Covenant require from those involved in the quest for unity a radical reappraisal of the whole course and purpose of the ecumenical movement?

Guiding principles

The Edinburgh Conference of 1910 marked the start of the ecumenical movement as we know it today, with three major guiding principles gradually emerging, to permeate the philosophy which was to govern the approach adopted by most ecumenical leaders.

1. The assumption that the words of our Lord in His High Priestly prayer quoted in John 17: 21 are directly and primarily to be understood in terms of church unity:

> '. . . that they may all be one; even as thou, Father, art in me, and I in thee, that they also may be in us, so that the world may believe that thou hast sent me.'

2. The so-called Lund Principle, originating at the World Council of Churches' Faith and Order Conference in 1952, by which the Churches are urged to do together all those things which differences of conviction and conscience do not compel them to do separately.

3. The belief that it is the *visible* unity of the Church which is the will of God.

How far a too-slavish adherence to these three principles has bedevilled the work of the ecumenical movement in recent years is the primary question to be answered in any reappraisal of the direction in which ecumenism should travel.

The biblical evidence

That all mankind 'may be one' is clearly and unequivocally the prayer of Jesus in John 17: 21; but the nature of the unity to which He points needs examination if it is properly to fulfil the divine purpose 'that the world may believe that thou hast sent me.' It must for instance be read in context, and in verse 17 Jesus also prays, 'Sanctify them in the truth; thy word is truth'; and continues (verse 19) 'For their sake I consecrate myself, that they also may be consecrated in truth.' Yet the floundering and foundering of more than one scheme for church unity has been through the ready acceptance of doctrinal statements couched in such forms that they might be interpreted in different and contradictory ways. A deliberate formulation of ambiguity is hardly an indication that one is 'consecrated in truth'!

The nature of the unity of which our Lord speaks is demonstrated in the qualifying clause which follows the plea, 'that they may be one': it is for a unity which is 'even as thou, Father, art in me, and I in thee'. That unity is well-expressed in the words of the Athanasian Creed, which demands that 'we worship one God in Trinity, and Trinity in Unity; neither confounding the persons nor dividing the substance'. For while the Godhead is 'all one', there is nevertheless 'one person of the Father, another of the Son, and another of the Holy Ghost'. Save that the Son is 'inferior to the Father as touching his manhood', He is at the same time 'equal to the Father as touching his Godhead', and the difference and differentiation of person is in no way seen either as damaging the unity or as a declaration that one Person is inferior to another within the Godhead. Some ecumenists need to learn the lesson that *difference* is synonymous neither with *inferiority* nor with *superiority*.

This understanding of unity is surely reflected in Paul's Letter to the Galatians (3.28): 'There is neither Jew nor Greek, there is neither slave nor free, there is neither male nor female; for you are all one in Christ Jesus.' Diversity is of the very nature of God's creation and that diversity is reflected in the Church which is His Body, both in the varieties of gifts and responsibilities He gives to the members (Eph. 4), quite out of proportion to their rights and expectations and also in the diverse range of race, social background and sex within that membership. It is only a peculiar quirk of our own generation which demands that the fulfilment of equality can only be in a clone-like identification, and that the acknowledgement of difference carries with it the implication of inferiority. Both assumptions are totally contrary to Holy Scripture.

St Paul carries us to an infinitely higher plane of understanding when he speaks of the unity which the Son enjoys with the Father: 'In him all the fullness of God was pleased to dwell'; of the unity which he prays should be granted to the Christian: 'that you may be filled with all the fullness of God' (Eph. 3.19); and of the unity which is of the nature of the church 'which is his body, the fullness of him who fills all in all' (Eph. 1.23). It is to this unity which Jesus refers in his High-Priestly prayer, rather than to the healing of ecumenical divisions by means which so often seem to deny the diversity which is the glory of creation, while at the same time compromising the truth in which the Church is required to be consecrated.

Differences between Jewish and Gentile Christians as well as those between Jewish believers in Jerusalem and Jews of the Dispersion arose in the early days of the Church, and issues were sometimes resolved with verbal force. 'At Antioch', claims Paul, rather proudly, 'I withstood Peter to his face!' (Gal. 2.11) Jesus himself was aware of the deep differences within Judaism and does not hesitate to proclaim the truth without fear or favour. 'The Sadducees say that there is no resurrection, nor angel, nor spirit' (Acts. 23.8), and Paul on trial before the Council is ready to play one against the other. Jesus on the other hand when questioned by the Sadducees in the hearing of the Pharisees is concerned neither that his assertion of the fact of resurrection will anger the Sadducees nor that it will please the Pharisees. He simply makes a flat and absolute assertion of the truth: 'You know neither the scriptures nor the power of God. . . . He is not the God of the dead but of the living; you are quite wrong.' (Mark 12: 24, 27)

There was also the much deeper division between the Jews and the Samaritans. Although initially descended from the Twelve Tribes (and to this day keeping Jewish festivals and accepting a slightly divergent form of the Pentateuch, though no more than this of the Old Testament), they had intermarried with many other nations and tribes, not least because of their geographical location on the east-west trade routes. By our Lord's day, 'the Jews had no dealings with the Samaritans', regarding each other with undisguised hostility and sometimes open conflict. There is more than a hint of this when, after telling the story of what to his hearer must have been a contradiction in terms, a *good* Samaritan, Jesus asked the lawyer which of the three characters in the story had 'proved neighbour to the man who fell among the robbers'. The reply was of only grudging acknowledgement: 'The one who showed mercy on him'.

Yet Jesus himself clearly shares none of the customary Jewish antagonism (as in the good Samaritan (Luke 10.33), or in the leper who gave thanks for his cure (Luke 17.16)), and appears to be at pains to avoid controversy with them, forbidding the disciples to preach in their villages (Matt. 10.5). He is ready to pass through Samaria when travelling from Judea to Galilee, rather than take the customary detour, and this leads to the encounter with the woman of Sychar at Jacob's Well.

Is not this a unique ecumenical encounter, where Jesus, a prophet of mainstream Judaism, faces one whom He must regard as belonging to an unorthodox sect, yet towards whom it would be anathema to Him to display traditional Jewish hostility? In that fascinating conversation which John records (John 4), Jesus disarms the woman's prickly antagonism ('How is it that you, a Jew, can ask a drink of me, a woman of Samaria?'), by his immediate respect for her religious integrity and by pointing to that which they might share: 'If you had known . . . he would have given you living water.' She remains suspicious and asserts her credentials: 'Jacob . . . gave us the well', but Jesus presses her to look beyond the slogans towards God's purpose and promise. When he questions her personal morality, she responds by means of a Samaritan 'ours-is-better-than-yours argument', contrasting the huge mass of Mt Gerizim which towers over them with the little hill of Jerusalem: 'Our father worshipped . . . yet you say Jerusalem. . . .' Again Jesus takes her beyond contemporary controversies, leading her to see God's ultimate purpose, 'when true worshippers will worship the Father in spirit and truth', and even to wonder if he is not the Christ.

Superficially this appears to be an exact parallel with the hopes and methods of modern ecumenical endeavour, but in fact there are three highly significant contrasts with the efforts of our own day. While he points to a future in God's purpose in which Jew and Samaritan will have moved beyond current divisions, he

79

nowhere rejects them as unimportant and unnecessary *for that age*; although he never questions the religious integrity of the Samaritan women he does not hesitate to assert the pre-eminence of his own beliefs: 'You worship what you do not know; we worship what we know, for salvation is of the Jews.' (Can we imagine a modern ecumenist saying to another of a different denomination, 'Because we believe God has shown us this way, we believe also that we are right and you are wrong!'?) And throughout the encounter what he seeks is not compromise but reconciliation.

The Lund Principle

The conviction that the Churches should do together all those things which differences of conscience do not compel them to do separately dominates, not surprisingly, the thinking of the British Council of Churches, for it is at the same time the Council's *raison d'être* as well as its hope for expansion and therefore influence. Carried to a logical conclusion, the Lund Principle would demand that member Churches abandon their own separate central departments, dealing with such issues as education, youth work, social responsibility, international affairs, mission and evangelism, whose work would then be continued ecumenically by the departments of the BCC. The Churches would be seen to be working together, thereby (so it is argued) witnessing to the world their unity; there would be saving of financial outlay through the pooling of resources; and the BCC would be able to 'speak for the Churches' with an influence and importance which at present is almost entirely lacking.

While the Lund Principle has certainly had its rightful place in the development of ecumenical understanding and co-operation, does it represent an immutable law rather than a concept undoubtably appropriate to a stage in the life of the ecumenical movement? Is it not right to ask if the Churches are not now ready to move into a relationship which represents a greater trust and growing maturity?

There are certainly areas of work which will be better done ecumenically by the BCC, than separately by the individual Churches, such as the oversight of Local Ecumenical Projects, the continuation of the work of the now defunct National Initiative in Evangelism, and the present work of the BCC Community and Race Relations Unit. But can it not also be acknowledged that it is a better contribution both to Christian thinking and to the life of the

Churches if controversial areas of social thinking – for example on abortion, sexual ethics, disarmament, nuclear war – where individual Churches tend to lean towards strongly differing conclusions, are left to the appropriate departments of the individual Churches? With only the BCC, the statements made would either be of such bland compromise that no-one would be helped or satisfied, or else simply an echo of the prejudices of the liberal establishment to which the Council sometimes appears to be as wedded as the Church of England has been in past days to another Establishment. The Church as Feminism or the Militant Tendency at Prayer is no less offensive and dangerous than the Church as the Tory Party at Prayer.

There is a third area of activity in the BCC where the Lund Principle could be challenged: where the work is already being better done by others. When there is an adequate department of the World Council of Churches which deals with international affairs, can the expense of its duplication by the BCC really be justified? Even though the BCC's offerings in this field have been criticised as being pretentious and naive, it cannot be denied that some of its contributions have been of the highest quality, but careful stewardship of limited resources rather than quality or quantity should be the criterion. Certainly when the BCC's Education Department was closed, this was regarded as an abdication of responsibility, yet the individual Churches needed separate education departments, while an effective ecumenical agency already existed in the Christian Education Movement.

In necessarily advancing beyond the Lund Principle, there are two lessons to be learnt: firstly, that big is not always beautiful and a huge monolithic body in the form of an extended British Council of Churches could well be a poor servant of the ecumenical movement; and secondly, that the effectiveness of a reformed BCC will depend on a greater commitment by member churches, not least in financial terms. It would probably help the major churches – and would certainly benefit the smaller – if more staff assistance were provided within existing church departments (for example, the Youth Department of the Church of England sharing all the necessary resources with a number of small churches which simply cannot provide separate youth departments). And in those areas where the BCC must expand if the highest calibre of staff cannot be obtained, the blame lies firmly in the member churches and not in the BCC when proper financial demands are refused or resisted.

The quest for visible unity

At the Autumn 1982 Assembly of the British Council of Churches, there was strong pressure for a considerable extension of the Council's involvement in the practical and theological programme of ecumenism in Britain, following the failure of the English Covenant and the demise of the Nationwide Initiative in Evangelism. However, the Council's absolute and total commitment both to the Covenant and to a single interpretation of church unity ought to suggest that wherever a springboard to future ecumenical thought and action is to be found it is not and cannot and should not be centred on the BCC.

At an earlier meeting of the Assembly (Spring 1980), Dr Kenneth Greet successfully proposed an amendment to a motion on ecumenical affairs, to add the words:

'. . . expresses the hope that the Churches' Council for Covenanting will bring its work to a successful conclusion'.

Both Catholic and Evangelical representatives from the Church of England pleaded with the Assembly not to follow this path, not least because it seemed to reject any prayer for the guidance of the Holy Spirit in decision making on the Covenant and assumed that the success of the Covenant was the only possible way forward. But the Assembly accepted Greet's lead, and the same attitude was reflected at the Autumn 1982 Assembly, in a paper by the Divisional Secretary, Martin Conway. In it, he asserts categorically that only one understanding of unity – even only one of visible unity – is acceptable: 'the reconciliation of different churches . . . to form a single, *organically functioning* body at God's service'. Contrasting the Christian quest for peace and the Falklands episode (of which the BCC disapproved) as a parallel to the contrast between the quest for unity and the 'acquiescence in the failure of the General Synod to achieve a sufficient majority on the Covenant', Conway, representing the dominant thinking of the BCC, clearly cannot conceive of any circumstances in which there could be God's will in the Covenant decision. He does, somewhat hesitantly, acknowledge that 'all have sinned and fallen short' and that there is hurt on both sides, but the underlying message is of the 'shame of many Anglicans' and of 'the sense of so much time and spiritual energy wasted'. One BCC critic has spoken of 'leading our Anglo-Catholic brethren in the Church of England out of their fears', as if disagreement with the ecumenical party line can only indicate mental or psychological disorder. Dissidents in the Soviet Union have the same problem. Others would wish to change the rules, and in an immediate response to the Covenant vote in the General Synod, Methodist Kenneth Greet demanded that the 'undemocratic' voting methods of the Church of England should be reformed and the right to vote by separate Houses of Bishops, Clergy and Laity be abandoned (thus also preventing the Laity from overruling the two clerical Houses as they have since done). In fact, the total Synod vote failed to reach the necessary two-thirds majority – while in the Methodist Church and the URC, the other major participants in the Covenant, no less than a 75% majority had been demanded. This was denied to the Synod, even though it was the requisite majority for the Anglican-Methodist Scheme in 1972. Martin Conway quotes with approval a demand that local churches should move 'ahead, steadily, determinedly and indeed aggressively into the kinds of practical ecumenism . . . *which the General Synod – thank God – has no power to block'*. So we learn that for the British Council of Churches, organic union is the only way forward, God's will is known so there is no need to be open to His guidance, representative bodies which reject this must undergo constitutional change, opponents are suffering from psychological disorder, and the General Synod (and anyone else) in rejecting the party line is outside God's providence. Far from being granted a major role in future ecumenical endeavour, such an attitude from the BCC points to a new bigotry which is at least as unpleasant as that which in ecumenical affairs it has sought with thankful success to remove.

The essay by the chairman and secretary of the Council for Covenanting ('The Failure of English Covenant') is in marked contrast, for though it naturally reflects a deep and understandable disappointment and frustration, it is nevertheless remarkably open in its admissions. There is immediate recognition of a diversity of views on the nature of the unity sought, and no rejection of those for whom 'visible unity' is not synonymous with 'organic unity'. It records how the haste encouraged by Methodists resulted in misjudgements on the measure of agreement and understanding between the Covenanting Churches. Assurances which had been given, in all faith, to questions from some Anglicans about lay celebration of the Eucharist – that this was not a problem, that it was a rare occurrence in the Free Churches and would be phased out – were clearly wrong and a cause of continuing unease on both sides of the argument. Even though a Covenant in scriptural terms is a declaration of God's final achievement, the essay records a number of major ecclesiological and fundamental theological issues which remained unresolved when the Churches came to vote on the Covenant. It is hardly surprising that one of the many areas of unease for opponents was that it had far too much of the character of a blank cheque.

That the Covenant's failure caused deep hurt is beyond question, but it was by no means confined to those who were hoping for it to succeed. Opponents were, throughout the months of debate at local and national level, accused of being 'against unity', of 'resisting the Holy Spirit', of 'frustrating the will of God by deliberate intent'. Even their doubts about the proposals for the reconciliation of ministries were presented, quite falsely, as a denial that God's grace could work through non-episcopal ministries. Had the Covenant been achieved, it is clear now that there would have been major difficulties for those who dissented from it. There were conscientious provisions, prepared with much thought and pastoral sensitivity, but they remained inadequate, and the deeply censorious attitude of some of the leading supporters of the Covenant towards those who, in all conscience, felt they must remain in opposition has made it only too obvious that dissidents would have been subjected to intense pressure to conform to the Covenant. Indeed the greatest hurt suffered by opponents since the Synod vote has been the growth of an (albeit incredulous) awareness that there were not a few proponents of the Covenant who would have been ready, if all persuasion failed, to 'lose' the non-Covenanters from the Church to which many had given a lifetime's service. This claim will meet with vehement denial (justifiably, in the case of many supporters) but in the light of the sustained and occasionally vicious obloquy which has been heaped upon those who refused to accept the Covenant as the way forward, the sad conclusion must be drawn that the pressure to conform would have been absolute.

A 'yet more excellent way'?

The recognition of ministries has been the Achilles heel of so many schemes for unity, often in a mutual confusion of ambiguity about what was actually taking place. The recent Proposals included an act of 'reconciliation of ministries' within the initial Covenant Service, both at the national and at the local level. It was certainly not intended to be ordination to the historic threefold ministry by some kind of subterfuge, and nor, quite properly, was there an implication of any basic inadequacy in the non-episcopal ministries as channels of God's grace. At the same time, it was more than a solemn acknowledgement of an inherent validity in the separate ordination of participating Churches. It was to be understood that after the service those who had taken part (and in some cases those who had been absent but who were nonetheless in sympathy) had orders which were interchangeable, and that all future ordinations would be within the episcopal pattern as practised by the Church of England. If the *visible* unity of the Church is God's will, organically or not, then it is clear that an essential element must be a mutual recognition and interchange of ministers. But is it not at this very point that God may be indicating a new way forward? If the conversation between Jesus and the woman at the well can be seen as a type of ecumenical encounter, there will be guidance here for the Church.

In the account, it will be recalled, Jesus firmly and without equivocation proclaims the pre-eminence of Jerusalem against the woman's presentation of the credentials of Mt Gerizim. At the same time, Jesus points beyond the present reality towards God's ultimate purpose 'when true worshippers will worship the Father in spirit and in truth'. Archbishop Fisher's seminal proposal in 1946 that the Free Churches 'take episcopacy into their systems', of such immense importance in the development of ecumenical understanding, should be seen as one stage in a process rather than as a final word.

Those Churches in the episcopal tradition can rightly claim that it is to this form of ministry that God has led them, and from which they cannot faithfully turn away if they are to honour the truth as revealed to them. In the face of the woman's claims Jesus could assert that 'salvation is of the Jews' without denying the integrity, under God, of the Samaritan claim and, at the same time, with a firm acknowledgement of the transience of all human understandings. Cannot an episcopal Church, while attesting to the episcopal form as God's revelation of what is of the *esse*, the *bene esse* and the *plene esse* of the Church, at the same time be ready without qualification also to recognise God's hand in the integrity of another's understanding of ministerial order, an order which will contain within itself, wider insights into the nature of *episcope* as part of God's total revelation?

The Church, which is the one Body of Christ, can be seen as a

crown of many jewels, in which episcopal and non-episcopal forms
of ministry have an equal value within the purpose of God. While
it is true that God, through the Holy Spirit who guides mankind
towards the Truth which is his very nature, may indeed lead the
Free Churches to move away from the patterns of ministry to which
He had formerly guided them and to 'take episcopacy into their
systems' (or for that matter the episcopal Churches to reject their
present forms), cannot the Church learn to contain both as expressions of the will of God, and moreover as a demonstration of the
diversity which is part of the glory of God's creation? Though it
may not be until we move from the limited comprehension possible
to mankind on earth, where we see only as 'through a glass darkly',
there will come the time in the future, maybe in eternity when
we join the great company of the Church Triumphant, that 'true
worshippers will worship the Father in spirit and in truth'. Then
we shall either see the error of our ways, or we shall be led to
understand that the very differences which appear to divide us are
no more nor less than part of the fullness of God and a true
expression of the glory of His nature in creation.

This is surely closer to that pattern of unity which is demanded
by our Lord, a unity which is in his words, 'even as thou Father
art in me, and I in thee'. Reconciliation is required, but not of the
kind which looks for acquiescence or submission nor that which
seeks to present a brave face to the world by a compromise which
only papers over the cracks. Compromise anyway is the solution of
the politician and bears within it the unspoken qualification of
future persuasion to another view. It has no place in Christian
reconciliation, which, at any rate in human terms, is best expressed
in the loving acceptance of that which can sometimes be mutually
irreconcilable in the relationship between husband and wife. A
marriage which bears this is all the stronger for it, and presents, to
a world which seems to prefer an easier path, a unity in diversity
in which, through true reconciliation, love is deepened to become
more like the 'unity betwixt Christ and his Church'. Truly it is a
harder path, demanding an acceptance of the total integrity of
another's incompatible position. But there are clear signs that it is
in this direction that God is leading the Church as the next stage
in the journey to a unity which is according to His will. One
need only look at the documents of the Anglican Roman Catholic
International Commission, the World Council of Churches' Lima
statement, 'Baptism, Eucharist and Ministry', and the new under-

standings reached between **Roman Catholics** and Lutherans on the Augsburg Confession to become aware of radically new urgings of the Spirit, directing the minds and efforts of Christians into uncharted waters.

Dr Kenneth Greet has commented:

'The way marked out by a whole generation of ecumenical leaders has proved to be a *cul-de-sac*. We must pray that a new generation will succeed where we have failed, for in the end a way must be found. The Holy Spirit does not declare a moratorium just because we temporarily lose our way.'

Perhaps like many a prophet before him, Dr Greet has, with unwitting prescience, signposted the way to God's new reality. For the blind alley becomes a new horizon when we allow God to remove the scales from our eyes: failure exists when we imagine in our pride that it is we whom God has chosen to succeed; and we lose our way only when we are so foolish as to imagine that we can have reached the end of the journey.

SEVEN

STRANGE GIFTS

THE REVEREND PETER MULLEN

'CHARISMA' IS THE OLD Greek word for gift; so Charismatics are the gifted ones. The particular spiritual gifts most frequently associated with them are speaking in tongues, healing and exorcism, all of which are practised by Charismatic Christians but not significantly by the rest of the Church. Charismatics claim that they are being true to the original New Testament pattern of Christianity and that their worship and their lives have been greatly enriched by the fact that they have taken the promise of these gifts seriously.

If you visit a Church which practises Charismatic Renewal, you will be struck by the liveliness of the worship; often the atmosphere resembles that of the theatre as a sense of excitement and anticipation is evoked from the start. Though the particular theatre I have in mind is the Old Tyme Music Hall rather than the Royal Shakespeare. At Easter I went to St Michael le Belfry, a famous Charismatic Church in York, for an evening celebration of Holy Communion. Before the service began, the Church was already full of worshippers; though the atmosphere was not one usually connected with worship – not, at any rate, with the sort of reverent, discreet and sober worship to be found just across the road in York Minster. In fact the place was filled with rather noisy chat. Charismatics would not take this allegation for criticism. They would insist that the worship of God by his chosen people is a very lively business and that a congregation which knows the meaning of true fellowship and which is in anticipation of spiritual excitement to follow is bound to seem rather noisy.

At one minute after half-past six, one of the clergy came in and began the service by making one or two jokes which, I thought, received rather more laughter than they deserved. The next item concerned a dog which belonged to two members of the congregation – Pat and Dick – who were going away for a few days: would any other members of the congregation look after the dog, please? After this, the service took a more religious turn as the clergyman in the lounge suit announced that everyone was welcome to join in the service whatever his religious denomination. Next minute we were singing a hymn.

The service proceeded fairly normally for a while according to the Order called Rite A in the Alternative Service Book – except the clergyman would pronounce the prayers in a rather over-exhilarated tone, as if the words themselves lacked meaning and needed to be supplemented by an injection of enthusiasm. My comparison of St Michael's with the Music Hall seemed to be borne out by events, for it soon became clear that the parson who had begun the service with his smiling exuberance and shaggy dog stories was only the warmer-up. The Rector, respectably dressed in cassock and surplice, came on and preached a longish sermon about Christian responsibility in the community.

We reached the point in the service where the minister says, 'The peace of the Lord be always with you.' At this word of peace there was an outbreak of ersatz jubilation and raucous chumminess. People turned to face one another. They smiled, clasped hands, embraced and generally greeted one another in a very noisy style. As one brought up in a rather more staid Anglican tradition, I found this outburst acutely embarrassing, but, I am bound to admit, I seemed to be the only person in the Church who did find it so. The service proceeded in this high emotional fashion up to the words of consecration and the administration of the bread and wine. There was a rather restrained example of speaking in tongues, a sort of corporate humming as a background to the more specific babbling practised by one or two. This babbling and jabbering is entirely unintelligible except to the individual who is blessed with the gift of interpretation. The accusation of unintelligibility would not be taken as an insult; Charismatics prize the general unintelligibility of these utterances as a sign of special blessing; the voice of the Spirit is not constrained by the ordinary rules of grammar and syntax. He speaks only to the Elect.

Speaking in tongues is a phenomenon difficult to describe: it reminded me of nothing so much as *Stimmung*, the tantric choral work by Stockhausen. Those caught up in the experience seemed ecstatic. They resembled the entranced swaying crowds at pop-concerts; their movements were similar to those of moved football supporters singing 'You'll Never Walk Alone' – not a bad epitaph for a group of Christians who pride themselves on their togetherness. Whatever the real cause of speaking in tongues, there is no doubt that it is closely connected with many other forms of mild hysteria produced by the carefully generated emotional atmosphere typical among large gatherings met in a common cause and aroused by their leader's admonitions and much corporate singing and chanting. As such, it is no worse than the football crowd in its extra-time ecstasy or than the excitable adolescents at the pop-concert; but Charismatic Christians assert that when this behaviour is exhibited by their members it is a gift of the Holy Spirit of God and therefore an experience of the same type and importance as that recorded in the Acts of the Apostles when, '. . . they were all filled with the Holy Ghost, and began to speak with other tongues, as the Spirit gave them utterance'. I cannot prove that so called 'tongues' of the sort I have heard in Charismatic services are *not* a special visitation of the Holy Spirit, but it seems to me that the real problem here is not mine but the Charismatic Christian's: for if the behaviour which accompanies speaking in tongues can be exactly replicated by other groups whose intentions are far from praise and worship, it is not possible to maintain that any one incidence of this phenomenon is 'genuine' without admitting the authenticity of all other incidences. Sincerity of purpose is no criterion, since pop-concert-goers and football fans are also noted for their utter singlemindedness and devotion to their own idols. In short, if the experience itself is taken as proof of its own validity, then the similar experiences enjoyed by spectators at pop-concerts and at exciting football matches must be regarded as equally significant.

On the other hand, it must also be admitted that Church services generally are not renowned for their liveliness and that if Charismatic Christianity can bring some sense of natural joy and spontaneity to its worship then this is to be welcomed. The emotions, as well as the intellect, make up the whole man and as such they must form part of worship, of man's total response to God. It is perhaps true that traditional Anglicanism has been rather cerebral and fairly staid – though I myself do not find the hymns of Tallis, Byrd and Orlando Gibbons unexciting nor the prose of the Book of Common Prayer and the Authorised Version dull. But the emotional dangers of Charismatic exuberance leading to speaking in tongues is great, for when a person is in an ecstasy of excitement, his critical awareness is lessened and his susceptibility to all kinds of suggestion is increased. This is a fact known to all persuaders and demagogues. And there can be nothing but instability and erratic judgement coming from states of emotional abandonment. It does not matter so much when the subject is football or pop-concerts where the material is not connected to moral prescriptions about how one ought to live. But it matters very much in the field of religion where not only morality but also truth forms the subject of experience. An abandoned, uncritical and irrational state, a state of low resistance and high suggestibility is not one in which anyone ought to form the religious and moral principles to guide his life. We know that this happens in the mindless religious cults from which distraught parents will do anything to rescue their gullible offspring; nothing that happens in the repetitive chanting of 'tongues' persuades me that these dangers do not apply to Charismatic Christianity also.

Whatever the final verdict on Charismatic worship and speaking in tongues, there are other aspects of the renewal movement which are even more disconcerting. Principal among them is the phenomenon of so-called 'Divine Healing'. As a parish priest I have had direct experience of this and my experience has made me extremely wary of Charismatic claims to heal the sick. I will recount just one of many disturbing experiences.

I once visited a parishioner who was suffering from cancer of the liver. She was in a state of shock because she had just discovered that she had only three months left to live. At first she was sceptical; 'But I feel fine. The doctors must have made a mistake.' Then, as her symptoms worsened, she grew belligerent: 'Why me? What have I done to deserve this? It's not fair!' This woman had been a lifelong Anglican and church-goer of the conventional type; she did not have a strong faith in the supernatural aspects of her religion such as the life of the world to come. Finding herself, then, with only a few months of life left to her, she quite naturally became very dejected and depressed.

We met every week for an hour or so and gradually I found out more about her deepest joys and passions, chief among which were poetry and music. So we talked and we prayed all that autumn. Very slowly my friend's attitude changed from one of bewilderment and anger to that of quiet acceptance and thankfulness for a good life now drawing to its close. This was a great encouragement to me and it served to strengthen my own practical faith. Christmas that year seemed suffused with a deeper significance than any other I can remember.

Early in the New Year, after a gaily enthusiastic telephone call, three Charismatic Christians turned up at my friend's house to pray for her healing. They told her that it is *always* God's normal will to heal'. She should repent of all her sins and have faith in the redemptive work of the Lord Jesus Christ. He would heal her. There occurred some prayer and praising at the bedside and the Charismatics administered the Laying on of Hands and then they left. The effect upon my friend was startling. She became elated – you might almost say she was manic. She was convinced that her sins had been forgiven and that her healing was imminent. She even chastised me for not being able to bring about the dramatic change which had at last been wrought by the peripatetic healers.

One week later she took a turn for the worse. She realised that, after all, she would not be healed. She was going to die. Three weeks after that she did die, in a state of terror and confusion from which I could not retrieve her spirit; for now added to the ordinary tortures of terminal cancer there was guilt because she had not been able to summon enough faith to save her own life. She actually blamed herself, her own lack of trust, for the fact that the disease had got the better of her. The healers did not turn up at the funeral. They were not on hand to comfort my friend's sister and the other members of her family who had had insult added to the injury of their grief by the outrageous events of the New Year.

I wrote about this incident in *The Guardian* newspaper and in the next two weeks I received sixty letters from all over the country from people who had also had unfortunate experiences at the hands of the Charismatics. Some time later, a Charismatic Bishop called to see me and to suggest that my article in *The Guardian* was an exaggeration, a distortion of Charismatic practices. He went further: he described my writing as 'pure vitriol'. He tried to convince me that such misfortunes as befell my friend at the hands of the healers were merely 'excesses'; they were the sorts of occasional misfortunes which are bound to occur in a spirit-filled church where there is so much spiritual power in the air. But I told the Bishop that I did not consider this experience as in any way excessive; it is just the sort of thing we should regularly expect when emotions and hopes are irrationally raised in the face of imminent death. I questioned the meaning of the Charismatic doctrine that 'it is always God's normal will to heal'. How can this be true when so many people die in awful pain and distress and when we all die eventually anyway? He replied that 'death itself can be a kind of healing'. In that case why go through the horrific pantomime of the promise of physical healing and the attempt to bring this about by the Laying on of Hands and a lot of emotional overkill when the great healing of death itself will soon be on the way?

The Bishop said that Christ had commanded his followers to preach and heal and that Charismatic Christians had rediscovered this command and were carrying it out. So the justification of their activities was the commandment of Christ. They saw their faith confirmed in the many healings which, they alleged, took place every day. But, as always in cults of irrationality, the logical point is missed or else deliberately ignored. For if *their* healings are taken to be a validation of their doctrines about God and Christ, then the healings wrought by other groups – Spiritualists or Voodoo practitioners for instance – must also be regarded as validations of their doctrines. However, Charismatics wink at mere logic which they regard as only an example of being clever, of the misguided wisdom of this world. They themselves believe they have access to a higher way than logic; through their fundamentalist interpretation of Scripture they claim a hot-line to the counsels of God. And, as with all forms of sectarian demagogy and ideological extremism, the real and down to earth concerns of mortals are always subordinated to dogma and doctrinal purity. In the end it does not matter how much evidence or argument anyone adduces against the doctrines of Charismatic Christianity, they will not shift their opinions because they believe that these opinions – however illogical and inconsistent and to whatever cost in terms of personal human distress – are guaranteed by God. Indeed, they see any and all criticism as a sign that they are on the right lines. Did God not say that they were to expect persecution? Very well, all criticism is construed as persecution and blasphemy and all who challenge the truth of the Charismatic doctrines are guilty of sin against the Holy Spirit. It is the old dodge approved by all religious and political chauvinists and power hungry paranoiacs: the quick route to infallibility by the claim that God is on our side.

There was another incident, even more distressing, connected with the Charismatics' doctrine of exorcism. I was teaching my

Evening Class in York when a middle-aged man burst in. He was in a state of extreme anxiety, even panic. It turned out that he had only recently moved into the area and he had looked for a Church to which, as a conventional Christian, he might attach himself. The Anglican Church which he found suggested that he might like to go along to one of their mid-week Prayer Groups. In due course he found a Prayer Group in the sitting room of an ordinary suburban semi. There were about a dozen people present, some in armchairs, others sitting on cushions on the floor. There were a few choruses to guitar accompaniment and then the main matter of the meeting began: it was a discussion and Bible reading about the nature of evil and the person of the Devil. My friend, when asked for his opinion, said that while he did believe that there was much appalling evil in the world he did not believe in a personal Devil – the Devil as an individual being in his own right.

The reaction of the Charismatics was swift and devastating. They reasoned that, since they themselves were quite certain that there is a real, personal Devil (is he not to be found in the Bible?), then anyone who denied his existence must be in league with the Devil – a sort of Satanic fifth columnist come to disturb the faith of the Group. My friend was guilty of such a denial. The remedy was simple and straightforward; they performed an impromptu exorcism. The recipient of this ministration was utterly distressed and disorientated. What is an ordinary intelligent twentieth-century man to conclude when he goes along out of interest to an Anglican Prayer Group only to find that, within three quarters of an hour, he is having the Devil cast out of him? The result was a short stay in a mental hospital, further attendance at a psychiatrist's clinic and the prescription of tranquillisers. When I last saw him – a whole year after this event – he was at last beginning to make some movement towards recovery.

I related this incident in the *Church Times* but I was met only with the same abuse and castigation as I had encountered after my recollection of the 'healing' episode. It is no use challenging the Charismatics with these real life tragedies; they are certain that they are God's front line troops against the supernatural forces of evil in which there are bound to be occasional casualties – the 'excesses' of which the Bishop spoke. Their minds are so disturbed by their own disorienting dogma that they cannot see the obvious: that it is they themselves, their beliefs and practices which are responsible for these catastrophes.

Underlying Charismatic practices is a theology of a particularly repressed sort; all their doings must be seen in the light – if 'light' is the appropriate word – of what they believe. For underneath the cheerful singing, the warm handshakes and the liturgical embraces lies a literal theology of damnation. God made man and man became disobedient. God sent his own Son, Jesus Christ to die on the cross to save man from the consequences of his sins. Those who believe in Christ – in the jargon, 'accept him as their own personal Saviour' – will, when they die, go to heaven and live forever with God; those who do not so receive Christ and the Charismatics' interpretation of Christ's work will go to everlasting punishment in the fires of hell. One of the most famous of all the Charismatic leaders, Canon David Watson, wrote:

> Most people, by being the centre of reference for their lives, are saying in effect to Christ 'Depart from me. I want you to leave me alone. I don't want you to interfere with my life. I want to be king of my own castle. Therefore depart from me.' If a person says that now, and goes on saying that, is it unfair that Christ should say to that person on the Day of Judgement: 'Depart from me'? It was surely the man's own fault.
>
> (DAVID WATSON *My God Is Real*, P. 35, FALCON, 1974)

This is the Gospel then, the good news specially vouchsafed to the Charismatics and guaranteed to be beyond criticism. But this is not the Christian Gospel; it is a caricature of the Gospel. Note those words 'king of my own castle' and the appeal to fairness as if not only the battle of Waterloo but Armageddon itself is fought on the playing fields of an English public school. There is more to the eternal Gospel than this crude, literalistic vengefulness. Even I in all my imperfection – and, I suspect, even David Watson in his – would not send another human being to endless torment no matter what he had done. How much less would Christ do such a thing!

To this summary scheme of redemption, the Charismatics add and import the whole mythology of the ancient middle east without criticism, without reinterpretation, without understanding. So the ordinary world of the park and the garden and the journey to work is peopled by demons of every kind. The most trivial event is taken to be evidence of demonic activity; if a Charismatic misses his bus on the way to a Prayer Meeting it is likely to be construed as the Devil's work. I am not exaggerating. I am not even joking. I know Anglican Charismatics of the most impeccably bourgeois connections and appearance who pray for a parking space; I have been in the car with them as they did it. These attitudes, as any psychiatrist will testify, are the symptoms of psychotic dissociation.

The superstitious supernaturalism of Charismatic doctrine would not be so worrying if it did not carry with it emotional and moral consequences of an immensely destructive kind. The preaching plays upon natural human feelings of guilt and inadequacy. It defines and accuses men and women as worthless until they have accepted Charismatic attitudes and beliefs. In other words it creates a false-consciousness of guilt and then goes on to produce a quite spurious concept of redemption. The whole experience is conducted in a highly-charged emotional atmosphere in which the critical faculties are diminished and despised. Emotional attention is directed on to the hearers' sense of inadequacy and, not infrequently and by implication, on to the prevailing sense of sexual guilt – among adolescents this is, of course, easily identified in terms of masturbation and heavy petting.

This whole mistaken spirituality and psychology thus damages in two ways: first it caricatures the real nature of sin and secondly it distracts our attention from the only real method of making progress in the spiritual life, that is by genuine self-knowledge. All that supposed identification of demons active in the world is nothing other than a psychological projection of the dark side of the personality in a misguided attempt to be rid of it. It is only by facing our nature as it really is, as we really are, that we begin to make honest progress in our spiritual life, psychological development or whatever description you choose for the gradual process of maturing. Such progress does not come through a spurious identification of the offences against bourgeois niceness which make up the revivalist's notion of sinfulness.

If the Charismatic Movement is really as facile and as spurious as I have suggested, it might reasonably be enquired as to exactly how it generates its appeal. The answers are complex. First, it attracts by its immediate image of liveliness; young people are apt to contrast it favourably with the rather staid old C. of E. The Charismatics make much of what they call 'fellowship' and 'sharing' – concepts which they derive from the New Testament experience of 'koinonia'. Young people, perhaps away from home for the first time at college or university, often find in Charismatic fellowship an antidote to loneliness. It is the old appeal to 'come and join us' and 'safety in numbers'. Moreover, the pattern of Charismatic worship is not radically dissimilar from the rest of the pop-culture which the young these days imbibe through the mass-media. There is the pop-chorus, there is the liturgical guitar; the whole format is like Bruce Forsyth's *Generation Game* transferred to the nave and the chancel. This liveliness is itself seen as a mark of the Holy Spirit. But there are those who think that the pale pastiche of *Godspell* and *Jesus Christ Superstar* musical entertainment is rather more banal than inspired when set beside J. S. Bach or even Samuel Wesley. And so, from the aesthetic point of view, the question arises of why, if Charismatic worship is meant to represent the Holy Spirit's inspiration, is it all so third rate.

Secondly, the renewal movement attracts people because it claims to offer a simple certainty, a scheme of spiritual progress that resembles painting by numbers. Literalism and Fundamentalism present complex religious ideas in an easily digestible but caricature form. It is well known that human beings, given the choice between two courses of action, one of which requires the effort of a long slow grind and the other requires nothing more than the recital of a brisk formula, will be tempted to take the easy way out every time. The Charismatic leader, unlike say the teacher of English Literature or Mathematics whom young people also meet at the university, offers a simple message. This message does not demand of the recipient hours of intellectual spadework before he begins to make progress; on the contrary, the light shines instantly. In fact, the Charismatic preacher will often misapply such biblical texts as 'God confuses the wisdom of the wise' in order deliberately to disparage criticism and mental effort. Such an approach will hardly fall on stony ground with a particular sort of student who finds himself oppressed by the demands of his academic studies.

In short, Charismatic Christianity appeals because it offers certainty and togetherness, the comforts of sectarianism against the naughty world. Its adherents therefore frequently turn out to be those who feel uncertain, insecure, inadequate and alone. These are often, as we have noticed, the young, teenagers and college students; but they also include a high proportion of lonely and distressed people in middle-life, the widowed and the divorced. I have seen cases in which divorce has been the result of Charismatic involvement by one partner in a marriage. Perhaps the wife becomes attached to a Charismatic Church; she encourages her husband to attend as well; he does not wish to do so. Well, any organisation whose members are quite capable of defining a non-believer in the

Personal Devil as possessed are also capable of persuading a wife and mother that her husband belongs to the synagogue of Satan if he will not join their company. After all, they have only to wax fundamentalist on the text 'If any man come to me, and hate not his father, and his mother, and wife, and children, and brethren, and sisters, yea, and his own life also, he cannot be my disciple' (Luke 14:26) – and the job is done. I have seen it happen.

Thirdly, the Charismatic Movement is popular with the hierarchy of the Church – or at least with a section of it – because it brings in the young people, it builds up the congregations. It takes moral courage to denounce something that is thriving especially where money and influence are involved. Besides, it all looks so nice on the surface – the songs, the dancing, the clean-cut middle class kids ('Such a change from those awful Punks!') with their guitars and their psychobabble. The average Bishop is not likely to become much involved with Charismatic Revivalism (unless he wants to become involved) until a healing or an exorcism goes wrong. And then he will be persuaded that such a misfortune is an aberration, an excess.

Finally, it is depressing to notice that few who become deeply involved with Charismatic Christianity ever succeed in escaping its influence. This is because of its strong emotional appeal and, of course, its definition of all criticism as the work of the Devil. In this respect, it resembles any other eruption of fanatical sectarianism and the widespread cults of unreason. There will be a lot more damage caused to human personalities before the image of Charismatic Christianity begins, like all other manifestations of trendiness, to pall. Perhaps on that day, those who out of pastoral concern and that priestly duty which they owe to the public at large dare to speak against Charismatical vapours will no longer be castigated as 'negative critics' by a gullible hierarchy at last coming to see where illusion fades and honest, unspectacular, workmanlike Christianity begins.

EIGHT

CHRISTIAN MORALITY AND THE CHURCH OF ENGLAND

O. RAYMOND JOHNSTON

I

MORALITY IS NOT about what men and women do; it is about what they ought to do. This essay therefore begins with a brief look at the nature of morality in general, and of the Christian moral ideal in particular. The second section begins to set the discussion in a contemporary context, but opens with a quick historical glance at our traditional Christian morality in Britain, and at some of the changes it has undergone; we note the recent shift of interest from individual morals to social morality, and the way in which the Church of England has followed the trend. The third section indicates how the Church of England has tried to grapple with these broader issues in recent years, and introduces some criticism of our emphases and priorities. The fourth section deals with post-war developments in individual morality in the nation as a whole, and the responses of the Church of England. Considerations of space preclude the use of many examples, but this essay is intended to provide a framework in which readers can further reflect on the way in which society and church are moving, and a measuring rod by which the performance of the Church of England can be measured.

Moral debate and moral judgements are part of human existence. Only homo sapiens has an 'ought' dimension to his thinking and his discourse. Religious awareness too is uniquely human. Christians move easily in their thinking from religion to virtue and back again; faith and morals inter-penetrate in Christian experience. God commands certain types of behaviour, and Jesus is Example as well as Saviour. The godly man sees the good more clearly and strives after it more energetically. But even without a religious frame of reference, the mid-twentieth century philosopher wrestles unceasingly with the close analysis of the language of duty, the world of obligation, the nature of goodness, the relation of 'is' and 'ought'. Whether we think of the plain man faced with an agonising personal decision, or of the philosopher trying to make sense of the slippery concepts of ethical discussion, the conclusion is the same. Morality – the principle of right conduct – is indissoluble. Morality is a fundamental constituent of our humanity.

Moral assessments appear to be judgements of behaviour which refer to rules or broad principles about what is right and what is wrong. There is more to morality than bare rules, but rules there are. Moral excellence can be discerned or demonstrated by the fact that an outstanding achievement conforms to the standard, or approaches nearer to such conformity than the majority of men have been able to attain. Moral leaders or moral authorities are those who enunciate the principles most clearly, or most cogently, or with renewed insight and fervour or who help to sharpen the moral awareness of those who follow them, and who succeed in living accordingly, to the ideals or rules themselves, sometimes to an unrivalled degree. The good life that is set before the Christian in the New Testament is seen in different terms by different Biblical writers – sometimes as rules, sometimes as inner dispositions or attitudes (virtues), sometimes as a consistent direction of the believer's life godward, ever conscious of existence as an earthly pilgrimage. Correct observance of behavioural rules does not constitute the whole of Christian morality; if regarded as such it can lead a man into hypocrisy and Pharisaic harshness. But neither is it adequate to call Christian morality no more than a cluster of particular attitudes to God, neighbours, the material world etc. There are specific demands which give cash value to the desired attitudes or qualities of character – to the call for love or justice, for example. We shall return to some of these later. Such general problems were explored at some depth, if rather untidily, in the illuminating collection of essays *Christian Ethics and Contemporary Philosophy* (SCM 1966).

From what has been said above it must be clear that the writer believes that there is a distinct and unmistakable Christian morality – a set of principles and a vision of goodness which are uniquely bound up with the emergence of the Christian church. This morality was enjoined upon the community of believers in the first century by the Man they worshipped as God manifest in the flesh. Thereafter it was taught by His accredited representatives, the Apostles, whose teaching has been adequately recorded, by Divine providence, in the Scriptures of the New Testament.

Building upon (and often assuming without stating) the ethical precepts of the Old Testament, Jesus applied them more deeply than contemporary teachers, pressed them home until they hurt, and then announced that only those who saw themselves as inadequate transgressors of the Divine Law could enter His Kingdom. But those who fell to their knees in true repentance, despairing of their own efforts, were by the mercy of God 'justified'. Pardon for transgressors is the greatest gift of grace. Indeed, it was to 'seek and to save the lost', to give 'his life a ransom for many' that Jesus came. God so loved the world that He sent His Son to die and rise again for our justification, as the Apostle Paul was never tired of reminding his readers. The justified sinner lived a new and distinctive life, obeying God from sheer gratitude because he had been forgiven for Christ's sake and freed from the slavery of sin. The Christian was called joyfully to obey all the moral demands of Old and New Testament in terms of outward behaviour. If the inner reluctance or coldness of his heart often gave him pause, the believer was made conscious thereby of his need for daily repentance and daily forgiveness. He hungered and thirsted after righteousness. He was *simul justus et peccator* – righteous yet a sinner at the same time, as Luther often explained.

In the light of the story of salvation completed at the Cross and the empty tomb and of the future return of Christ in glory, the first Christians lived their lives. These great events still form the deep driving force in Christian morality. The new energy within the child of God ('born again' as he is so often described in the New Testament) shows itself in a recognisable pattern of living. The joyful response of Christian obedience to the Gospel weans a man or woman from certain characteristic deeds and dispositions, often called 'the world'. There may be more than seven deadly sins, but the mediaeval array of vices is pretty comprehensive and fits in well with the New Testament lists of the 'works of the flesh' which Christians are urged to steer clear of. Likewise the virtues. There was a radical difference between the lives Christians were called to live and the life tolerated or praised in official Judaism on the one hand, or in the pagan world of the first century on the other. The combination of joy, peace and certainty with energetic striving, self-discipline and daily repentance is unique.

Any standard work on Christian ethics will take the reader further into this matter. But there is a balancing truth to be mentioned also. The Christian conception of the good life is not totally fresh. It did not burst upon the first century world newly minted, as some strange new vision of human fulfilment. It corresponded to much that the best thinkers of the pagan world dimly apprehended, so much so that it was once fashionable theology to assert that St Paul was really only a kind of highly polished Stoic! There are analogies with the precepts of moral teachers from many different continents and in many different centuries, as C. S. Lewis pointed out first in his brilliant essay 'The Poison of Subjectivism' (1943) and then later the same year in his Riddell Lectures *The Abolition of Man*. Lewis showed how 'the same indispensable platitudes will meet us in culture after culture' ('On Ethics' in *Christian Reflections* p. 55); these he called 'the primary platitudes of practical reason' (ibid. p. 78). The Christian maintains that he would expect men everywhere to recognise the desirability of the sort of life Jesus lived, and which He taught his followers to adopt. It is the life enjoined upon us by a loving Creator for our own good, because he knows how we can most happily function and develop in the world he has made. Mankind being constituted in His image, we have an innate response to His commands; our consciences echo what He requires. Through human sin, this response since the Fall has been imperfect. We only see our way dimly by conscience alone, and our pride and selfishness often cause us wilfully to misinterpret the voice of conscience and the demands of practical reason. But in Christ the vision of goodness is dazzlingly renewed, the rules of rightness written again in characters none can mistake.

The outlines of Biblical morality are clear. Christian morality simply clarifies what we suspected was true all the time. The adult convert to the faith in our own increasingly pagan age often stresses this ancient familiarity. The demands made upon him now as a believer, though dauntingly comprehensive and searching, are not alien. They are what he had been groping for in his better moments for as long as he can remember.

II

The setting for our consideration of Christian morality is, however, the Church of England, and the Church of England at a particular juncture. The writer has neither the space nor the competence to trace the Church of England's official voices and documents down the centuries in the light of the given principles of the New Testament ethics.

There have been periods of moral decay and ethical stagnation. There have also been eras of great moral development, as in the burst of creative energy under the first Elizabeth, when William Perkins established the rich vein of Anglican casuistry based firmly upon Scripture. This was made possible only after the more famous Reformers had purified Anglican theology from the accretions of centuries which so obscured the Gospel. Perkins and Ames started a tradition which lasted until well into the seventeenth century, and whose peak may well be seen in Baxter's *Christian Directory*. In the succeeding century, optimistic views of human nature led to neglect of both the vibrant New Testament Gospel and the demands of Apostolic morality; it was the Evangelical Revival which returned the churches to their foundation documents in more ways than one.

In the nineteenth century, the impact of the Oxford Movement led naturally to an increased study of the early fathers and the unbroken tradition of Roman moral theology. The reintroduction of private auricular confession by the Tractarians, together with certain Romanising tendencies, introduced some Anglican clergy to the tradition of Roman casuistry.

'Casuistry' is to many a dirty word; in fact it simply means the determining of particular 'cases' (problems) of conscience or conduct in the light of Christian principles. It has always been needed. During and after the Reformation casuistry gained a bad name, since some of its Roman practitioners were adept at avoiding the plain meaning of divine demands and standing apostolic morality on its head. Rightly used however, the art of the casuist does not undermine, but increases our appreciation of the riches and wisdom of God's revelation. Baxter's work is an outstanding example.

In the nineteenth century, the impact of evangelicalism in all denominations had a profound social impact. It was the evangelical apprehension of the demands of Christian morality which lay behind the freeing of the slaves (Wilberforce), the amelioration of the factory conditions and child labour (Shaftesbury), the obtaining of Sunday as a day of rest for most workers, the reform of the prisons (Fry), the founding of what has become the probation service and much else. The suppression of child prostitution, blasphemous language, swearing, obscene publications, drunkenness and other lewdness which disfigured the eighteenth-century life were also targets of the Anglican evangelicals in the last century. Wilberforce, it should be remembered, had two aims: 'the suppression of the slave trade and the reformation of manners'. And 'manners' meant morals.

The twentieth century has seen a shift of emphasis. The cluster of areas popularly considered as the principal field of moral discussion and action is altered. Briefly put, this shift has been away from matters of personal decision, problems which face all or most people as individuals in the course of their ordinary lives, to broader issues of social concern where decisions and policies made by leaders, governments and other groups are examined.

This shift is related to the positivist views of man and society which began with the eighteenth-century Enlightenment, and the heady optimism of the rationalist thinkers before, during and after the French Revolution. Science, for them, was about to banish error and superstition, reason would break the immemorial chains of habit and despotism, so that humanity would at last begin to construct the perfect society where all men would be free and fulfilled; the good of each mean would necessarily be consistent with the good of the whole community.

The heir to these currents of thought was Karl Marx. Accepting a dogmatic materialism, a fixed (and forced) view of the 'key' to history in economic inequality and ownership, playing upon class antagonism and inequalities, Marxism has increasingly taken the stage in our own century. Despite its rejection of religion (a mere metaphysical anaesthetic to buttress the status quo in unscientific societies) and of all moral absolutes (the good is merely that which advances the revolution, or the hegemony of the disinherited urban proletariat), Marxism is fiercely moral in its constant stress on injustice and the wrongness of exploitation. Marx and his followers thunder like Old Testament prophets against capitalist abuses. They champion the oppressed (economically) with a certainty that is strangely at odds with their own theory of the relativity of all moralities and their derivation from economic conditions. But, despite philosophical incoherence and a record of cruelty wherever Marxist regimes have been in power (world deaths through

Communism are reckoned conservatively at 143 million since 1917 according to Professor Brian Griffiths in *Morality in the Market Place* Hodder, 1982, p. 62), the secular, egalitarian and essentially economics-orientated mind-set of Marxism has become incredibly pervasive, even among thinkers and writers who would repudiate dogmatic adherence to Marxist or Communist theory. The rise of sociology, and in particular the fluid but useful shorthand concept of social class, has seemed to open up new areas of seminal thinking about societies past and present, and to offer an analytical tool of great power to 'explain' historical change. Since World War II, the spread of the Marxist cast of mind has meant a quite new emphasis on what might be called macro-moral judgements. Nations and states are judged as good or bad, corrupt or progressive, enlightened or wicked in more dogmatic and assured tones. Within nations, whole classes of people are more easily stereotyped, praised or blamed. We all develop noses for sniffing out 'vested interests'. There is much talk of oppressed minorities (women, blacks, homosexuals, unmarried mothers, prostitutes etc.). Correspondingly, certain 'rights' are said to exist for everybody, or for certain classes of person, and the fire of righteous indignation is fuelled by the supposed injustice when the various groups are being (it is asserted) denied these 'rights'.

In addition to the historic rights asserted at the times of the French Revolution and the American Revolution – life (personal security), liberty (choice of employment, freedom from arbitrary arrest etc.), property, association, voting for a representative government, publication, new rights are now asserted – privacy (especially from police surveillance and computerised data recording), free public education, free public medical care, the right to work, the right to a living wage, etc. It is beyond the scope of this short essay to list them all or to evaluate them all. What stands out is the tendency to moralise almost every social issue in a secular sort of way ('monstrous', 'obscene', 'oppressive', 'exploitation', etc. are the sort of words used, each with a strong moral overtone). Nuclear warfare is the latest big issue in the macro-moral field.

The list of issues for moral indignation today omits precisely those items which our grandfathers would have regarded as 'moral questions'. These are the areas where each man *does* decide for himself alone, as distinct from those decisions made by his government or his international alliance (e.g. NATO) or his trade union or his professional body or his district council, etc. Though the dictionary often mentions sexual morality as one particular and narrow meaning of the word 'morality', and though it is not the writer's conviction that this restricted sense is justified, the usage itself points to the whole area of what might be called micro-morals. It underscores the fact that previous generations have thought of morals as largely those principles which help Everyman to discern the good life for himself in the spheres where his decision counted, and his life and that of his immediate neighbours and relations were affected. The modern trend has been to regard these matters as secondary at best, or as not a proper subject for moral discussion or moral guidance at all. They are, it is said, matters of individual conscience – by which is meant very often simply individual preference. This approach removes them from the sphere of moral judgement altogether – they become matters of mere taste, like the fact that I prefer tea rather than coffee or Beethoven rather than Bach.

Thus in Parliament, certain issues are not party matters. They are left to MP's to vote for as matters of individual conscience to be determined by what is called – perhaps significantly – 'a free vote'. It is bad form to raise them too often, and the government cannot, of course, be expected to grant them much parliamentary time. They concern (it is alleged) only what a man does with his private life, and as such are no business of the state. They are, it is said, insignificant beside such great concerns such as employment, taxation, foreign policy, economics or defence. The conclusion is irresistible – they are not really very important. Ultimately, they do not matter.

The Church of England is the Church of the nation. She is by law established and there are dozens of ways, both obvious and hidden, in which her life is woven in with that of the total community in which she exists. It would be surprising if she had not moved in the same direction as the rest of society (in particular the mass media) and become convinced that the real moral issues are the macro-moral questions. By contrast the micro-moral items from traditional lists are contentious, divisive issues, better left to private guidance and interpersonal discussions rather than for Church Commissions, strong sermons, bold statements by Archbishops and weighty episcopal pronouncements.

It is not necessary to go the whole way with the Rev. Dr Edward Norman in his famous Reith Lectures (subsequently published as 'Christianity and the World Order', OUP, 1978) to see how far the Church of England has accommodated herself to the priorities of secular society. In one sense this is not only to be expected; it is to be praised. For anything that concerns and puzzles large numbers of our fellow-citizens must engage the attention of serious Christians. The Church has no business to refuse to consider *whether* the law of God and the Gospel shed any light on current preoccupations. But the agenda for Christian moral witness is not to be set by the world. This must be insisted upon.

When it comes to items like what our government should do about South Africa, or about unemployment in the United Kingdom, or about the economics of international trade, either the Christian tradition has no unambiguous moral answer, or (more usually) there are indeed guiding principles of morality clearly found in Scripture (more often the Old Testament), but these are of the utmost generality. Quite often bishops and church committees know far too little of the details of a contemporary problem to know just where or how to apply the principles. Sometimes, rightly, we call a halt after simply re-asserting the principle, in the hope that those more immediately concerned with the problem situation will hear us and work and pray for its right application. At other times however, the church may injudiciously lay down the law. We then make unnecessary enemies at best; at worst we end up months or years later looking stupid because our preliminary knowledge was defective or our analysis of the situation faulty for some other reason; time shows our intervention – whether in praise or blame – to have been ill-timed, or intemperate or even mischievous. To enter these caveats is not to say that the Church of England has always been mistaken in devoting resources of time, money, committees and expertise to these macro-moral questions. It is more a matter of proportion and priorities. In some of these fields the wisdom of experts outside the Church surpasses anything the Church of England can produce. On occasions matters are so complex that it is not immediately clear which Christian moral insights, if any, are to be applied to the problem under review. Let it be said again: the world's moralised agenda ought never to become the Church's agenda of moral priorities for work, discussion and pronouncement. But that is not to say that we ought never to accept the challenge of the wider social agenda as an induction that we ought to pay some heed to a particular issue. Caution is needed. That is the warning that needs to be given.

III

For guidance on social morality, the Christian ought naturally to turn to the Old Testament. Though it is of course impossible to make immediate contemporary application of the framework given by God to a national community in a pastoral age in the Near East three millennia ago, there are reasons why the Old Testament is obligatory reading for those seeking an outline of Christian ideals. Firstly, Jesus took the moral precepts of the Old Testament with utter seriousness. He stressed that He had not come to destroy them. Secondly, the dangers and blessings of living in a community are in many respects the same throughout history; the way man exploits man has not changed much in essence, only in degree, over the centuries. Thirdly, actual study of the Old Testament law reveals surprising topicality to a host of twentieth-century problems – work and leisure, punishment and restitution, care for the aged, for the alien resident, for animals, for plants and the land, for the due process of law and justice in the courts, hostility to accumulated riches and the holding down of wage levels, and so on. In their different ways both the law and the prophets reveal a surprising number of moral principles, which have relevance to any society. It is certainly the duty of the Church of England to remind the nation of these enduring guidelines.

A glance at the index of debates in the General Synod of the Church of England during the most recent completed five year period shows the range of topics which the central bodies of the Church have tried to tackle (1975–1980). The Board for Social Responsibility presented reports on the following subjects: defence and disarmament, human rights, Chile, South Africa, the Irish problem, humanity and sexuality, homosexual relationships, euthanasia, Britain as a multi-racial society, prisons and prisoners, the economic crisis, unemployment and world development, marriage and divorce. In addition there were debates on under-developed countries, Soviet imperialism, Namibia, sexual ethics, the 1967 Abortion Act, the cost of funerals, the death grant, child benefit, a special fund for race relations, pluralism, capital punishment, the police, blasphemy in broadcasting, rural housing, the closed shop and animal welfare year.

While the range of topics is commendably wide, indicating a breadth of outlook and a willingness to engage in almost every topic emerging at the top of the secular agenda, three critical comments might be made. The first is that with its limited time and resources, the central bodies of the organised church are trying to do far too much. In some ways it is amazing that its reports and debates, mostly the work of gifted amateurs, reach the standard they do. The second comment would be that there is a disturbing similarity of approach in these documents and debates, with a tendency to reach quite predictable, eminently 'progressive' conclusions on most topics. Many churchmen find the reports and the discussion insufficiently aware that the Christian is called to view all temporal events and responsibilities in the light of eternity, and that the principal task laid upon the church is to preach the Gospel to all mankind – a Gospel demanding a response of repentance for the forgiveness of sins and faith in Christ as the only Saviour, a message concerned with heaven and hell. The transcendental reference is missing in these discussions. They therefore tend towards a self-righteous moral attitude, a worldly certainty, lacking spiritual awareness. Thirdly, underlying our second comment, we note the tendency to sit loose to the plain teaching of Scripture. Sometimes where Scripture is silent, there seems a desperate need for the church to chime in authoritatively with the views of the *Guardian*-reading intellectuals of the period. Christian uncertainty at these points might have been a wiser stance. At other times, when there *is* Scriptural material which is relevant, it is only cursorily examined and on some occasions actually ignored entirely.

IV

When we turn to the field of what we have called micro-morals, we find the area of the Church of England's greatest failure. Too little has been said, and what has been said has either been too late or even painfully misguided. Yet the need for clear counsel was never greater – both for ordinary church people and for the nation as a whole. Never since the early eighteenth century has the community been in greater need of Christian standards of personal morality. The need and the church's failure must be seen in the light of four considerations.

The first is the acceleration of the process called secularisation, though readers should be warned that the term is more a description than an explanation. It denotes the drifting (or the forcing) of religious considerations to the margins of individual decision-making and public discussion. God is no longer mentioned, rewards and punishments in the next life no longer relevant to chosen good or evil in this life. Increasingly the church is ignored as even a possible repository of divine wisdom which men ignore at their peril. The assumption is that we are on our own and we make up our own morals as we go along. As one Anglican writer has put it: 'Since the Second World War ended, the good life for man has been under constant discussion in terms of permissive Western secularism: in terms, that is, of the assumptions that self-exploration and self-discovery is our prime task, and any means to that end which does not violate others' freedom or destroy their well-being should be thought allowable, and that toleration of deviant behaviour should be practised up to the limit as being both a civilised virtue and a universal duty.' (J. I. Packer in the Preface to *Law, Morality and the Bible* (IVP, 1978), a most useful symposium which deserves to be better known; all the writers are Anglicans).

The second aspect is the vastly increased vulnerability to manipulation of the modern citizen, thanks to the constant exposure of almost every member of the community to the impact of mass media – newspapers, advertisements, magazines, radio and television. Culture is homogenised, individualism becomes a more difficult option, Christian thinking almost unheard of. Morality, if acknowledged at all, is materialistic and utilitarian. The models of a desirable life-style are sports people, entertainers, actors and actresses and media figures. In these circumstances, Christian morality is either presented as the path of distant unattainable and incomprehensible sainthood (Mother Theresa), or as something slightly comic (Lord Longford, Mrs Whitehouse).

The third fact is the actual social damage resulting from the trends noted above. The worst side of permissiveness is seen in its effects on those who have taken its tenets to be the only option, or the most fashionable option. Individual standards of conduct slid disastrously downwards as the apparent moral certainties of earlier generations melted away during the 1960s. The personal virtues of sobriety, thrift, truthfulness in speech, financial integrity, diligence at work, abstention from arbitrary violence, respect for the property of others (or of the community), acceptance of the rule of law, public decency, chastity and family loyalties (fidelity and obedience) – all these were widely ignored and frequently sneered at during the 'swinging sixties'. Yet these ideals – prosaic or even Victorian as some of them may sound when listed in this way – are the hidden foundation of our fragile and precious democratic way of life. They constitute the bedrock of civilised living. This cluster of values offers the only possible basis for a community which wishes to be both orderly and humane. Two other states of society are possible. If we abandon civic virtue and do nothing else the most likely result is anarchy. The other option is the police state – a population held to conformity by terror. The Church should have been reminding the nation that the bonds of society in a democracy are the intangible attitudes of respect, those individual values and ideals formerly taught in home and school. We first learned them from the messengers of Christ. The alternatives to personal and neighbourly goodness are seen in present day Uganda and the Soviet Union. There are no *civilised* alternatives to Christian morality.

Every index of moral deviance and disintegration in personal life now shows the same depressing downward trend – crimes of violence, financial malpractice, theft, rape, divorce, alcoholism, promiscuity, sexually transmitted diseases, illegitimacy, abortion, homosexual activities. Each of these events can mean the shattering of a family or the disintegration of a personality, a scarred heart, a torn life.

The fourth factor in the situation is the one which highlights the failure of the Church of England. This factor is not new but enduring. It is the blazing clarity of what God demands of men and women in the field of personal morality. On these matters the Bible speaks with one voice from Genesis to Revelation. There is a continuous and consistent picture of the good and godly life. At its very heart lies the love of God – our Creator, gracious sustainer and above all Redeemer. Flowing from this is our love of God's Word – the Scriptures he has given to guide this people; in the Old Testament it was rejoicing in the law (see Psalm 119), in the New Testament it was a desire to know more of the Gospel, to be fed by the 'milk of the Word', to be nourished by all the Old Testament Scriptures and to continue to be strengthened by the Apostle's doctrine. Love of God means we love and keep his Word – read it and obey it. The Church exists to proclaim a Biblical gospel and to teach a Biblical pattern of living.

Now in the field of what we have called micro-morals, the pattern set for us by our loving God has been abundantly clear since Israel became a nation. Speech must be truthful and controlled; marriage involves exclusive lifelong fidelity for both partners, and is the place (the only place) where sexual union is meant to be enjoyed; children obey parents; families are outward looking in their support for elderly relatives and sojourners as they are able; human life is a trust from God and can only be deliberately ended under certain strictly defined circumstances; the property of others is to be respected; any individual in genuine need whose path crosses mine I am bound to help, if I can.

Such are the practical consequences of following Christ. Injunctions to this life lie scattered in profusion across the New Testament. The main features of this ideal cannot be mistaken.

In the 1960s there arose the so-called 'new morality', an attempt to invest the essentially negative and destructive character of 'do-it-yourself morals' with the dignity of a title which sounded fresh, exciting and positive. It was of course a parasitic system, living off the great moral injunctions of the orthodox Christian system which it denied. It was brilliantly described and pungently criticised by Lunn and Lean in their two books *The New Morality* and *The Cult of Softness* (Blandford 1964 and 1965) though sadly this pair of hard-hitting paperbacks did little to reverse the trend. Too many clerical figures desired to be 'progressive' in doctrine and morals, too many media people lived off their denials and re-formulations. In his useful background study *The Permissive Society* (Cassell, 1971) publisher and MP John Selwyn Gummer found himself obliged to entitle his ninth chapter 'Meanwhile, where was the Church?' At the centre of the controversy was – and is – the Christian family ethic.

In an increasingly pagan society, Christians find themselves in a position which is more reminiscent of their predecessors in the first-century Roman Empire. Then, as now, Christians are – or should be – distinguished by their level of consecrated obedience to Christ in the matter of sexual behaviour. 'Paul lays special emphasis on this particular aspect of practical holiness because it was in the sphere of relations between the sexes that even the highest pagan ethic of the time fell short of the Jewish and Christian standard. Fornication was widely regarded in the Graeco-Roman world as almost on the same level of ethical indifference as food and drink' (F. F. Bruce in *The New Bible Commentary Revised*, 1970, p. 1158).

The importance of this field of human experience and moral decision is not asserted here simply because it provides the most marked contrast between pagan and Christian, nor because it has been the clearest case of churchmen misleading many of their own flock and much of the wider community in the last two decades (though both are true, in the writer's judgement). It is also, and most importantly, because this is an area of human experience and human fulfilment open to everyone. Nobody is outside the field of family life (it took a man and a woman to make each of us!), no one is without the potential for friendships with others in which a sexual element almost always plays a part. A majority of us will marry, and most of us need the stable basis of a home life at least until we reach adulthood. These are common needs – they touch us all at our deepest level. What the rules are for the right ordering of human sexuality and family potential is therefore a question of fundamental significance for every individual.

We ought briefly to chronicle the way in which some Anglican influences have unwittingly contributed to the contemporary anarchy in the field of personal morals. The confusion afflicts most of our fellow countrymen today, and not a few of the members of our own church. Space permits only the briefest of treatments, but three issues will be chosen. In each case, though we are in the area of micro-morals, we need to recall that the behaviour of individuals has been for centuries shaped by social attitudes having their expression, and also their support, in the law of the land.

1. The heart of Christian family and sexual ethics is marriage. Covenant connects the unitive and the procreative. In English law there is only one form of lawful sexual intercourse – that between husband and wife (though other forms are not thereby automatically criminal offences). Marriage has always been for life, and even today the only lawful marriage possible in Britain is that in which promises of exclusive lifelong fidelity are made. This is the Christian position. Divorce is envisaged in Scripture but never commended or enjoined – indeed, there are powerful dissuasives against it in both Testaments. Hence, a society in which, for example, serial marriage is made possible, or widely practised, has radically departed from the Christian ideal. A healthy society will find divorce seldom necessary and provide for it in extreme cases only. For the highest moral concept of marriage to be maintained, a community will make divorce a difficult option, as befits a major tragedy in the serious disruption of at least two human lives.

Except for the rich, divorce had always been difficult or impossible in Britain until 1937; prior to that adultery was the only ground for the legal termination of marriage obligations. A minority of three led by the Archbishop of York opposed the increase in the number of permitted grounds for divorce proposed by the majority of the Royal Commission in 1909–12. A. P. Herbert's 1937 Bill however finally enacted the majority recommendations of the Commissioners' Report, though the concept of fault i.e. that one or both partners had committed a matrimonial offence – was still central. In the 1950s the alluring idea of no-fault divorce raised its head. Surely a marriage could 'break down' or 'die' without the attribution of blame, it was suggested, and this breakdown could properly be the basis of legal divorce without further enquiry, or any investigation of guilt or innocence? Then, in July 1966 an Anglican Committee appointed by the Archbishop of Canterbury produced *Putting Asunder*. Almost devoid of theological argument, the group proposed that the idea of 'marriage breakdown' should replace 'matrimonial offence' as the basis for divorce; in the spring of 1967 the Church Assembly gave their approval to the proposal. After efforts by private members to get Parliament to legislate, a Government Bill became law in October 1969 – our present divorce law. In the House of Lords five bishops had voted in favour and three against while the Archbishop of Canterbury abstained.

Though widespread fornication (extra-marital sexual activity) has been made possible by the availability of contraceptives and thus provided a powerful alternative to the Christian setting for sexual union (marriage), there is no doubt that easy divorce is also now a factor in the social consciousness which works against the centrality and desirability of marriage. Many couples still marry, but what do they *mean* by marriage? The number of divorces each year since the 1969 Act speaks more eloquently than any argument. From 58,000 in 1970 the figure rose to nearly 120,000 in 1972 and to over 170,000 in 1980. And the Church of England is now in the process of considering whether divorcees might not properly be re-married in church during the lifetime of a divorced partner. Divorce by consent after two years' separation is in the 1969 Act, and the alteration of this period to one year is being powerfully canvassed by lawyers' groups and others. In retrospect, we can see that the Church of England has assisted the crumbling of the concept of marriage as an exclusive, lifelong commitment. We have helped to marginalise the moral ideal which God has proclaimed as the way to human fulfilment and stability for all men and women.

2. From divorce we turn to the inviolability of infant life in the womb – the problem of induced abortion. In traditional Christian thinking, life is given by God (through the means of human procreation) in His time, not ours, and likewise its end is decreed by Him

(we may only kill intentionally in certain well-defined circumstances involving threat or harm to individual or community). Innocent life is sacred. Doctors are to care and to heal wherever possible. Abortion and infanticide were widely practised in Ancient Greece and Rome as well as in primitive societies, but Christians (as Scripture and the writings of the early centuries show) were unanimous in their evaluation of life as sacred from conception. Abortion in English law was therefore a serious crime from the earliest times; the Common Law offence was well known and spoken of with the utmost gravity. Saving the life of the mother was the one case where English law had contemplated, since the mid-nineteenth century, that abortion might not always be wrong and need therefore not be criminal; this became law in 1929. The Christian position stresses that from conception the individual is genetically complete, launched upon a unique journey to full adulthood and requiring thenceforth only food and oxygen and loving care. Furthermore, Our Lord was made man from the moment that He was conceived by the Holy Ghost of the Virgin Mary. The same must be true of all of us. So intentionally to destroy an embryo or a foetus is to destroy an unborn child, which is in principle the same act as to destroy a child after birth. This is the moral theology accepted by the Church of Rome, and increasingly (though belatedly, as we shall see) by Protestants.

In 1965 the Church of England Board for Social Responsibility produced a document *Abortion: An Ethical Discussion*. Steering clear of too much theology, it acknowledges a widespread demand for abortion. Rather than the sanctity of individual life, the mother's health and well being moves into the centre of the picture.

In 1966 John Robinson, Bishop of Woolwich of *Honest to God* fame, was calling for the abolition of abortion as a criminal offence, despite his view that it was an evil thing and 'a scourge to be removed from any civilised society'. Almost unbelievably, Robinson discerned only one person able to make a proper moral decision in the question of abortion – the mother herself. (*Christian Freedom in a Permissive Society*, SCM, 1970, pp. 57, 64). The personhood and rights of the unborn never appear; Robinson's arguments would justify infanticide after birth. No authoritative answer was given to Robinson from Anglican sources. The Church of England thus assisted a speedy shift in the focus of moral concern from the danger to the *life* of the mother to the *health and well-being of the mother* and towards the *well-being of the rest of her family* and eventually to the *social convenience* of the mother (e.g. income, job, housing, desire to have no more children, etc.).

David Steel's private member's bill to widen the grounds for lawful abortion was launched in the Commons soon after the 1966 general election; it received massive government help in terms of time and drafting (Roy Jenkins was Home Secretary). Its passage throughout the Upper House was facilitated by Lord Silkin, who had introduced an abortion bill in that House in 1965, and was coincidentally the father of the government chief whip in the Commons. Bishops in the Lords did not oppose the Steel Bill in its passage and it became law as the 1967 Abortion Act.

Since that date the number of abortions in England and Wales has risen dramatically. The Act has in fact failed to fulfil the promises of gain which its proponents made in the 1960s. Illegitimate pregnancies continue to increase, rather than decrease (as predicted). Illegal abortion has not been eradicated. The health of women has not improved, but rather runs further risks consequent upon abortion (and sterility has increased due to the direct effects of abortion); there are more battered babies rather than fewer. Towering over all these facts, however, are the statistics themselves. We now have, thanks to the Steel Act and in contrast to his stated intentions, abortion on demand, with a child being surgically destroyed in its mother's womb every four minutes round the clock, somewhere in Britain, day in day out. From 50,000 abortions in England and Wales in 1969 the number rose beyond 100,000 in 1972 and has never dropped below that figure since; in 1981 the figure was nearly 140,000. Most abortions are done for social convenience.

Since the 1967 Act, Anglican opinion has been slow to change. As late as 1978 the Dean of Liverpool contributed a chapter to a book published by the Birth Control Trust to celebrate the passing of the Act. Dean Patey suggested that the Act was a 'hard-won compromise' and maintained that all the non-Roman churches believed that 'this is an area where God has put a moral choice into men's hands' and that 'there can be no moral absolutes'. He believes that this 'moderate viewpoint' . . . seems to accord with the down-to-earth compassion which the New Testament commends'. The article is remarkable for the complete lack of any theological base, scarcely surprising when we read the words 'We welcome the first ten years of the 1967 Act.'

Organisations leading pro-life opinion have gradually found, however, that there are those outside the Church of Rome who are waking up and joining them; this is the experience of the Society for the Protection of the Unborn Child and LIFE. In the late 1970s, evangelicals inside and outside the Church of England have been stirred by the testimony and the films of Francis Schaeffer, the American philosopher-theologian whose stand against abortion has been on Biblical grounds but with a strong human rights emphasis. It was an Anglican layman who proposed the first modest amendment to the 1967 Act in the House of Lords (at least seven attempts had been made in the Commons) in December 1982. It failed by sixteen votes though five out of the six bishops present voted for it.

3. The perversions of human sexuality are not a pleasant topic. But Scripture and Christian tradition are clear about most of them, and we can therefore be sure that they are not simply objectively wrong and sinful – i.e. against the express command of God – but also harmful, i.e. against our best interests and human happiness. This is certainly true of homosexual genital activity, as we must call it (since the word 'homosexuality' can refer either to a disposition or to the practice of physical, sexual stimulation and/or conjunction practised by some homosexuals). In Scripture these acts constitute the ultimate perversions of the divine intention in sexual matters, for they overturn the order of nature as created by God. They were characteristic of paganism and attracted the death penalty in Israel. They demonstrated the ultimate end of godlessness; the language employed by the writers of Scripture is extreme and uncompromising. Both in the ecclesiastical courts of the middle ages and in the statute of 1533, sodomy and sexual conjunction with animals (bestiality) were offences deserving the death penalty. In 1861 the penalty for buggery (bestiality or sodomy) was changed to life imprisonment.

In 1952 the Church of England Moral Welfare Council set up a private and informal group to study the matter of homosexuality; their report was published in 1954. Public discussion was stimulated, and parliamentary activity also; the result was the appointment by the government of the Wolfenden Committee in August 1954 to examine homosexuality and prostitution. Its terms of reference avoided any clear reference to the moral basis of the law, mentioning only the law and its practice. By far the most influential submission to the Committee was, it was acknowledged, the evidence of the Church of England Moral Welfare Council – *Sexual*

Offenders and Social Punishment (C.I.O., 1956). In this study, largely the work of Dr D. Sherwin Bailey (whose research was also published separately and had lasting influence), homosexual acts were regarded as undoubtedly sinful in the Christian moral tradition but at the same time (it was stated) it is not the proper purpose of the law 'to safeguard private morality or to shield the mature citizen from temptation to do wrong'. Though not condoning them, the Anglican Committee believed that 'the present legal proscription of homosexual practices is an anachronism' and hence they recommended that homosexual acts by consenting adults (i.e. those over twenty-one) in private should no longer be criminal.

The Archbishop of Canterbury gave general assent to the approach of the Wolfenden Committee's Report, but the Church Assembly only approved the path of liberal reform by a narrow majority after a long debate (155 to 138). Eminent legal men – in particular Lord Denning and Mr Justice Devlin – called for caution, since the distinction between crime and sin was not, in their view, quite so obviously clear cut as Wolfenden or Sherwin Bailey suggested. But the Homosexual Law Reform Society set to work, and gradually public opinion was changed, assisted (despite controversy) by *Towards a Quaker View of Sex* (1963) and the new theological and moral liberalism flowing from the publication of *Honest to God* in the same year. After Parliamentary campaigning had begun in earnest in 1965, the reform of the law was achieved in 1967 without significant Christian opposition, with the passing of the 1967 Sexual Offences Act. 'The moral aspect of their [those opposing reform] case had been badly eroded because the Church of England . . . had accepted the principle that the state should deal with crime but not with sin', comments Professor Richards in his book *Parliament and Conscience* (Allen and Unwin, 1970, p. 81).

By 1975 a Methodist minister, Leonard Barnett, felt able to produce a book entitled *Homosexuality: Time to Tell the Truth* in which he wrote of 'homosexuality being as natural as toe-nails and hiccoughs . . . as left-handedness, tone deafness or ginger hair' (pp. 66–67) and described sodomy in full anatomical detail. He called for the minimum age for non-criminal homosexual activity to be reduced from 21 to 18, and for the social acceptance of authentic stable homosexual partnerships; he put the case for the acceptance of 'gay marriages'. The book was commended in a warm Foreword by the Dean of Liverpool, Edward Patey.

The most recent stage in this trend has been the Report *Homo-*

sexual Relationships by a Working Party set up in 1974 by the General Synod's Board for Social Responsibility, the chairman of the group being the Bishop of Gloucester. Several members of the working party were known for their particular interest in the problem from one point of view or another. The Report of the Working Party caused long and anguished discussion in the Board which had set it up, and finally it was published ten months later (C.I.O., 1979) with a disclaimer by the Board who had requested it. The General Synod debated the matter in February 1981, and the Bishops of Gloucester and Lincoln spoke in favour of the conclusions of the Working Party – in particular their conclusion that 'there are circumstances in which individuals may justifiably choose to enter into a homosexual relationship with the hope of enjoying a companionship and expression of physical sexual love similar to that which is found in marriage' (p. 52). The Bishop of Lincoln subsequently moved a motion which precluded any expression of the Church of England's traditional moral stance in this matter by the Synod.

It is widely known that homosexual propaganda was rife in certain theological colleges in the 60s and 70s. Young ordinands were recruited into the ranks of practising homosexuality by others, and a large number became morally confused and silent about the rightness and wrongness of such behaviour as a result of what they saw around them during their training. Fear of public scandal in the eyes of the church and community kept many lips sealed, and it is amazing that so little was publicly said.

The position now is that the Church of England can be quoted as 'not having made up its mind about homosexual behaviour'. There is no episcopal consensus as to whether practising homosexual priests are to be reprimanded, disciplined, warned or even encouraged. Certainly tender loving homosexual acts are free of all moral guilt in the eyes of at least two of the diocesan bishops. The former morality of the church, to the enquiring outsider or the puzzled man in the pew, lies in ruins. Homosexual activists and pressure groups in church, in the media and in the trades unions press for increasing acceptance of their distinctive practices and self-conscious lifestyle. And the recruiting of the young continues with increasing effectiveness. More than half of the new cases of sexually transmitted diseases in the London area are now caught through homosexual practices.

V

The relationship between theology, morality and the criminal law is an area which needs to be explored sensitively. The answers are not always obvious, the connections rarely easily discerned. Much of the field has been thoroughly mapped out in Basil Mitchell's *Law, Morality and Religion in a Secular Society* (O.U.P., 1967). What is clear is that the Church of England has been unable to speak clearly and unambiguously either to its own members or to those who frame or amend the law. Law shapes behaviour. It can strengthen or destroy moral convictions. But when those who appear to be the most authoritative representatives of the church do speak, their pronouncements have not infrequently confounded the moral confusion of society and misled those outside and inside the church as to the nature and demands of Christian morality.

The root cause of the problem is not hard to discern. It is a failure to take the teaching of Scripture seriously, which means failure to take the teaching of Jesus and the Apostles as normative. Not all our Christian moral principles can be translated into legal form, and it is not always best to obtain outward conformity to Christian standards by legal prohibition or coercion. But the commands of God are clear.

Though it has not been possible in this essay to deal with the detailed content of Christian morality (apart from in three outstanding social issues), there is one point which must be made about the foundation of Biblical ethics in the Decalogue. The Ten Commandments are not a code of law; they are a statement of basic religious and ethical principles. They encapsulate the whole field of religious and moral obligation as Jews and Christians see it. They encompass attitudes and actions, family and society, duties to God and man. All but one recur in the New Testament at least once.

Until recently the Ten Commandments formed part of the Church of England's one statutorily permitted Communion Service. They were *not* an optional part (whatever the practice of many churches might have been). They were, and remain, a fitting reminder of God's standards and of human need for forgiveness. At the initiative of the House of Bishops during the process of liturgical revision in the 1960s, they lost this place. They are now available as a second alternative in the appendix in the Alternative Service Book (p. 163) and in an emasculated form at two other points (pp. 161 and 207). Such ill-advised steps have contributed greatly to the moral uncertainty and superficial situational ethics of so many members of the Church of England. Such a departure from Apostolic tradition explains the stark contrast between recent Vatican pronouncements on morality (comprehensive, sensitive and always showing respect for Scripture) and most recent Anglican statements.

The Ten Commandments were once displayed, with the Creed and the Lord's Prayer, on the walls of every parish church. One way to restore Christian morality to our congregations would be for the Bishops and the General Synod to encourage their restoration to such a place of visible honour.

What is tragic is the slavish following of secular trends, especially in the moral field, by so many writers and groups who purport to be expounding a Christian position on behalf of the Church of England. J. A. T. Robinson's enthusiastic espousal of 'freedom' as the sole, over-riding interest of Christian morality deforms the Christian ethic almost beyond recognition, for example. Yet in 1979, more than a decade later, a diocesan bishop was happy to sign the Report of a Home Office Committee on the future of the obscenity law which saw no reason why those who wished for pictures or other descriptions of buggery or bestiality should not be able lawfully to obtain them. The predominantly secular cast of the Williams Committee Report (H.M.S.O., 1979) led, as might be expected, to the same theory of freedom as the one over-riding value, consciously following J. S. Mill. The break with Christian thinking was complete, but the bishop seems to have been unaware of the fact.

One encouraging feature of the Anglican scene should be mentioned to complete the picture. The emergence of intelligent vocal lay leaders in the moral field deserves comment. Towering above them all is C. S. Lewis, all of whose works in the field of apologetics and Christian morality are still in print, and selling well on both sides of the Atlantic. In an age when the beginnings of the drift of the churches from revealed Christian faith and morality were only barely discernible, the writings of Lewis during and after the war until his death in 1963 were a powerful support for orthodox ethics. Lesser but influential figures have been Harry Blamires (*The Faith and Modern Error*, 1956, reprinted as *The Secularist Heresy* 1981 and *The Christian Mind* 1963) and the many books by the evangelical Anglican lawyer, Professor Sir Norman Anderson. Similarly in the House of Lords, lay Anglican peers have recently shown an active and clear-sighted interest in the legislative dimension as it affects Christian morality; the names of the Earl of Lauderdale, the Earl of Halsbury, Lord Nugent, Viscount Ingleby and Lord Robertson will be known to Christians who study parliamentary proceedings. The Church of England should be grateful to these men, especially since other duties prevent most of the bishops with seats in the Lords from attending regularly, and when present they are often unable, for a variety of reasons, to speak and to offer a clear Christian lead.

Again, with Bishop John Robinson praising the influence of *Playboy* magazine and the Rev. Chad Varah regularly debating and writing in favour of the positive value of pornography and the blessings of complete 'freedom to publish', it has been largely layled and lay-inspired groups such as the Festival of Light that have paid serious attention to the matter of obscenity, and raised the level of consciousness of Christians in all churches to the moral danger of such material.

At the beginning of this essay we sketched in the outlines of Christian morality. Neither Church nor nation will regain anything like a state of moral health until the Gospel is once more being confidently preached from our pulpits. The result of such a renewal in the Church of England would be a fresh subjection to the Lordship of Christ, and hence to the teaching of Scripture on moral matters. We should become a prophetic church, calling sin by its proper name, warning our fellow countrymen of its deadly influence for love of our neighbours in Christ's name.

There are larger areas of our public life than we might think which suffer from the breakdown in the area of micro-morals. Promises broken in the bedroom will lead to promises broken in the boardroom. Moral corruption has always been linked with financial and political corruption. Some of the most disastrous defectors in the security services in recent years have been drunkards and sexual perverts.

It should surely be the prayer of every Anglican that our church may be renewed in faith, in evangelistic zeal and moral vigour so as to proclaim by life and by word – whether in pulpit or in print – the whole counsel of God, in whose service is perfect freedom. That is the paradox of the morality whose heart is Christian obedience – it liberates us from slavery to current trends and contemporary fads. Christian morality substitutes the firm guidance of the Word of God, gratefully accepted, for the modish and self-serving ethic of 'relax and do as you please' which the permissiveness of the 1960s introduced, and for which so many in our nation have paid so dearly.

NINE

COMMITTED TO THEIR CHARGE

ANTHONY KILMISTER

'Glory be to thee O Lord my God, who hast made me a member of this Church of England, whose faith and government and worship are holy and Catholic and Apostolic, and free from all extremes of irreverence and superstition and which I firmly believe to be a sound part of the Church Universal and which teaches me charity to them who dissent from me.'

THIS EIGHTEENTH-CENTURY prayer by a wise and holy man of God – Thomas Ken – is one I like to be able to offer in thankfulness, for like Bishop Ken, I love the Church of England. I am conscious of the values Anglicanism has given Englishmen over the centuries. About the Church of England's current preoccupations, however, I am considerably less enthusiastic.

A Christian culture cannot be static but excessive change can be a sign of spiritual and intellectual confusion rather than deepening insight. While I do *not* for one moment hold a fundamentalist view I am dismayed by the tendency, which has been only too apparent in recent times, to call in question the general reliability of the New Testament record and the traditional doctrines associated with the divinity of Our Lord. Furthermore one is on a slippery downward slope if one believes that the Church can afford to underplay either sin or the concept of the sacred or indeed to 'de-mythologise' the central tenets of the faith.

The surest way to undermine a religion is simultaneously to denude it of mystique and to cast doubt upon it as a vehicle of abiding truth. Commitment, for the simple majority, is related to conviction. An excessive emphasis upon social reform rather than spirituality and a confusing of the Third with the Next World leaves little room for personal *faith*.

For the simple majority, hanging on to conviction and thus to commitment is far from easy especially when one recalls that an Anglican bishop, Professor R. P. C. Hanson reported in *The Times* of 2nd August 1980 that 'a year or so ago both the Regius Professors of Divinity in the Universities of Oxford and Cambridge had declared publicly in print that they could not believe in any form of the doctrine of the Incarnation and one of them had expressed doubts as to whether any practical norm of Christian doctrine was attainable'.

During the July 1982 debate on 'The Use of Scripture' in the General Synod a University representative, Canon Professor Barnabas Lindars said, inter alia, and after first asserting 'the central importance and continuing validity of the Bible':

It is easy to exaggerate the differences between the liberal critics, who sometimes seem to use their learning to evade the Bible's message, the fundamentalists, who claim a proprietary right over the Bible but do not stop to examine their own presuppositions and the common or garden churchmen, who hanker after a pre-critical plain man's view of the Bible. We should all agree that all three attitudes are wrong, when they are set against each other in such bold and unfair caricature. . . . A responsible attitude to Scripture . . . demands self critical awareness of our methods of interpretation. *The certainty that we are right is the surest sign that we are likely to be wrong.*[1]

If anything were calculated to confuse 'the common or garden churchman' it is surely this last sentence. Stated another way it seems to say that the less certain we feel, the more likely we are to be right! Is not the 'common or garden churchman' being denied by some of the 'experts' a rational basis for his faith? Even if he had the time, education and learning (in a specialist's field) to discriminate, at the end of it all, the certainty that he was right would be the surest sign he was likely to be wrong!

It has been claimed over the years that the great majority of Anglicans in the parishes are neither Anglo-Catholics nor Evangelicals but are a solid centre dependent upon no extreme position. This may well be true but authority cannot rest with what some people care to call the 'liberal' tradition if the principal appeal of 'liberalism' is to 'reason'. Glorying in *uncertainty* is not Scriptural, Traditional or even Rational. Presumably each man who appeals to 'reason' makes his own analysis or evaluation and so constitutes his own 'authority'. No 'common or garden churchman' can have other than a buzzing head if there are no constants and he has to fabricate authority. It is, in fact, a blatant misuse of the word (or concept of) 'authority'.

This 'liberal' approach to Anglicanism entails the endurance of perpetual weighing, checking and speculation but then agnostics argue similarly that it is more mature to face life without religious 'props'. One would think a Christian must accept that there have to be *some* constants. Do Bible and Tradition set *limits* for 'liberals'? One has to presume not – in which case it is difficult to see *how* the excesses of false liberalism are to be avoided. Describing the 'liberal' stance the Dean of Durham, Dr Peter Baelz wrote: 'Its special witness stems from a firm conviction that the revelation of God to man, the communication of the gospel, is a matter not only of the declaration of the gospel by God but also of its reception and appropriation by man.'[2]

It is no accident that the source book of the doctrine of the Church of England is the Book of Common Prayer. But 'liberals' – good or bad – both reject and deride it (whatever Canon A5 might say) making it clear that they cannot forsee a settled liturgy (like the BCP) ever again.

Writing of Anglicanism's special contribution Dr Baelz says its Catholic, Evangelical and liberal traditions (to each of which he denies a precise definition) are interdependent and *not mutually exclusive*. His article had made it clear that 'the special temptation of both the catholic and the evangelical traditions is to echo without criticism the voices of previous ages'.[2] It would appear that in his eyes the only person fit to sit in the seat of judgement is the 'good' 'liberal'.

The liberal tradition as we have seen 'appeals to reason'. It really is very hard, however, to see how the 'common or garden churchman' can retain a rational basis for his faith when 'experts' – even scholars in the same field of study – wildly disagree and some, like the former chairman of the former Doctrine Commission, even deny the *possibility* of fixed *criteria* in the determination of theological truth and error.

In some senses it is a relief that a new Doctrine Commission has replaced the one which produced *Christian Believing* – in my view a breathtaking misnomer – and yet that report from the former commission was not debated by the General Synod and remains unrejected by them.

If *Christian Believing* was officially to be endorsed by the Synod one wonders where real believers would find themselves. The answer suggested by Francis Moss, whose essay on 'Authority in the Church' appears elsewhere in this book, would be that the *orthodox* would be the modernists and the *heretics* the traditionalists, on the lines that *if treason should succeed who would dare to call it treason?* It is not too fanciful to ponder over what has already been achieved. The late Canon J. B. Phillips whose modern translations of the New Testament are widely read gave the following account of what compelled him to write his little book *'The Ring of Truth': A Translator's Testimony*:

> What triggered off my anger (righteous, I trust) against some of our 'experts' is this. A clergyman, old, retired, useless if you like, took his own life because his reading of the 'new theology' and even some programmes on television, finally drove him, in his loneliness and ill-health to conclude that his own life's work had been founded upon a lie. He felt that these highly qualified writers and speakers must know so much more than he that they must be right. Jesus Christ did not really rise from the dead and the New Testament, on which he had based his life and ministry, was not more than a bundle of myths.[3]

I am *not* suggesting that there are 'experts' who are hell-bent on driving Christians to suicide. Of course the 'experts' and many of today's parochial clergy are, in the main, well-intentioned, good living folk who are very far from being callous. But despite their work for unity, the concern they show for the poor and underprivileged and perhaps a hundred positive attributes, all too often when compassion for and understanding of the disenchanted (suicidal or otherwise) is required they do not live up to their achievements elsewhere. There appears to be a blind spot in these matters which surfaces as indifference. There are not just retired clergy but layfolk also – men and women in the autumn of their lives – who are desperately unhappy and yet are ignored. Young persons and middle-aged people stay away from church in droves too. But the

Shepherd – the Church – in these matters seems singularly uncon-
cerned about the lost sheep.

There is the danger that this will breed a new type of heresy –
if indeed it is not already with us. It can produce a denial that the
Church is necessary at all. A substantial number of people now
think of Christianity merely as a sentiment. They forget or have
never been taught that the Church is a communion. It has been
said many times before that the terms Church and Christian are
correlative. One can no more have a Christian without a Church
than one can have a citizen without a city. The Church of England
must persuade the average Englishman that the Church is an essential part of the Gospel and in doing so must cure the disillusion of
its nominal adherents by demonstrating that it cares about their
distress.

There is no escaping the fact that there are all too many Anglicans
who have lapsed – who now sit in front of television sets rather
than on church pews. Some were driven away by the banalities of
the new liturgy and voted with their feet. Others find some of
today's hard pressed clergy unresponsive.

The priest, by virtue of his calling, his ordination and his special
liturgical function during church services is the embodiment of the
sacred as opposed to the secular – he is the personification of that
which is 'set apart'. It is he who, 'as of right', functions in the
sanctuary – an area to which the laity are bidden only at given
moments.

Sadly many clergy appear to be undergoing a crisis of identity
today. They appear to discard that sense of being 'set apart' so that
they might meet their own people on their own ground and on
equal terms. Some modern priests strive to prove their secular
strength and potency, by the tugging of the altar a few feet away
from the east wall. In a strange way these demolition engineers are
deluding themselves into thinking that this sort of architectural
vandalism is making a significant contribution to the Kingdom.
The mystery and majesty of God is cast aside. Instead one can
discern the development of a 'cult of personality'.

The westward position for the altar favoured by those priests
anxious to develop this 'cult of personality' introduces the face of
the celebrant to the congregation at times when hitherto priest and
people had all faced the same way – towards the altar where they
believed God was. Thanks to the new orientation the priest no
longer appears to lead his people towards the holy mysteries but

now faces his customers like a bar-tender in a cocktail lounge – an unquestionably secular occupation.

The old dispute over whether the celebrant should officiate from the north end or with his back to the people can be argued elsewhere. But whichever stance used to be adopted *neither* involved 'facing the people' in the way which the 'cult of personality' style now dictates. One is tempted to conclude that 'facing the people' encourages the thought that the people are praying *to the priest* rather than to God.

Before the revision of the Prayer Book in 1662 the Puritans lodged certain 'Exceptions' against the church services pleading, among other things, that 'The minister turning himself to the people is most convenient throughout the whole ministration.' The Bishops replied that:

> The minister turning to the people is not convenient throughout the whole ministration. When he speaks to them, as in Lessons, Absolution and Benedictions, it is convenient that he turns to them. When he speaks for them to God, it is fit that they should all turn another way, as the ancient church ever did, the reasons of which you may see in St Augustine, lib. 2 de Ser. Dom. in monte. (Cardwell: Conferences Connected with the Revision of the BCP, pp. 320 and 353.)

In fact the modern practice of facing the people whilst celebrating is quite without canonical precedent. In most of the early basilicas the communion table was placed at the west end of the building and the celebrant stood behind it, facing the people and praying to the east. But the people also prayed facing east *and thus had their backs to the celebrant for most of the time.* Jungmann (*The Early Liturgy*, Longman, 1960, p. 138) remarks that 'it was probably this inconvenience which finally led to the change in planning the church building. As early as the fourth century, some churches were built with the apse towards the east, in accordance with what became the general custom later on. Now the priest is standing at the altar, generally built of stone, as the leader of his people; the people look up to him and at the altar at the same time, and together with the priest they face towards the east. Now the whole congregation is like a huge procession, being led by the priest and moving east towards the sun, towards Christ the Lord.'

Removal of the altar to a more central position in the body of the church may well conjure up the feeling of Christ being 'in the midst' but where does one stop once one launches into this sort of advocacy? If it is wrong to make a distinction between the sacred and the secular, can it possibly be right to make a distinction between priest and people? For the ordained minister is, as I have suggested earlier, a literal embodiment of that which is 'set apart'. Ian Thompson has suggested in *Ritual Murder*[4] that there are grounds for thinking that the crisis of identity which seems to be afflicting many clergy at the moment – particularly apparent in a tendency to denigrate their own ministerial function – owes at least something to the influence of books like *Honest to God*. The coffee-table type altar is one thing (and nothing so destroys the visual sense of God's presence as the closed circle) but another is the practice of encouraging (or requiring) communicants to administer the sacrament to one another. In this way (i) the priestly role is reduced to a bare minimum; and (ii) the individual relationship between priest and communicant – so pregnant with overtones of a personal communion – ceases to exist.

In use of the Alternative Service Book yet more ceases to exist. It would be absurd to suggest that the quasi-modernity of Rite A appeals to no-one. Clearly many people like it and many more uncomplainingly *endure* it. But with this the liturgy ceases to be *Common* Prayer. (It is worth noting in passing that there are, including one in the appendix, no less than five alternative Eucharistic prayers or canons within that single rite – an ecclesiastical form of Russian roulette.) Not even the authors of Rite A would claim it was beautiful and the Bishop of Durham (Dr Habgood) in a speech to the House of Lords said 'Let me frankly admit to your Lordships that I believe that the General Synod has made a bit of a mess of the Lord's Prayer and that we now have something which combines the worst of all worlds.'[5] If they could not get it right why ever did they recommend the 'mess' for use in the first place? It seems that those who pull the levers of organisational influence in the Church cannot or will not see that in the 1662 Book of Common Prayer – every Englishman's birthright – they have an incomparable treasure and an inalienable part of contemporary life. After all if they had wanted to make certain 'improvements' to it they could have sought to do so without 'throwing the baby out with the bath water'. What they have done instead is to inflict upon the Church damage unequalled since Cromwell's fanatical troopers slighted the ranks of medieval statuary and left little beside eloquent, aching stumps.

In recent times it has not been necessary to justify changes – only to be seen making them. It is nevertheless strange that modernists should declare sixteenth-century texts to be archaic and then find in Hippolytus (i.e. by going back to the third century) a disputed and fragmentary text which they believe to be an absolute model of 'relevance' for today's needs. The definition by Christopher Derrick, in a Roman Catholic context, of the role of a modern-day liturgist helps to throw some light on them: 'A liturgist is an affliction, sent by God in order that at a time of no direct persecution no Catholic need be denied the privilege of suffering for his faith.'[6]

Ian Robinson argues in *The Survival of English*[7] that the new versions tend to reduce what is supernatural to the level of the merely implausible. Stella Brook has drawn attention to the widespread and deeply held belief that there is irreverence in addressing God as *You*.[8] According to Neville Ward much modern liturgical writing is interesting – 'and marvellously forgettable'.[9] The trend, writes Ian Thompson, is 'not towards but away from glory, transcendence, transfiguration. Manifestation gives way to "message" and "situation worship" – the former arguing a one-dimensional view of religious truth as of something immediately accessible in terms of content and therefore requiring extreme simplicity of expression. From being richly implicit the language of worship becomes startlingly, often embarrassingly, explicit.'[10]

The glory of language intended to uplift us to God is, in the view of many, replaced by condescension to the former Liturgical Commission's conception of the average church-goer. In traditional Christian worship there is an element of mystery which uplifts one to God. Among the more serious effects of the new are the injuries done in the presentation of God and the restatement of the Christian life.

The God of Cranmer's masterpiece was indeed worthy of our worship and obedience. In the Book of Common Prayer we meet God across the full range of his biblical character: He is the 'Maker of all things', the 'Judge of all men': it is against His 'Divine Majesty' that our 'manifold sins and wickedness' and to this Majesty that our prayers are offered: yet for the penitent His 'property is always to have mercy'.

The marvellous act of reconciliation between the faithful and their God for which the Prayer Book service of Holy Communion provides, gives way in these days of 'alternatives' to what is predominantly a social occasion. (If there is a choice of times, the Alternative Service Book is given the more convenient hour and the Book of Common Prayer is relegated to an 'off-peak' timing.) In 'modernised' services the meeting of the faithful with each other at best complements the encounter with God: at worst it obscures it. The occasion of the sign of 'the peace' becomes the pretext for handshakes and hugs and the renewal of acquaintances; the text repeatedly emphasises the 'all one body' idea and the sharing in one bread is used to demonstrate not the common object of our faith but the social solidarity of those who adopt it. At the same time, the being of God is relegated to the level of the sociable. He is addressed as 'You' (on the peculiar assumption that the modern *You* is the equivalent of the ancient *Thou*) and the sense of otherworldliness is discouraged.

A 'de-mythologised Christianity' was the central plank in the construction of the new American Prayer Book. Just before he died The Very Rev. Urban T. Holmes, Dean of the Seminary at Sewannee, Tennessee wrote one of the most revealing chapters in a book entitled '*Worship Points the Way*'. In it he boasted that the theological basis of Anglicanism was being comprehensively overturned because in his view and those of his colleagues on the Standing Liturgical Commission classic Anglican theology had been obsolete for the last few hundred years. Dean Holmes disclosed how the initial revolution was achieved by stealth, double-talk and a refusal to meet criticism. He did not see the choice between the 1928 and 1979 Books as a matter of taste. 'It is', he wrote, 'more a question of truth for our time. Two standard Books of Common Prayer would be theologically naive, to put it kindly. The task that lies before us is to show how in fact *lex orandi* is *lex credendi* and to rewrite our theology books in the light of our liturgy.'[11]

One is driven to consider the position of the English Liturgical Commission and the General Synod. Unless they can refute the assertions made by Dean Holmes then either the Church of England has also been hi-jacked or the English and American Churches are now radically at odds. Furthermore one cannot help but wonder what value to place upon the often stated reassurances that the Book of Common Prayer remains in the terms of Canon A5 the Church of England's identity card. One is faced with the possibility that it constitutes a politic facade on the American model. It seems unlikely too to say the least, that the de-mythologisers have not left their mark on the ASB.

Significantly a generation of children is growing up who have never been exposed to any forms of liturgy but those in the Alternative Service Book. This is doubly tragic for they are at once being corralled off from the Anglican doctrine enshrined in the Book of Common Prayer (as American revisers intended Episcopalians should be) as well as being robbed of their heritage. For as one of the leading poets of today, C. H. Sisson, has put it: 'There is no such thing as passing on profound truths in superficial speech.'[12]

A diocesan bishop (the Right Rev. Vernon Nicholls) wrote: 'I cannot help thinking that had we, as a Church, spent as much time on the evangelism of England and her conversion to Christ as we have on liturgical revision, the nation would, in my view, be much nearer to God and many of the evils now facing us would have long been conquered.'[13]

The changes which have taken place in the Church of England in recent years have gone beyond a change in the language of the liturgy. There has been a profound change of ethos and the fabric of the Church is crumbling at numerous points. One major problem is the need for a proper understanding of 'Authority', dissension between theologians on the grand scale is a self evident problem too and the gradual break up of the parochial system (and thus the strengthening of the bureaucracy) is a yet further contribution to the current malaise.

A shortage of both clergy and money has resulted in pluralism being forced on clergy. They, in turn, are becoming both more remote and more able in such circumstances to dictate terms to the laity. For example if the congregation in a particular locality want services at reasonable times then there is a need for them to keep on the right side of the peripatetic parson. He, on the other hand, is probably only being paid for one benefice and the erosion of his freehold is causing him concern. Understandably few parsons like their actions being questioned by their laity nor equally understandably do they like adopting anything but a 'safe' line. They know that promotions – canonries and the like – are most likely to go to those who toe the diocesan line. Parish tension is a frequent result. Team Ministries *can* be successful but often they are able to promote no greater parish spirit than the lone parson who is caring for four or five flocks. There is a widespread fear that the whole 'parish' concept is under attack and the fear is well founded.

No parish can remain stable if it is subjected to heavy external pressures. Yet the appointments system seems geared to prevent continuity of churchmanship. For example when ill-health forced the resignation of the traditionalist no-nonsense Bishop of Chester,

Victor Whitsey, there appeared to be a deliberate snub in store for him and a desire to overturn his work. In his place was appointed Michael Baughen, a man understood to be devoted to 'pop' styles, a leading light in the (then) forthcoming hymnal sporting a new national anthem and apparently an advocate, if the press are to be believed, of guitars and a variety of 'way-out' forms of musical praise. The new and old bishops of Chester could hardly be more different. Similarly there would seem to be a deliberate replacement in the parishes (outside those enjoying party patronage) of catholic by evangelical clergy or evangelical by catholic or traditional by radical. Even if insufficient data has been collected to prove this latter point, examples of such changes are numerous enough to make one uncomfortable. They would seem to point to a desire to keep the Church's structure and organisation in these ecumenical days thoroughly fluid.

For church leaders to claim that the Worship and Doctrine Measure has been a step towards parochial democracy is pretty bizarre. 'By the Spring of 1981 indisputable evidence' existed, a leading member of the General Synod, Dr Margaret Hewitt, has written in *Tracts for Our Times* (C.L.A., 1983) 'that pressure was being exerted by local clergy to ensure the adoption of the "new" services and the abandonment of the old.' Congregations are often wary of arguing about this or anything else with their vicar, fearing that if they press their point too hard the incumbent may retaliate by deciding, at a time of high diocesan quotas, to move elsewhere. The parish might then find itself with no replacement in prospect. If a replacement *does* materialise parishioners could well find the appointee is someone who *has* to sit on the fence. In today's Church the pressure which bishops and Deanery Chapters (with their 'group mind') can exert is enormous.

Indeed these days Bishops (or those specially deputed) have an increasing ability merely to appoint a priest-in-charge once the patronage has been suspended and unlike a Vicar or Rector a priest-in-charge has no security of tenure at all. Whether the system of lay patronage can survive the war being waged upon it remains to be seen. Certainly there is the danger that the independence of the parish and of the incumbent will suffer in a major way if patronage wholly and entirely passes to committees dominated by bishops.

In saying this no slight on the principle of episcopacy is intended. The retention of that historic ministry of bishops, priests and deacons which has been the hall-mark of the Church of England is central to my conception of the Anglican Church as a *bona fide* part of the Holy Catholic Church. It is that Catholick and Apostolick Church to which we pledge allegiance in the Creeds. Peter Moore, the Dean of St Albans, has said: 'The argument that there have been bad bishops and heretical bishops does not take away from their essential functions. There have been bad and heretical priests, but this does not invalidate the priesthood. There have been bad Kings, judges, politicians and statesmen. It is lamentable, but it does not argue that their offices should be abolished.'[14] One could wish however that more of today's bishops would act, as they should, as true Fathers-in-God and not with the qualities theatre audiences see attributed to Mothers-in-Law.

A large number of bishops are hot for unity. Foiled by the failure of the Covenant for Unity to achieve the necessary majority in the General Synod they are encouraging Local Ecumenical Projects which promote the effects of Covenanting without actually having a Covenant. The Covenant had blandly assumed a basic unity in Faith and Order where manifestly no such unity exists. The L.E.Ps do much the same thing. One questions their good sense. At home each of us tends to our own garden often chatting to neighbours over the hedges and fences in between. We borrow each other's lawn-mower or power drill when necessary and have a happy and thoroughly friendly relationship. None of us would want, however, to pull down our hedges or fences so that the gardens might be merged and turned into a typically uniform municipal park with one of the garden sheds at the end turned into a public convenience. We should have lost the individuality of our own gardens and made neither our neighbours nor ourselves any happier or any more friendly towards one another.

This analogy is necessarily imperfect and in no sense do I offer it as a justification of our historical divisions. Unity *must* be the aim of all Christians but the unity we long for is the unity of plenitude and not an attenuated and merely bureaucratic unity. True ecumenism is organic: a gradual growing together in love and mutual discovery; it is not to be achieved by the denial of personality and historical tradition. Given the increasing fragmentation of life in all its aspects it is, perhaps, understandable that society now displays a well-marked tendency to opt for collectivist solutions; yet these solutions are more apparent than real. Bureaucratically-devised unity schemes are, in themselves a disguised form of coercion and as such they offend against Christian freedom and the life of the Spirit. To hasten reunion artificially is to exalt time above eternity and structure above life itself. It is to suggest that the answer to our problems lies in the natural rather than in the supernatural order of things.

Local Ecumenical Projects are a backdoor form of coercion – gentle perhaps but coercion nonetheless. Perhaps mergers still appeal but frankly big is not necessarily beautiful.

Size would seem to be dear to the Synodical heart. The organisation of Synodical government has led to increased bureaucracy in the Church and proved extremely expensive. Year by year more and more money (much of which has to come from the ever-suffering parishes) is frittered away on commissions, reports and all sorts of expensive trendiness claimed to have a high degree of 'relevance' though this is not always discernible as central to the Church's mission. 'Ecumaniacs' are usually ready to reconsider selected subjects time and time again presumably in the belief that by such tactics unthcological, unjustified and unwanted change can eventually be accomplished. There is, for example, the matter of the controversial proposal to 'ordain' women to the priesthood. Eric Mascall has pointed out that: 'Those who dismiss the Church's past practice as socially conditioned and obsolete should seriously ask themselves whether their own proposals may not fall under the same condemnation.'[15] Surely it is more than questionable whether the Church of England can rightfully alter the universal tradition of East and West in this respect. Indeed can it *really* be within the competence of a national church, which claims to be catholic, to ordain women to the sacred ministry thereby initiating a major change in the concept of the priesthood which could prove to be a corruption rather than a legitimate development of Christian doctrine? Furthermore, all this its General Synod would be strangely claiming to do by a special vote! Some years ago a novelist stated in the title of a book that '*God is an Englishman*'. But to claim that a special vote can settle the issue of women 'priests' is to suggest that He resides in Anglican division lobbies.

Votes counted in those division lobbies which lead to changes in the ordering of the Church are very readily paraded as revealing the mind of the Church. What is much more revealing is the unusual franchise upon which the General Synod's House of Laity is built.

Aside from the parishes the lowest tier of Synodical government is the Deanery Synod – a talking shop of parochial representatives over whom sometimes the Rural Dean presides and sometimes the

Lay Co-Chairman. The duties of a Deanery Synod are not, by
and large, onerous and with a few exceptions its decisions are
unimportant. (Whenever a really important issue arises the Deanery
Chapter – a caucus of clergy meeting behind closed doors – can
decide how to guide the hand of the Deanery Synod.) Though it
has few, if any, teeth a Deanery Synod tends to take itself seriously
and to be sure that its debates on the affairs of this or the Third
World are of vital importance and the greatest 'relevance'. Despite
that self assurance, however, most men and women in the parish
pews are unconvinced that their Deanery Synod is an exciting and
scintillating forum and have often to be begged to serve on it. The
composition of a Deanery Synod often reflects, many times over
therefore, the character of a typical Vicar or Rector who has persuaded, cajoled or begged the two or three people required to
serve as representatives of his parish. However reluctantly then it is
usually the Vicar's hand-picked few who venture forth to Deanery
meetings and somewhat naturally they tend to vote in the way he
might have suggested or in a way of which they know he would
approve.

Deanery Synods have one major and supremely important
function. Every five years they act as the Electoral Colleges for the
General Synod. Contrary to popular belief the General Synod is
not elected by Diocesan Synods still less by the people. It is elected
by these Deanery Synods in an energetic exercise of ecclesiastical
leap-frogging. If, then, for no other apparent reason, the importance
of the Deanery Synod on the Church scene cannot be overlooked.

Indeed if one attempts to liken the General Synod (which is
the Church's parliament) to the House of Commons incongruities
immediately show themselves. Pursuing the analogy one would
find Members of Parliament elected to Westminster not by their
constituents but by their local Mayor and Borough Council.

Those on parish electoral rolls, therefore, play no part in electing
the national assembly of the Church. It may well be that direct
elections would be too cumbersome and too expensive to arrange.
Nevertheless an electoral college which all too often gives the
appearance of being composed of those who have succumbed to an
ecclesiastical press gang (or were otherwise 'hand-picked') is not
representative enough an electoral system for one of the great estates
of the realm. For good or for ill the responsibility which rests upon
the clergy who do the 'hand-picking' is great.

Yet there is so much else to be done. If strings could only be left unpulled the task of preaching the Gospel could proceed. When the author of the Fourth Gospel by a stroke of genius or divine inspiration – they amount to much the same thing – made use of the term 'logos', 'the Word', to express the person and work of Christ, he translated his teaching into current philosophical phraseology. These days the rich imagery with which the first chapter of St John's Gospel opens (so majestically illuminated by the Book of Common Prayer as the Gospel for Christmas Day) needs some explanation. It is a compelling statement upholding the truths of the Incarnation and when explanation and instruction are required then the clergy should provide these. If the man in the street does not at first comprehend St John's message he deserves no blame – that attaches to the man whose vocation, ministry and duty it is to preach the Gospel and provide the comment.

There are all sorts and conditions of men in the ministry. There is the priest who, at the whim of a determined wife or at the drop of a hat, is forever disappearing on holiday – whether this be convenient to the parish or not. There is the priest who believes himself indispensable, never takes a holiday and thus becomes tired, irritable and wearily resigned to every passing difficulty. There is the over-enthusiastic minister, to avoid whom one dashes into the nearest shop doorway. Of these the middle one may be the least superficial but none of them is doing the best for his flock. All need to take stock of their ministry.

Then there are Vicars who can be so introverted that they no longer see any joy in bringing back to the Church someone who for several decades has shown scant interest in it – or any guilt if such a person slips through his hands into the oblivion from whence he came. There are those who take no steps to prevent parishioners who have spent a lifetime as active Anglicans from joining the ranks of the lapsed.

Happily there are yet others among the clergy who lead quietly sacrificial lives bringing, under difficult circumstances, the message of the Gospel to eager listeners. These are truly wonderful people on whom the future of the Church of England depends.

Hopefully the Church will one day concentrate on the gospel rather than on politics. For the moment one cannot help but notice the way that zealots inside and outside Church circles are claiming that their political aims are supported by Christian teaching whereas those of their opponents are not. At one time the Church of England, perhaps as a jibe, was described as the Tory Party at prayer. Today there are those who think of it as the SDP at prayer. But the further along the political road some people travel the more vociferous they are in claiming to be the sole guardians of the Christian conscience. Some of today's Church leaders lean towards the seemingly cosy pronouncements of an increasingly Left-Wing Labour Party, others towards CND and most towards the latest radical consensus.

Political power and leadership of the Church are these days divorced from one another and for this one can only be grateful. When combined in the past they have by themselves rarely, if ever, advanced the Kingdom of God. On the contrary such a combination often lowered the tone of the life of the Church and accommodated it to the level of the world. It would be a profound misjudgement of the role or mission of the Church if it were to form an alliance with any one political party. In the same way it would be very wrong for the Church to endorse the manifesto of any such party or any association of people pledged to acts of controversial 'reform'. 'Thy Kingdom come, on earth as it is in heaven' expresses the purpose to which the Church on earth must be dedicated and for which it is 'the light of the world' and 'the salt of the earth' (St Matt. 5. v. 13–16).

Whether a nation be a monarchy or a republic, whether it be collectivist or individualist, socialist or conservative is not, so long as democracy itself is not endangered, of direct concern to the Church. Christianity bids sovereign and parliament alike to be guided by Christian principles and to exhibit righteousness and charity in the conduct of affairs. The Church's duty is to proclaim to those who govern, whoever in a democracy they may be, these truths so that they can be guided by those principles. It is not, except in the rarest of circumstances, the duty of the Church to formulate national policy in the secular field. Anglicans are distributed among all political parties and are to be found on both sides of every issue. Government is best left to democratically elected politicians. The Church has a large beam in its own eye requiring urgent attention and would do well to concentrate upon the removal of that beam rather than on playing politics. The present unease, uncertainty and bewilderment in Church circles cry out for remedy. The treatment and the cure are for church leaders to provide.

For my part I do not feel I could conclude this contribution to debate any more effectively than by quoting from a letter to the

Daily Telegraph from an octogenarian pillar of the *Church Times*, Miss Rosamund Essex. From her home in St Albans she wrote:

I am pleading that the Church of England shall be the Church of England fearlessly and unequivocally; that it shall teach and preach the gospel unreservedly and without apology about the birth, life, death and resurrection of Christ and his universal claim (for if Christ did not rise 'we are of all men most miserable'); that it should reiterate the laws of God and warn against their abuse – the old Ten Commandments were never a wholly satisfactory code, but they were something to go on with, and we are the worse without them.

I want the Church to be the Church of the land and not bend itself over backwards to show that it is only one of many religions. For heaven's sake what makes the Church so hesitant when it has the best Good News in the world? It has all the treasury of historic Catholic and Apostolic Christianity.

I should hope bishops would spend less time on committees and more on pastoral work, and that (if they must have them) they would keep their theological wrangles among themselves and not air them to the confusion and bewilderment of worshippers with less technical training. It would be good if parish priests would be more steadfast fathers-in-God, less disseminators of doubt; teachers of the young, builders of belief according to the creeds and Church formularies which they profess. Is not all this what the Church of this nation is for, to lead men and women out of doubt into faith, to righteousness and to God?'

And only this is needed: that to herself the Church should be true.

References

1 General Synod, *Report of Proceedings*, Vol. 13, No. 2.
2 'Reconciling Anglicanism's interdependent traditions', an article by Peter Baelz, Dean of Durham, in *The Times*, 27th November 1982.
3 J. B. Phillips' *The Ring of Truth: A Translator's Testimony*, Hodder, 1967.
4 I. R. Thompson's 'The other liturgical revolution', *Ritual Murder*, Carcanet Press, Manchester, 1980, pp. 157–8.
5 Official Report (*Hansard*), House of Lords, 8th April 1981, Vol. 419, No. 66, Col. 623.
6 Quoted by Joanna Bogle in 'The changing faith of the clergy' *Daily Telegraph*, 17th September 1982.
7 Ian Robinson, *The Survival of English*, C.U.P., 1973, pp. 35–9.

8 Stella Brook, *The Language of the Book of Common Prayer*, André Deutsch, 1965, pp. 53–4.

9 J. Neville Ward, *The Following Plough*, Epworth, 1978, p. 113.

10 I. R. Thompson's 'Gospel Message/Gospel Manifestation', *No Alternative*, Basil Blackwell, 1981, p. 30.

11 U. T. Holmes in *Worship Points the Way: Celebration of the Life and Work of Massey H. Shepherd Jr.*, ed. Malcolm C. Burson, Seabury, U.S.A.

12 C. H. Sisson, *Poetry Nation Review*, No. 2.

13 Vernon Nicholls, Bishop of Sodor and Man, in *The Sodor and Man Diocesan News*, No. 70, October 1982.

14 *Bishops: But What Kind?* ed. Peter Moore, SPCK, 1982, p. 163.

15 E. L. Mascall, *Women Priests?* Church Literature Assoc., 2nd edition, 1977, p. 25.

TEN

MACHIAVELLI AND THE SACRED MINISTRY

DOCTOR ROGER HOMAN

Who moved the stone?

THE PLAIN REDBRICK Primitive Methodist chapel, with its walls chequered by grey foundation stones and bricks engraved with the initials of benefactors, provides an example of an essentially nineteenth-century phenomenon. The slabs were laid by various constituent bodies of the circuit, the local preachers, the Sunday school and neighbouring chapels: and the two largest of them are on the front wall, one of these having been laid by the pastor. Thereby the minister of God commits his name to posterity and the tangible achievement of building a chapel is for ever associated with his ministry.

It was the same in the Church of England. By the nineteenth century the extension of churches by family chapels was more or less a thing of the past. The inspiration to build and restore churches, which was a response to the decadence and decay of the late eighteenth century, was less a matter of lay initiative than of official management. In 1818 parliament granted a million pounds for church building and the Church Commissioners came into their own as the custodians of that fund. While heirs of manors, prosperous ladies and even local employers who hoped for discipline and sobriety among their workers made substantial contributions, the credit and satisfaction on the occasion of opening a new or restored church was the incumbent's: and to him was due the gratitude of the congregation.

The death of Queen Victoria in early 1901 marked a turning point downward in the rate of church building, and since the end of the 1950s when the war-damaged churches were being rebuilt, there have been more redundancies and demolitions than consecrations. The sites occupied by the early Commissioners' churches in many cases now command high prices from developers and the temptation to sell all or part of a central site is often overwhelming.

Simultaneously the educational status of the clergy has changed relative to that of their laity. The time was when the parson was peerless in his parish. By contrast, the parochial church council on which I have served over the last fifteen years has included four members with theology degrees, three civil engineers, and various numbers of teachers, company secretaries, accountants, solicitors, business managers and administrative grade civil servants. In management of money, people and plant, then, each of the traditional roles of the incumbent corresponds to the sphere of professional expertise of one or more of his lay members.[1]

The modern clergyman has not lost his predecessors' instinctive desire to lead the people, but he is without the material resources they commanded and he is aware of the limited personal satisfaction to be derived from teaching his grandmother to suck eggs.

The headteacher cannot hope for a new school building but it costs relatively little to play around with the curriculum. So too in the Church: rumours round chapters and questions from bishops to incumbents are not about new boilers or leaking roofs but about family worship and Rite A. The new vicar at my own place of worship issued a sheet on his first Sunday with some directions for 'slight' changes in posture, the sanctus bell disappeared and the altar was shifted a couple of feet westwards so that the celebrant could go behind it and face the people. The liturgy is widely regarded by clergy as the subject of their prerogative power and the domain of church life in which they can make some impact upon the parish and some impression upon the hierarchy.

The Worship and Doctrine Measure, it has to be said, does not share this view. The Measure is intended to prescribe relationships between incumbent and laity in the negotiation of an acceptable liturgy. It is, however, open to interpretation, and the Standing Committee of the General Synod has made at least three attempts at providing 'A Guide for Parishes': the fourth edition, which attaches the greatest importance to the desires of the church council, was produced early in 1982 as a response to votes cast in the Commons and Lords in April 1981. In all interpretations, however, it is clear that the Prayer Book form must be available for the main services if *either* the Parochial Church Council *or* the incumbent desires it.

The letter of the law, then, instances yet another deprivation of traditional clerical influence. But there is among clergy a general reluctance to comply with their new-found impotence and the rest of this chapter documents their resistance and the opportunities they find between letter and spirit.

The power of prayer

One of the most potent managerial skills available to the clergy is the appeal to reverent behaviour. There are certain habits of deference and senses of occasion which are formed early in the lives of Christian people, upon which the clergy can trade.

The eucharist, for example, is not generally regarded as the place for a showdown. Very few people are inclined to lay their political hobbyhorses at the altar: the Movement for the Ordination of Women is an exception. The man on the Hyde Park soapbox counts on his lot of hecklers and disputants but the preacher in the pulpit expects a quiet ride. The preacher announces himself and his message 'in the name of God, Father, Son and Holy Spirit' and there is no answer to that: to contradict what follows would be to expose the human element in the sermon which the introductory prayer is worded to conceal. Sermons are, at least while being uttered, indisputable. So are prayers. If there is an intercession for striking railwaymen, it is not for the man in the pew to chip in the employers' point of view. Even prayers for the sick and departed or requests to include particular names are politically charged if the individuals concerned have been prominent campaigners within the parish. A new priest in charge of a moderate-to-low parish church resolved to introduce the reserved sacrament and encountered opposition to this practice among the conventional worshippers there: so he announced a month of prayer about it at the end of which the decision was taken to reserve. Another familiar use of prayer as a means of prevailing upon the faithful is in respect of ecumenical schemes: the appeal is to the will of the Holy Spirit and he who resists church unity is made to feel very guilty and very brave to cast his vote against that of the Holy Spirit.

The charge to pray amounts to an instruction to comply. To the request 'Pray for renewal' one cannot reply 'No: I don't think it's a good thing.' Prayer derives its power from the inappropriateness

143

of conflict or flippancy in respect of it. Theologically, it purports to be the means of reference and submission to a greater than human power: sociologically, however, it is a technique for the control of one or more human beings by another, normally of the laity by the clergy. The following chorus, for example, is apparently addressed to God but its intended effect upon a disruptive element in the congregation will be, if at all, direct:

> This meeting, Lord, control;
> Thy richest grace display,
> That those who come to ridicule
> May hence return to pray.[2]

One of the more insidious functions of prayer consists in its assumption of commitment to particular views or courses of action among those on whose behalf the petition is being offered. A congregation having mixed feelings about a series of liturgical innovations is urged:

> Pray for these changes, that they may be made a blessing to us and a source of enrichment in our worship.[3]

Conflict of view invariably attends change of any kind: in the church, prayer is the method of begging critical questions and moving on quickly to the execution of policy.

Respect for the host

A certain traditional deference attends the clerical role. Customarily, the laity refrain from explicit disagreement with clergy and from causing any unpleasantness which would embarrass the vicar as well as others present. Meetings of the parochial church council are supposed to be polite occasions free from animated conflicts, motions of censure, votes of no confidence, premature termination of business, expulsions and slammed doors. Likewise, during religious worship a degree of decorum is preferred.

If the avoidance of conflict is agreed to be desirable by all parties, the strategy of declaring one's view at an early stage in negotiation is a potent one. The priest who faces the people before intercessions and asks in a nice gentle voice 'Will you please stand?' is in fact behaving in an extremely autocratic manner. To call it a rhetorical question is an understatement. He or she who in conscience prefers the kneeling posture for prayer must either abandon such scruples or must risk the reputation of defiance and the personal disapproval of the priest who regards his leadership to have been challenged. In the context of public worship, the matter of posture is non-negotiable. The incumbent is not legally required to consult his parish council – though he would be wise to do so as a matter of good management and diplomacy. Stage directions without prior consultation put clerical authority to the test: they may take worshippers by surprise first time but in my own experience there was gradual reversion to the kneeling position until the persistent appeal 'Will you please stand?' was immediately followed by a shuffle of hassocks and visitors to the church thought they had misheard the priest.

Such is the potential of worship as a means of influence, however, and of the sacrament in particular, that it is sometimes used to set the tone for business meetings. In my own former parish, the eucharist was imported to the PCC: we started at 7.30 in the vestry, ran through the service until the communion, then moved to minutes of the last meeting, apologies for absence and the rest of the agenda, and after any other business we picked up the service books again and had the final prayers. Being in the consecrated vestry, smoking and eating were not allowed: and if any member raised his voice in dissent, the chairman would switch to his role as celebrant, tap the service book and say 'Ahem, we've not yet had the blessing.' Once again, the vicar's expressed or implied intention was difficult to contradict. If a motion was put which he disliked, he would estimate the support it had and only call for a seconder if he reckoned it would be defeated. Sometimes he would say 'I think we need much more discussion' or 'The council would really need notice of a motion like this' in order to avert it being put to the vote. When the mood of the meeting was apparent, he would judge a vote otiose, but then it would not feature in the minutes, which successive secretaries reported to have been drastically edited by him before typing. When heavy snow prevented the attendance of a passive group of elderly members, the meeting was judged incompetent to make decisions: but when holidays prevented by the same measure the attendance of his opponents, no such judgement was made. All these are standard tricks for the chairmen of any meeting and it is up to members, if they wish, to point them out. It is particularly difficult to censure the vicar, however, to challenge his 'massage' of the minutes or to call him an autocrat, in the presence of the Host which he has just consecrated. There is a kind of spiritual blackmail about business meetings in the church and the clergy enjoy effective immunity when the going gets heavy.[4]

Insulated walls

There is a popular playground game variously called 'He', 'It', 'Tag' and other names in which children run around trying to 'catch' each other by touching: players may avoid being caught by crossing their fingers and declaring themselves thereby 'vanes'.

This provides the model for various kinds of constraint upon lay-clergy interaction. In the case of Moses in his legislative role, he took himself up into a cloud, the *shekinah*, where he would not be seen and his transactions could not be scrutinized. In the case of the Orthodox liturgy, the priest disappears behind a screen, the *ikonostasis*, and shuts out the laity by closing the holy door.

In the Church of England, the shutting of the door takes various forms. In particular, a pious language is used to signal to the curious that they are about to trespass by persisting in discussion or that they are not possessed of the expertise that would enable them to understand. A priest challenged about a reportedly discourteous telephone conversation he had conducted with a local personality says 'Clearly I can't go into my pastoral relationships here.' On another occasion, the parochial church council is assured 'There are very good liturgical reasons but obviously we can't discuss them here.' To discussions on censorship of letters in the parish magazine and on directions for posture in worship, he contributed 'I must do what I judge is right to build up the kingdom of God: you think what you like but that is my duty and my calling.' And he discerns as the work of devils the independent views that prevail on matters of stewardship, posture and the Book of Common Prayer. Whereas in the pentecostal churches the spiritual gift of discernment is recognized among lay members, in the Church of England it tends to be a clerical prerogative. Similarly, it falls to the priest in his command of definitions like 'pastoral' and 'liturgical' to remove from the arena of negotiation those matters of business on which he would prefer to make the decision himself.

The trend which these instances suggest concerns the accountability of the modern clergy. Like Moses and the Orthodox priest, they may retreat at will from many of the kinds of business – the day-to-day running of the church – which in theory belong to the institutions of synodical government from the PCC upwards.

The privatization of subject matter is complemented in larger parishes by the adoption of industrial forms of management. The simplest method is for the Director to appoint one or more deputies or associates to whom are delegated the responsibilities of converting the people to the wisdom of his policy decisions. A couple to be married ask for the Prayer Book: the request goes up to the top, is declined, and the curate visits the couple to tell them it is not possible, there is nothing he can do about it, it is one of those things, they mustn't blame him because it is not his fault and so on. The incumbent writes a blacklist of those who are not allowed to read lessons: appellants are referred to his deputy who has nominal responsibility for the conduct of worship.

The prospect of resurrection

The clerisy is in crisis. The clerical profession in the Church of England now fails to command the authority and respect to which it has at times aspired. The complaint of the vicar upon the opening of an adult video shop in his parish is confined to the pages of his own monthly magazine: and sex shop proprietors are uninhibited by still small voices like his.

The modern clergyman has lost the kudos that formerly belonged to his office: like King John in the Wash. The insistence upon leadership of God's people, however asserted, is not a function of the diminution of his influence in the world.

It is not suggested that Machiavellianism is now universal in parish management. Indeed, there are many pastors in the Church of England who are deeply sensitive of local needs and customs and who respect the capacity of lay people for wise judgement. There is one extreme of management, barely more desirable than clerical autocracy, in which the incumbent defers to lay opinion and suspends his own contrary preferences. At the other extreme the incumbent persistently prevails over the laity, whether by legitimized authority (as often in Catholic parishes) or through his unrivalled piety; or else he may so teach and publicly pray that his flock internalize his intentions and end up actually believing that they themselves want women priests or gifts of the spirit or Rite A. In all these cases the leading role of the clergy is secure and the parishes are reported to be conflict free, because conflict has by various means been pre-empted. Problems only arise between these extremes, where there is no consensus about authority, where wisdom is recognized to be the endowment as well of people as of priest, or where the sheep will not close their eyes while the wool is pulled over.

The devious management skills alleged in this chapter are not so much taught in theological college as caught in practice. From Carlisle to Chichester, the clergy who massage minutes or manipulate church councils with cunning opportunism are not practising the transmitted expertise of a conspicuously conspiratorial profession: they are merely succumbing to the temptation to play the system that is faced by all chairmen of committees, from staff meetings in schools and colleges, trades unions, political parties to local government. High Machiavellianism is the common disposition of the insecure leader. Those for whom leadership is the attracting feature of the clerical profession are frustrated to find their role compromised by the higher education and enfranchisement of the laity.

A little knowledge is a dangerous thing. One way to avert the danger is to keep the laity ignorant of the powers to which they are entitled by, say, the Worship and Doctrine Measure. When, a few months after its publication, I asked at the bookroom of Church House in Hove for a copy of the third edition of 'A Guide for Parishes', I was told that there were copies in stock but that the Bishop of Chichester had given instructions for these not to be released. At the time of writing the General Synod claims to have circulated 22,000 copies of the fourth edition but in my own PCC the vicar is declining to have it discussed and says he doesn't know of it.[5] There are, then, conspicuous cases of the assurances given at national level not being allowed to penetrate to the parishes. But perhaps these cases are not numerous: the Archdeacon of Reading's survey revealed that only five incumbents ('only') in his sample had introduced ASB without any consultation with the people.

To recognize machiavellianism as the defence mechanism of a professional group under threat or in demise is not to excuse it. The alarming aspect of endeavours by clergy to recover within the management of church affairs the importance they once enjoyed in the world at large is the subordination of the sacred domain to the political will of the professionals: prayer, the eucharist, postures in worship are made the means by which the clergy jockey for positions of control. This devaluation of the sacred is rationalized in a new theology of Christian worship which explains the eucharist as the social gathering of the faithful rather than as primarily an encounter with the Almighty.

Recent reports, such as that of Towler and Coxon, refer to a continuing lowering of the academic qualifications of ordinands. Yet the participation rate in higher education is at its highest ever. The secular professionals, it seems, are leaving the clergy further and further behind. On present trends we may look to a continued loss of confidence and authority by the clergy. There are two possibilities.

First, there may well develop a disrespect for the modern clergyman as a careless steward of the sacred domain, an unscrupulous manipulator of church business and an unlearned spokesman on current affairs. Chaucer's pardoner provides the archetype of this style. So we have armchair politics on Ulster or the Falklands uttered from the pulpit in the name of God, Father, Son and Holy Spirit: or the Bishop of Chichester pontificating on sociology. Clergy who trade upon traditional deference when making uninformed statements outside the spheres of their expertise weaken – not to say jeopardize – the authority due to them as a professional group.

Second, there is the prospect of an enhancement of clerical status within the dimension of the sacred. Many examples affirm that theological prowess and personal piety endear the clergy to their people while amateurism in secular matters and unscrupulousness in management are thought unworthy of the sacred vocation and bring it into disrepute.

References

1 See Robert Towler and Anthony Coxon, *The Fate of the Anglican Clergy*, Macmillan, 1979; and Anthony Russell, *The Clerical Profession*, SPCK, 1980.
2 Quoted in Roger Homan, 'The Society of Dependents', *Sussex Archaeological Collections*, 119, 1981.
3 Vicar's letter in parish magazine.
4 For further discussion see Roger Homan '*Noli me tangere*: management skills of the parish priest' *PN Review* 13, 1979; and 'Theology and sociology: a plea for sociological freedom' *Theology* 89, 1981.
5 ASB news-sheet, Autumn 1982.

ELEVEN

WHERE STANDS THE PRAYER BOOK NOW?

PROFESSOR DAVID MARTIN

IN THIS ESSAY, written at the end of 1982, I describe situations and attitudes which could be overtaken by events. It would be pleasant to think that real changes for the better might make it history rather than a contemporary report. I fear, however, that even if a few details alter, or one or two events become trivial with distance, the general configuration of attitudes described here will remain.

The votes in favour of the Prayer Book (Protection) Bill were intended as a symbolic gesture of disquiet.[1] I also know for certain that there were some people who shared the disquiet but did not make that gesture because they were uneasy about what the Bill implied with regard to relationships between Church and state. The debate in the Lords clearly shows the degree of unhappiness felt by parliamentarians of all political persuasions.

The House of Bishops met in the June following those debates and issued a unanimous statement. The statement contained three recommendations. The first, and most crucial, adjured the theological colleges to give proper weight to the Prayer Book in teaching and in worship. The second suggested that Bishops' Councils should consider how best to use the Prayer Book in the ordinary life of the Church. The third referred to a forthcoming revision of the pamphlet 'A Guide to Parishes' which sets out the legal and pastoral criteria to be applied locally.

Many people felt that the statement marked a new phase and constituted a considerable step forward in securing just treatment for those who wished to worship in a traditional manner. However, it was clearly advisable to monitor the response to the statement. One has to say that the results visible so far are disappointing. Next to nothing has happened in the theological colleges, many of which seem to have assumed that the statement was designed to gain time. Westcott House now has a Prayer Book Evensong, whereas previously the Prayer Book was entirely abandoned. Three or four colleges use the Prayer Book for about one third of the time spent on worship, but they are the same group as did so before the statement. The almost total neglect of Rite B in the ASB, which is in traditional language, largely along the lines of Series 2, is equally strange. One college chaplain simply informed me that Rite A[2] was regarded as the primary rite of the Church, adding that this was because of episcopal pressure. If he is right then the lack of response to the June statement is unsurprising. One episcopal visitor did indeed open his remarks by saying that there was no need 'to take too much notice of the statement'. At any rate, the answers to Sir John Colville's letter of enquiry[3] as analysed by Mr Ian Thompson make exceedingly depressing reading, and undercut the less detailed and more optimistic reports made to the General Synod.

Just how contumacious some teachers in theological colleges can be is illustrated by the circulated comments of the liturgist at Cranmer Hall, Durham. He says that 'it seems to me that the Prayer Book has had its day' and 'there is a tension between viewing chapel as the worship of Christians in the 1980s and using it to familiarise folk with an old liturgy'. He also says 'Although I think the issue is important, I personally share the view of Colin Buchanan that ... parliamentary action raises serious constitutional issues for the Church of England, that the Bill's supporters in Parliament showed little knowledge, learning or good sense, and that colleges should not, for a moment, let themselves be made "the whipping boy" for the "troubles" of Parliamentarians.' (The view of Colin Buchanan is taken from 'News of Liturgy', Issues 76–8, St John's College, Nottingham.)

As for the responses from Bishops' Councils, these are somewhat more varied. Nevertheless, the Master of Emmanuel College, Dr Derek Brewer, who analysed them, had to summarise the general tone as 'evasive or defensive'. Some dioceses did not think Sir John Colville's letter of enquiry worth even a reply, but of those that replied about four contained positive suggestions, for example concerning the publication of a shorter Prayer Book and the proper use of the Authorised Version.

The revised pamphlet, 'Worship and Doctrine – a Guide for Parishes' (April 1982) was both better and worse than its predecessor. Detailed criticisms have been made both by the Vice-Chairman of the Prayer Book Society, Mr Kilmister, and by Mr Frank Field, MP. These criticisms run along very similar lines. Frank Field asked in a letter to *The Times* and in correspondence with the Bishop of Southwark and the Secretary-General of the General Synod whether we have more than a surface improvement. For example, the *right* of the PCC (Parochial Church Council) to comment which is to be found in the third edition, is removed in the fourth edition and replaced by a phrase saying that the incumbent 'may well wish to take account' of any views of the PCC and the congregation. The fourth edition also omits reference to 'consultation between clergy and people about the option to be used' and in Mr Field's view this amounts to a real weakening of the influence of the laity. He points out that even Rite B can be so deployed as 'to bear little or no resemblance to Prayer Book material'. The laity in his view clearly need to have influence over the options within a given Rite.

Furthermore, both Frank Field and Anthony Kilmister argue that there seems to be a general tendency, in the pamphlet as elsewhere, to try and push towards a polarisation between the Prayer Book pure and simple and Rite A. Series 1, which in practice covered all variations between the Prayer Book and the Interim Rite, is, in the words of the new Guide, 'no longer authorised for use'. This is important, particularly, because perhaps the largest single group of liturgically displaced persons is comprised of 'Prayer Book Catholics'. Frank Field concludes by emphasising that 'a concern that the laity should not be dragooned into the exclusive use of Rite A should not be read as part of a campaign *to deny modern forms of liturgy to those parishes wishing to use them*'. The point needs to be underlined since some churchmen have preferred to read disquiet over the handling of the introduction of 'alternative' services as a desire to repress the new rites. There is not a single passage in the voluminous literature of the last four years which can be read in that sense, and the Prayer Book Society expressly disavows such an attitude. To think these rites unsatisfactory or unappealing, or merely 'quasi-modern' is not to embrace the absurd and indeed impossible aim of repressing them.

If the issue appears technical and confused to the ordinary layman, that is only a measure of the effort demanded of those who are forced to go into such matters simply to defend a service they know and love. Not merely can the matter be easily bogged down in technicality. Only a small proportion of the faithful want to spend their time fighting it out in the undemocratic apparatus of General Synod elections or arguing with the incumbent or gaining a grasp of how a very large and complex organisation works. When the Bishop in charge of C. of E. public relations said 'We are going to win because we are full-time and you are part-time. In a clerically led Church, we decide,' he spoke no more than the truth.[4]

Something needs to be said about the situation in the parishes. This has been obscured somewhat in the past by statements which claimed that X number of churches in the diocese of Y 'use' the Prayer Book. (Statements of this kind also obscured the situation in the theological colleges.) You can get the measure of the situation by careful local inspection and by reading archidiaconal returns. Some areas are almost bereft of the Prayer Book in any shape or form at any time. The Bishop of Lincoln, answering a traditionally-minded priest who wished to come to the diocese, said 'We have scarcely any parishes which still stick to the 1662 service as their main liturgy.' Three years ago I visited Louth Parish Church and read a notice 'All services are Series 3, except for holy communion on Tuesdays at 11.00 a.m.' My own parish Church has a Prayer Book Service on two days in the month, one a Tuesday, the other a Friday. Clearly this way of using 'alternatives' will ensure that the *next generation will have no option, since it has no experience on which to base a genuine decision. The Prayer Book has to retain at least the degree of symbolic salience and mainstream use which makes it available as a shared inheritance and ensures the continuing possibility of real choice.*

More usually the Prayer Book Eucharist is relegated to 8.00 a.m. The Archdeacon of Berkshire has recently carried out a survey reported in the *Church Times* for 1st October 1982. Somewhat less than a third of the priests who replied used the Prayer Book for their own daily office. Only one parish in ten used the Prayer Book for Sung Eucharist or Parish Communion. On the other hand, Morning Prayer and Evening Prayer were largely said or sung according to the Prayer Book. However, given the persistent down-grading of these services, this means that a large proportion of worshippers are not exposed to the Prayer Book. (The Vice-Principal of Ripon is certainly right in pointing here to the effects of the parish communion movement, as I believe he is also right in querying whether that movement has not reached the end of its usefulness.) The Archdeacon of Berkshire went on to claim, unsurprisingly, that his returns showed there had been full consultation and agreement about the introduction of the ASB in most parishes.

This last point requires some comment. I have myself been present at a large gathering of clergy in the Canterbury diocese where a clergyman lectured his fellow clergy on how to cozen a recalcitrant congregation to accept the new services. What interested me most was that nobody present remarked on the oddity of such a lecture. What very frequently happens is that the priest, without necessarily having any direct intention of subverting the preferences of his parish, suggests that it would only be fair to give the new service a period of trial. This is in itself quite reasonable, and very few would be inclined to oppose it. However, once the services are in use and the incumbent has in various ways made clear to the PCC what his own preferences are, it requires a very persistent layman indeed to organise an opposition to reverse the situation.

Dr Roger Homan in his entertaining contribution to PN Review 13 entitled 'Noli me tangere' gives an analysis of some of the techniques which can be brought into play to secure conformity. I myself sampled a large number of parish magazines in the latter part of 1980 and noted how again and again lay protest elicited a clerical counterattack. Even the pulpit can be used for one-sided propaganda. When I was at morning Eucharist in Lincoln Cathedral, the Dean declared that those who opposed the new services were 'like the trolls who die at sunrise', while a Bishop speaking in a church I attended on the coast of Maine threatened resisters with exclusion from the Messianic Feast.

Such examples are, of course, merely anecdotal, but I shall later revert to the massive disparity between institutional thrust and individual preference in some remarks on the situation in the USA It is very characteristic of large modern institutions, organised on bureaucratic lines (as is the Church of England) to develop a line seriously at variance with a large sector of their constituency. Only somebody willing to attend every meeting of the ecclesiastical equivalent of the trade union branch can hope to counter such a line.

It is only fair to notice certain improvements, some of which bear on a very crucial matter: the symbolic salience of the Prayer Book on important official occasions. The General Synod, for example, excluded the Prayer Book from its principal services for years, thereby signalling its real status to all its members. Now the Synod has held a service using the Prayer Book. The recent consecration of the Bishop of Salisbury and two other Bishops was according to tradition. The Royal Wedding was celebrated in a form which approximated to the 1928 service. These things may not seem important, but symbolic salience acts as a signal of the direction taken by those with ecclesiastical authority, and it is at least heartening that recent changes have partly come within the bailiwick of the new Archbishop of Canterbury.

It is also good that some cathedrals take seriously official statements to the effect that the new services are alternatives not replacements. I have not made exhaustive enquiries but Durham, Oxford, Wells, Coventry and (I think) Salisbury and Winchester maintain an unexceptionable balance. Guildford uses the Prayer Book for all services except Sung Eucharist, which is celebrated according to Series 2. Chelmsford also plans to use the Prayer Book to some extent in its main eucharistic celebrations. There are others which act similarly.

I understand that Southwark frequently uses a sung Latin (and Greek) text with Rite A, which not only presents a shattering shift of register, but wholly contradicts the expressed aims of liturgical change. However, one must be grateful that the threat to the treasury of church music is much less evident in the cathedrals and collegiate foundations than in the parishes. No doubt something is owed to the vigorous stand which most church musicians have taken in favour of the Prayer Book and traditional forms as, for example, Dr Herbert Howells, Dr Francis Jackson and Sir David Willcocks. The majority of masters of music signed the 1979 Petition.[5] (The Royal School of Church Music is not of this mind, and is distinctly well-disposed to the ASB.)

Another heartening sign is the appointment of Professor Douglas Jones as Chairman of the Liturgical Commission. Professor Jones is anxious to produce a shorter and less expensive Prayer Book, and an edition of the Authorised Version which rivals in attractiveness of format the Readers Bible of the 1930s. He also invited the Principal of St Hugh's to address members of local commissions, though this was an occasion which underlined the great gulf fixed between an articulate traditionalist and the liturgical activist.

This meeting of minds is important, since the Liturgical Commission has up to very recently totally ignored the Prayer Book Society and the strong body of protest found among Christian academics. This is surprising simply because quite a large part of the fundamental thinking of the Church has to be done by university teachers, most of them not in orders (as is also the case, for example, in the Orthodox Church of Greece.) Some churchmen have tended to dismiss the almost complete rejection of the new services among academics as the aesthetic tic of atheists who enjoy feeling superior at the expense of the Church. It is tedious to counter such dismissals in detail, but the citation of just a few of the names of those involved would be enough to show that somehow or another a huge gap had developed between the Christian intelligentsia and certain of the specialist organisations of the Church.

Too few people have asked themselves how such a gap could arise. After all, it is not really very likely that Christian members of universities should engage in (almost) united protest unless something had gone very wrong in the composition of the new services and in their organisational promotion. Even so, many such people have preferred to keep their despair to themselves. So judicious and careful a scholar as Basil Mitchell, Nolloth Professor of the Philosophy of the Christian Religion at Oxford, is not likely to engage in an unfounded public outcry. No-one can seriously contend that the Principal of St Hugh's, the Principal of St David's University College, the Master of Emmanuel College, The Professor of the Philosophy of Science at Cambridge (Mary Hesse) and the Principal of Westfield College, London University, would be aroused without due cause for concern. Moreover, so much of the theological confrontation with the twentieth century has had to be mediated through poets like T. S. Eliot,[6] W. H. Auden, Charles Sisson and R. S. Thomas that their sense of betrayal and unease at evident blundering cannot easily be put aside. A very deep sense of despair can grip the Christian intellectual who is seeking to re-present the resources of traditional Christianity and is, at the same time, deprived of the resources of the traditional liturgy. This is precisely why the opening of a conversation, however tardy, is important. The meeting between concerned parliamentarians and the Archbishop of Canterbury was important in the same way.

Before I conclude this brief survey of the situation, I should mention the situation in the USA, which is even more depressing than that obtaining here. I refer to the USA, since we are after all dealing with an inheritance which we in England share, to a greater or less degree, with all English-speaking peoples. Of course, in the USA, the Episcopal Church is privately owned in that there are no public checks through a link with the state, nor for that matter an extensive Anglican intellectual presence in universities to challenge the ecclesiastical bureaucracy to open debate. The apparatus works in a self-contained manner, and the result has been that the traditional book (i.e. the 1928 revision) has been officially replaced, though a certain amount of local option remains, with episcopal permission.

The late Dean Urban T. Holmes, in an account of how liturgical change was managed during his time on the liturgical commission of the American Episcopal Church, claimed that the intention was radically to alter Anglican theology at the top and then induct the laity into the new thinking by controlling the way they prayed. This is to give a new twist to the old tag *lex orandi, lex credendi*. He also said that protests had been met by careful silence since the protests were well-based. I do not know whether the silence maintained until recently by the English liturgical commission was based on a similar strategy. No Bishop or member of the Commission in England has been as frank as Dean Holmes (though one Bishop upbraided me for 'setting myself up against the mind of the Church and the Holy Spirit').

What is particularly interesting about the American situation is the way a supposedly representative central body utterly fails to represent its constituency in liturgical matters. Official opinion rated the opposition to the new liturgy as confined to a small minority. When Dr Gallup showed this was not the case, even among the most active church members, and among the young, he was subjected to precisely the same disbelief and contempt for fact which I encountered in my own small exercise with Gallup. Dr Gallup repeated his exercise two years later, with the same results, and he also showed not only that clerical attitudes were roughly the inverse of the attitudes of the laity, but also that protagonists of the change were less tolerant than traditionalists of a genuine plurality of options.

Having given a brief summary of the situation within the Church of England, I want now to look at one or two institutional areas outside the Church, notably the press, the schools and BBC religious broadcasting. I will take the press, the BBC and the schools in turn.

The press, in England as in the USA, has been solidly traditional in its affections. I have kept a record over the last four years and I doubt if there is any issue on which the serious newspapers have been more united. This is partly because the leader writers of three papers, the *Guardian*, the *Daily Telegraph* and the *Daily Mail* include in their number communicant members of the Church of England, who know what is happening in their own local parishes and feel deeply about it. (I presume the same is true of *The Times*, but the screen of anonymity hides these allies from my eyes. Certainly the previous editor, though a Roman Catholic, shared in the general unease, and personally researched some of the liturgical arguments e.g. concerning the use of 'We believe'.)

There is more to it than leader writers eloquent in defence of their traditional liturgy and of the Authorised Version from a secular pulpit. A unity has been forged between Christian and secular intellectuals on this issue, which brings together people of very varied opinions. Marghanita Laski and the Master of Peterhouse represent quite different poles of opinion, but they are united in shock over what has happened. Thus a huge and remarkable series of articles has appeared in the national press not to mention more specialist journals written by journalists, Christian academics and secular intellectuals criticising the substance of the new rites and the manner of their introduction. The letter columns, especially in the *The Times*, the *Guardian* and the *Daily Telegraph* have been particularly illuminating. Dr Derek Brewer carried out an analysis of newspaper correspondence which showed clergy three to one in favour of the changes and the laity three to one against. Only in some of the local papers was there a more equivocal voice.

The situation in the BBC shows a distinct gap between specifically religious broadcasting (though one must except people like Hubert Hoskins and Gerald Priestland) and broadcasting in general. No less than five people have used *Words* to express their disquiet. Both Radio 3 and Radio 4 have had several programmes on the controversy, only one (featuring James Fenton) being slanted in favour of the changes. Even BBC TV and ITV have screened debates. But the actual provision of worship, as decided by religious broadcasters, has been very disturbing. The Prayer Book has been almost entirely ousted from all services, except mid-week Evensong, which is now transferred to Radio 3 (Wednesdays and Fridays). I have sampled the month of October and *all* Anglican services are according to Rite A. Nor can one be happy about the output of *Sunday*. The previous editor of *Sunday*, having omitted all reference to the 1979 Petition, told me that it had already received enough publicity, as if his business were to rectify the news, not reflect it. Although *Sunday* included a reference to the forthcoming Prayer

Book Protection Bill, the following week this programme contained no mention of the favourable vote the Bill received.

So bad was the situation, in spite of the fact that the issue had been raised on the Combined Religious Advisory Committee by Professor Basil Mitchell, the Rev. James Bentley and myself, that a letter was sent to Sir Ian Trethowan from Sir John Colville, Lord Glenamara (Edward Short), Henry Moore, Earl Waldegrave, the Dean of Windsor and others. This letter asked that the Prayer Book have a share of Sunday worship consonant with its official status, the strong support indicated by Gallup, and the obligation stated in the Annan Report to reflect the main religious traditions of the country. This would mean not to stretch the point, that at least one Anglican service in three should be traditional. The reply received to this extremely moderate request was peculiar to say the least. It said that the BBC could not treat any group with favouritism.

Eventually, after a certain amount of rather sharp correspondence, a meeting was arranged between myself, Mr Kilmister and the Head (until recently) of Religious Broadcasting, the Rev Canon Colin Semper. This proved an amicable though revealing occasion. Canon Semper cheerfully conceded that the reply to Sir John Colville and his co-signatories did not meet the point at issue, and presumably was not intended to, since he had drafted it himself. He also explained that a major difficulty lay in his colleagues who, on hearing of the complaints, responded with 'They've lost.' He himself had plans for Choral Mattins to complement Evensong. However, he said it was next to impossible to find Prayer Book (or Series 1) churches which met BBC criteria i.e. good music, a 'lively' local fellowship and a good preacher, despite information we had given him.

Mr Kilmister and I then suggested a meeting with his Department. At the meeting, the same points about BBC criteria were made again, and a sort of informal agreement reached that if we could find churches which met those criteria they would be considered. We did, but looking at handouts and the *Radio Times* since I have the impression that not much has changed. In answer to a complaint from Professor Fryer, of Nottingham, the Bishop of Manchester said it was 'very important indeed that modern forms of service should predominate'. He, at least, is having no nonsense about them just being 'alternatives'. The situation has been particularly parlous at the great feasts (with the exception of Ante-Communion from the Temple Church on Good Friday). Television is even worse, if that be possible, and there is a considerable prejudice against formal worship as such, let alone the Prayer Book.

I have spent a little time on BBC religious broadcasting because it is an area, like the theological colleges, where decisions can be made without constraint, and where there is a definable pocket of power. The situation in the schools, including the independent sector, is not less alarming.

So far as the public sector is concerned i.e. 92% of all pupils, the situation is part of a general disarray in Religious Education (R.E.). In my view there is some good work done in the R.E. field, against a background of considerable denigration and neglect.[7] I would not for a moment criticise the use of modern translations of the Bible in schools provided they were used alongside the Authorised Version and provided at least the great passages in the A.V. are taught. But this is not how things usually turn out.

I should give a preliminary warning that there is now under way an attack on traditional hymnody,[8] which has so far made its greatest impact in the schools. Much of what is now offered consists of trite or contentless ditties beside which the A.S.B. looks like a work of imaginative genius. These ditties characteristically go to jig-a-jig tunes in pathetic emulation of outdated pop music. This is tragic, since there is, amongst a large amount of expendable rubbish, a corpus of classic hymnody central to the English religious inheritance.

As to independent schools, I have recently had some useful association with the Bloxham Project, concerned with R.E. in that sector, and this has allowed me to test the water. Professor Basil Mitchell, the Rev. Bruce Reid and myself have stressed the importance of the Prayer Book and Authorised Version in deepening the imaginative life of pupils.[9] We have argued that such masterworks act like powerful icons, touching the deepest layers of response, and, moreover, that these icons are set in the context of our literature and history. They are keystones in the arch of cultural continuity. Such arguments are listened to respectfully, though an appeal was made to me not to go all out along a line which would 'appeal to the natural instincts of headmasters'! All the same it is clear enough that most chaplains have pushed the new services. Replies to a letter of enquiry from Sir John Colville to heads of independent schools, were analysed by the Principal of St David's University College. Some of them illustrate a remarkable triumph of conformity over education e.g. 'We give them the A.S.B. because that is what they will encounter outside.'

Before some final remarks, it may be useful to summarise the arguments used in support of liturgical change. These arguments differ, of course, in their type and weight. Nevertheless, one may say that those who defend what has happened believe:

A. That the Church should not appear antiquated, at least in the key area of the spoken word.

B. That failure is in significant measure due to not being understood.

C. That 'cultural' concerns are middle class and these must be jettisoned if the Church is to widen its constituency.

D. That the established connection is an uncertain blessing. This feeling can be expressed in a considerable ambivalence towards the state prayers and the 'regalism' of the Prayer Book. It is also expressed by using the A.S.B. as a kind of totem of ecclesiastical independence and as part of a generalised resentment towards those who regard the Church as a walled-off enclave of the 'spiritual', a sort of biddable spiritual side-show.

E. That common texts, however poor, are useful in the politics of ecumenism and give a sense of common cause to Christians who are otherwise divided.

F. That the Church is not primarily connected to 'Little England' but to the ecclesiastical equivalent of the EEC and/or the Third World. The Prayer Book then suffers because of its distinctively English character.

G. That participation, even if mainly symbolic, is more easily congruent with the ASB, and that such participation is the most faithful realization of the reformers' intentions for our own time.

H. That the form of the traditional eucharist does not conform to primitive models: four-fold action etc.

I. That the renewal of theology, including a theology of the incorporation of new members and of marriage cannot avoid a break with the traditional framework.

J. That theology, both contemporary and primitive, is bound to regard the traditional form as over-emphasizing sin and atonement and under-emphasizing[10] Resurrection and the action of the Holy Spirit.

K. That there is a sharp division to be made between verbal form and the substance of meaning. The raw core of meaning is primary.

L. That the Church must adopt one particular (and rather Puritanical) view of the relation between the beautiful and the holy. Thus all criticism that fastens on the aesthetic aspect is not truly theological. Those who hold this view often argue that because it is possible to say a profoundly Christian prayer in a graceless hut or a prison then Lincoln Cathedral is a dispensable superfluity. Art is an extra to those things which are *real* or else to those attitudes which are *sincere*. Art is a seductive agency which leads humankind away from God, not a primary channel of divinity. This kind of argument is often developed to include the notion that art necessarily intrudes complexity where there should be simplicity. (The Rev. John Wesley and the Rev. John Newton objected to Handel's Messiah on the ground that they could not hear all the words.)

Obviously, critics of recent changes may be sympathetic to some of these arguments. Personally, I am sympathetic towards the argument which claims the Church is not a walled-off enclave of spirituality, and I know of people who care greatly about the Prayer Book, for example, the Dean of Clare, Dr Arthur Peacocke, yet see the advantages for ecumenism of prayers shared in common. Nevertheless, one has to say that difficulties often appear once one pursues the arguments listed beyond the level at which they can be used to blend the faithful either with liturgical science or with self-evident tags ('Isn't sincerity all that *really* matters?'). The logic of the argument about simplicity runs, for example, straight into the brute facts of Christian history, particularly the power of Baroque or (say) Mexican churches to induct simple peasants into the divine presence. But even if one regards a huge part of the Christian architectural inheritance as falling away from the proper Cistercian or even Puritan ideals, nevertheless, it is precisely the Cistercian and Puritan examples which show that art and simplicity are perfectly compatible.* Indeed, the Book of Common Prayer is 'artful' in the best sense but also very simple. The relationship of the beautiful and the 'artful' to the holy is a subject of amazing complexity which cannot be set aside with a few supposedly self-evident tags.

*I am thinking of the classic simplicity of early dissenting architecture, and the immense architectural deposit of New England from 1680 onwards.

It will be useful, perhaps, to give some other examples of how debatable the current wisdom becomes once examined a little more carefully. For example, those who do not care for the shift from 'I believe' to 'We believe', often argue, with W. H. Auden, that to say 'I believe' involves an assumption of personal responsibility for belief. They are countered by examples of primitive practice, which however turn out to be quite equivocal in their import. So equivocal are they that the Roman Catholic Missa Normativa retains Credo, and scholars translating that Mass into the various other vernaculars have often retained the first person singular. Exactly why those who translated the Missa Normativa into the English 'vernacular' were more impressed than other scholars by the arguments for 'We' is a puzzle. However, there can be little doubt that many people are influenced to accept the 'We' by the *gemeinschaftlich* (or, if you like, collectivist) overtone. In the same way it seems odd that R.C. scholars in Washington should adopt the bathetic 'And also with you' and that scholars in our own Church should thrust it upon us, while several other Roman Catholic language groups retain 'And with thy spirit' e.g. 'und mit deinem Geist'.

To take a quite different instance, objections to the N.E.B. as the sole vehicle for readings are often rebutted by reference to the faithfulness to the texts achieved by the modern translators. Yet, the Rev. Professor Kenneth Grayston (Methodist) in 'Confessions of a Biblical Translator'[11] which is to some extent an apology (in both senses) for the N.E.B. makes it clear that such vaunted accuracy is impossible. More than that it can be argued quite persuasively that the Authorised Version is often *more* accurate, as does Geoffrey Strickland[12] in 'The Holy Bible: translation and belief'. Gerald Hammond argues that part of the archaic and powerful texture of the Authorised Version derives from precisely its faithfulness to the original.[13] Ian Robinson in *The Survival of English* extends this point by relating the unconvincing tone of the N.E.B. to faithlessness at a deeper level i.e. the failure of men and women in our time to find a religious language which conveys either meaning or conviction.

I could give endless examples where the criteria adduced for a particular change are so debatable that one concludes that it was political considerations which were really decisive. The learned journal *Worship* published in Collegeville, Minnesota, USA, and a notable source of liturgical innovation, will provide a whole battery of examples, including the charge that the brutalism of the

Englishing of the Mass, so widely transferred to our own liturgical work, was partly based on mistranslation of an allocution of Paul VI defining the guiding criteria to be followed. Again, the fragmentary texts of Hippolytus Romanus are much cited as giving us guidance to early Eucharistic practice, and this primitive character is held to be authoritative for our times. But the same people who parade Hippolytus Romanus as an authority will quite calmly jettison the most primitive layers of the New Testament i.e. the Epistles, at any point where they prove inconvenient. I have no doubt that many people find the 1662 view of the reasons for marriage offensive, but the offensiveness has clear authority in the New Testament. Criteria of selection are entirely arbitrary: the custom of the Kiss of Peace looked attractive by the standards of contemporary Zeitgeist, whereas primitive directions concerning the display of female hair are conspicuously lacking in appeal. Of course, if the new reformers prefer what Kierkegaard rightly characterised as a Jewish view of the family and marriage to their own most authoritative sources (not to mention the fourth century Desert Fathers) then that is very understandable, but it means that all criteria invoking authority dissolve on inspection into arbitrary existential preferences and mere 'feel'. When scholars are picking their way selectively through the various authoritative layers of Christian tradition they can usually rely on the Holy Spirit to revoke His previous inconvenient revelations as 'culture bound', thus giving us full authority to select in accordance with the cultural assumptions of our own day.

Beliefs about the nature of modern speech are equally odd as are beliefs about what people can understand. Charles Sisson, writing in the T.L.S. said that the A.S.B. contained hardly a single modern sentence. Fraser Steel in his contribution to *Ritual Murder* (p. 122) comments 'In the *Te Deum*, for instance, what principle of consistency reconciles the functionalist unpunctuated, bluntness of "You are God we praise you" with the sham-antique of "Throughout the world the holy Church acclaims you: Father of majesty abounded".' The new *Te Deum* also includes respectable essays in Victoriana ('the white-robed army of martyrs' etc.). This is all right, but certainly not modern, or simpler than the traditional version. Professor Randolph Quirk has argued that the new versions often have a more difficult vocabulary than the old (which is perhaps why one Bishop told me that critics have the same trouble with the A.S.B. as musicians had with Wagner!). It may seem unbelievable, but the previous Vice-Principal of Westcott House told me that the Commission actually voted on a proposal to remove the image of the Lamb, since lambs are not part of our contemporary urban experience. So much for 'Little Lamb, who made thee', which presumably should be banned from schools as in archaic English and as referring to an unknown animal. The Principal of St John's, involved in so much of this, actually accused me of being the sort of person who thought people could understand the phrase in the service for the Solemnization of Holy Matrimony 'like brute beasts that have no understanding'. Indeed, I *am* that sort of person. People know what brutes and beasts are and they understand what it is to have no understanding. The lack of understanding is located elsewhere.

What then do I conclude? I think one must distinguish between institutional *mauvaise foi* and individual *mauvaise foi*. When you talk to an institution, you find that nobody is responsible. I mean both that you cannot trace a primary agent of what has happened, and that everyone refers to someone else. The ball is never directly in someone's court, but flying in the air. The buck never stops, not even with those apparently in authority. This is not to say, that once a line has emerged certain powerful agencies cannot be identified which maintain it in being. The Secretary-General of the General Synod, for example, has reacted to criticisms with comments which give clear indications of where the weight of ecclesiastical bureaucracy is placed. After the Gallup Poll, he said that he would be sceptical about any poll with which I was associated, and also said that critics had now 'shot their bolt'. Dr Blanch, Archbishop of York, has responded to complaints with public remarks which throw judicious neutrality to the winds and make clear where the weight of authority in the Northern Province lies.

Nevertheless, I do not conclude when talking to individuals, even the most open partisans of the new rites, like Canon Colin Buchanan, Principal of St John's, that they are engaged in deception, or even, in many cases, that they are insensitive to the issues. The Church of England has not suddenly become bereft of learned and godly men and taken over by crass Philistines. The logic of institutional change is more subtle than such suppositions allow. Some individuals who give assent to what has happened openly admit to a continual daily mortification of the soul when using the new rites. It only requires one mistaken supposition about why the Church of England is not succeeding, or one illegitimate inference from the success of some lively Charismatic congregations, for a man to do penance in this way or for a man to conclude that, however poor in content and expression, the changes must be supported. The Rev. Professor Kenneth Grayston openly argues that because modern English is slack, feeble and unimpressive, a truly modern translation such as the N.E.B. can only reproduce these characteristics. Just one mistaken inference can lead them to a personal stance which supports the enfeeblement of the word.

The institutional line, which constrains future generations to its pattern, with the weight of hands no longer active or even dead, is bad faith of a very clear kind. The previous deputy leader of the Labour Party is undoubtedly right in asserting that the collective entity we call 'The Church of England' has quietly stolen away from the understandings which lay behind the Worship and Doctrine Measure of 1974. The evidence of a disparity between provision and preference is too clear. There is an obvious lack of accountability to the wider community in general, and to that wider community of the faithful who do not engage in the internal politics of the Church, and who see no reason why faith demands a spell of ecclesiastical politicking. The quasi-democratic apparatus develops a momentum at odds with the constituency it claims to serve and the rules it claims to follow. Those who occupy key roles in that apparatus are forced to use formalistic defences which obscure the real injustice.

The situation is paradoxical. The Church of England is now a pocket of privatised spiritual power, which rejects admonition or pressure from public authority as 'Erastian'. The right of ecclesiastical authorities to order their own affairs and exercise what they see as a divine commission is, without doubt, important, but it can be too easily defended by an appeal to precisely that kind of privatised power which lacks responsibility to the wider community. That is why the American bishops, who are simply part of a private religious corporation, within the broader international consortium of the Anglican Church, are able to act in such an authoritarian way, and even to exhibit the unacceptable face of authoritarian liberalism.

When the Houses of Parliament made their gestures of disquiet in April 1981, there were some who confused the right of a Church (meaning the whole body of the faithful) to autonomy, with the exercise of clerical power over against a very large part of the laity. The participation of the laity let alone the dialogue with the secular world, was plainly understood as confined to areas where it did not inconvenience that power. Two smokescreens were sent up. One was a threat of disestablishment, which the Bishops mostly do not want and which a recent O.R.C. poll shows is confined to a minority of the clergy as a whole. The other was a battle cry of God against Caesar raised by the Rev. Canon Colin Buchanan. Plainly Canon Buchanan thinks that God has been pocketed by the ecclesiastical apparatus and himself, and his remark 'They will not change us from the outside' shows a sectarian view of the boundaries of the Church. That, in fact, is the problem: the definition of inside and outside which affects the contemporary Church of England, and turns it into a defensive denomination, aside from either contemporary culture or the continuity of the nation over time. What can be done about the situation I do not know. I am not an Erastian (or more correctly, I am not a follower of Marsiglio of Padua) and the appeal to parliament was a last resort when petitions, polls, remonstrances and the critical protest of the serious press had not produced a response, only resentful silence. Perhaps the institutional *mauvaise foi* admits no cure.

References

1 Introduced in the House of Commons by Viscount Cranborne MP and in the House of Lords by Lord Sudeley on 8th April 1981. The speeches in the Lords are excerpted in D. Martin and P. Mullen (eds.) *No Alternative*, Basil Blackwell, 1981.
2 Rite A is the modern, or rather quasi-modern rite which descends lineally from Series 3.
3 Sir John Colville, CB, CVO, former Private Secretary to Sir Winston Churchill, wrote as President of the Prayer Book Society.
4 The Right Rev. 'Bill' Westwood.
5 i.e. the Petition to the General Synod signed by some six hundred academics, writers, politicians, musicians etc. in favour of retaining the Prayer Book in the mainstream of worship.
6 As to the views of Eliot these are set out in the oration at his funeral in East Coker and further underlined by Valerie Eliot when she signed the 1979 Petition to the General Synod. Eliot described the N.E.B. as a work 'not even of distinguished mediocrity'.
7 I set down my own views on this in *Learning for Living*, 1977.
8 The main book is *Hymns for Today's Church*, published by Hodder, November 1982.
9 Cf. my *Alternative Visions* and Professor Mitchell's article in The Bloxham Project Newsletter.
10 Theological liberals omit the definite article.
11 *New Universities Quarterly*, Vol. 33, No. 3, Summer 1979.

12 *New Universities Quarterly*, Vol. 33, No. 3, Summer 1979.

13 G. Hammond 'The English Bible' in Poetry Nation Review, No. 24, 1981. Ian Robinson 'The Word of God Now', Poetry Nation Review No. 13, 1979, and Andor Gomme 'The New Religious English' in B. Morris (ed.) *Ritual Murder*, 1979.

Professor C. B. Cranfield of Durham has a sharply critical view of the accuracy of the N.E.B. and gives some examples in his 'Changes of Person and Number in Paul's Epistles' (*Paul and Paulinism*, eds. M. D. Hooker and S. D. Wilson).

TWELVE

DO WE WANT A NATIONAL CHURCH?

C. H. SISSON

'I N A FREE SOCIETY,' the Bishop of Salisbury is reported to have said (*The Times*, 19 October, 1982), 'the state is not identified with the party in power. Any individual or institution can criticise some aspect of the party in government. The Church of England has done it before, and will do so again.' What, one wonders, does the Bishop think the Church of England is? What does he think the state is? One might add, who does he think he is? The last question, as he would no doubt agree, is not important. The other two do matter.

The extraordinary *débâcle* of the Church since the Synodical Government Measure, 1969, and the Worship and Doctrine Measure, 1974, has made it clear that these questions, which lie at the root of the re-organisation and the subsequent setting aside of the Prayer Book, were not satisfactorily answered before the Measures were embarked upon. Were they indeed ever seriously asked? It does not appear so. The ecclesiastical authorities seem to have fallen in limply with what they saw as the drift of the times. Perhaps they believed all they read in the papers, if not in much else. There was democracy, they knew; there was the individual, theoretically sacred since Jean-Jacques Rousseau if in practice still treated much as usual; there were all those human rights which are historically the refuse of the eighteenth-century *philosophes*, now given a new lease of life by international and other institutions. The Church, it appears to be thought, should pull its socks up and run with the bearers of all these banners.

What, meanwhile, of the Church of England as an historical entity? It is very much in the spirit of the age to ignore the past as far as possible, so no doubt the ecclesiastical authorities thought they must be on good ground in doing the same. That is, however, a very odd and in the end surely untenable, point of view for churchmen. There are theologians so prophetic that they hardly stop to look behind them, but even for these fast runners it must be true that the Church is nothing – *nothing in the world* – if it is not some kind of historical succession. I hope, in this essay, to keep away as far as possible from theological controversy but, surely if the Incarnation did not take place in time, if the whole Christian drama is not played out in time, then the universal Church falls like a pack of cards. As far as the Church of England is concerned, one has to assume a true succession, on whatever theory. There one can leave these high matters, and look at the squalor of everyday life which is political history and which includes the ordinary doings of Popes, cardinals, bishops and lesser clergy as well as of mere laymen.

The political squalor of the clergy did not begin with the Reformation, and nothing more clearly shows the ingenuousness – or plain ignorance – of contemporary Anglicans at large than the readiness with which they have fallen in with the misconception – or lie – that ecclesiastical authorities look on the affairs of their day more responsibly than those who have to take the effective decisions. It is a matter of history that Popes have defended their political and economic interests as unscrupulously as anybody, and in proportion as they have meddled in the affairs of others have shown – or, in the case of the present Pope, does show – the same fallibility and the same self-interest as others. It is no great impertinence to ask the bishops and clergy of the present Church of England – to say nothing of the lay representatives assembled in Synod – to accept that they have the same limitations.

The defamation of the Book of Common Prayer which became the ordinary talk of the ecclesiastical authorities following the Worship and Doctrine Measure, 1974, has largely overlooked the constitutional and political elements of that volume. There has been an ugly, and it must be said childish, pleasure in what is taken to be the fact that not only has the state loosened its dirty grip on the Church but the Church's affairs are now *almost* entirely in the pure hands of bishops, clergy and elected laymen. What has really happened is that the Church has lately ceased to bother about

England and her institutions and concerned herself, however ineptly, more and more with the Church and its congregations. At the same time, fearing that the babies would go out with the bath-water – as most of them have been going out – it has bestirred itself more and more to make its voice heard on what the media have assured it are the great issues of the day, and to confine its gospel to matters which will be acceptable to the sort of democracy it is the nature of the media to pretend that we have.

The Book of Common Prayer could not be entirely abolished, for parliament had not left the Church free to abolish it. That, one can see, made things difficult. For, if it saved the authors of the *Alternative Service Book* the embarrassment of re-stating the doctrines of church and state implicit and explicit in the Prayer Book – an enterprise which would certainly have alarmed even their own public and brought to light difficulties which could never have been resolved – it meant that their own notions on the subject remained less than half-formed and had the character of little more than an innuendo. In the *Alternative Service Book* the Crown has been demoted and the bishops have been promoted, which if it does not exactly answer to popular sentiment at least flatters the ambition of bishops and clergy jealous of what some of them strangely consider to be the independence of the Roman clergy. Independent of the British crown and parliament, so far as that becomes British subjects – even a little further, perhaps, in the case of some of the Irish – the Roman clergy are the subjects of the most antiquated monarchy in the world. It seems odd to regard this as a peculiar liberty. The argument must be that the Pope is a spiritual power whose service is perfect freedom. Without entering upon the merits of that proposition, one must say also that he is a political monarch, not merely as the head of a Ruritanian state in Italy but because any large organisation which demands a measure of obedience is a political entity, whatever else it is or is not – and *a fortiori* one that exercises an international discipline as the Roman church does. The English clergy who envy their Roman brothers' independence of the state aspire to a comparable independence – national only at first but ultimately as part of a world-wide society standing over against ordinary legitimate governments. The vision is of a new version of mediaeval Christendom. There is perhaps one difference. In Rome there lingers on a memory of a Church which claimed – however ineffectively in practice – supremacy over all civil governments. The English clergy, a little more plausibly for the twentieth and no

171

doubt the twenty-first centuries, see themselves rather as a dissident organisation holding aloof from government by its moral superiority merely. They have forgotten that the Church's quarrel with the state, in mediaeval times, was about rights and privileges of the clergy, about territorial matters, wealth and its ownership and control, matters of *power* which are the ordinary concerns of governments. The notion of a conflict in which the church represents the spirit and the state the world is a pure fantasy.

The bishops, clergy and laity of the Church of England, in or out of Synod, live in a state in which the supreme power is vested in the Queen in parliament and any assertion to the contrary is a form of treason, however benign, not to say vague, we have become about matters of allegiance – and I am not suggesting that it is not better in practice, to be vague and benign rather than too insistent. Churchmen eat the same bread, drink the same water, use the same transport and run the same dangers as the rest of us. The once famous Three Alls puts the matter in a nutshell: the ploughman works for all, the soldier fights for all, and the parson prays for all. The conception of the Prayer Book, as of the mediaeval church before it, is that there is one church in England, *the* Church. Rome maintains a like fiction on a worldwide scale, as with the superstitions attaching to its monarchy it is bound to do. The Church of England has been so far from maintaining its own claim, in its restricted territory, that it has receded into a position of a sect, one of several 'churches', even though it cannot in practice agree to give full theological recognition to any of the other ecclesiastical bodies which are locally prominent. It is arguable that, as a matter of history, any wide uniformity of faith and practice has always been the work of strong-arm governments, and that since modern governments do not concern themselves with these matters the future of the Church at large is more likely to lie in fissiparousness than in re-union as hitherto conceived. However that may be, what the Church of England has done, in bowing out of its role as *the* Church in this land, is in effect to take its lead not from its previous history, or even from its theology, but from the practice of democratic government as here understood – that is to say, from the practice of regarding all opinions as equal, on the basis of one man, one vote.

In a sense this must be welcomed as a demonstration of realism. That is how things are, and any acknowledgement of privilege for a particular ecclesiastical body must be regarded as vestigial. If there is unrealism, it must be in the assessment of the nature and scope of the privileges enjoyed by the Church of England. The residual traces are not unimportant. There is the special relationship with the Crown, and the constitutional requirement that the sovereign be a member of the Church. This position many Romanists would like to undermine, and they look for an opportunity – such as might have been offered by the marriage of the heir to the throne – to upset it. A more radical attack, though not one more damaging to the political health of the country, comes from the logical democrats who say that in a democracy there can be no place for such a requirement; religion, according to this argument, is a matter for the individual conscience, like sexual morals. There is the place of bishops in the House of Lords, no longer very significant for they are there only so long as they keep their heads down. There is the privileged position of the Church of England in Oxford and Cambridge colleges. There is, most prominently of all, the vast inheritance of ecclesiastical buildings – cathedrals, parish churches, bishops' palaces, parsonages and so on. The burden of this heritage has already begun to sit uneasily on the shoulders of the Church, so that its more destructive members are beginning to ask why so much money is wasted on them when it could go to support some more fashionable humanitarian projects, and there is little recognition of the fact that if the churches had not been built the Christian religion would be much nearer to being forgotten than it is, and such prominence as the Church of England enjoys would long ago have vanished. If the Church of England really has nothing special to say, if it does not matter that Christianity in this country should be left to an increasing number of sects and to the agents of the Roman monarchy, then all the privileges of the Establishment are indeed a burden which should be humped off into a ditch at the earliest possible moment. If this is a matter of conscience – and perhaps in any case – the more prominent bishop's palaces should be changed at once for small handy houses nearby.

It is not for me to make a theological case for the Church of England, though an ordinary layman may express astonishment that almost nobody now thinks this worth doing. A non-theological case is as likely as not to be treated with contempt, but perhaps even bishops and eminent laymen should not so treat it until they have publicly examined its theological implications and told us why it is either nefarious or unimportant. The importance of there being only one church in one place is presumably not denied by anyone, even though such an objective is now completely out of reach. At an earlier stage of the argument, in the sixteenth century, the religion of the prince was the religion of the people, and this fits with the notion of an irrevocable creed such as could be imposed with the support of the feudal system. The equivalent in a democracy would be an official religion which was the lowest common denominator of the beliefs of the people at large. There could hardly be a church for which that was enough; indeed, it would have to be accepted that religion on those terms could not be Christian at all. The religion of democracy to which appeal is now universally made, by clerics as well as politicians, would be the only serious candidate. Any case for maintaining the Establishment would have to be made in the name of this other religion, perhaps on the grounds, which might pass now though quite the contrary of what has been taught for most of the history of the Church, that Christianity is the real *source* of democracy and should therefore be maintained even though most people would not bother with its theology or worship – rather as in the Communist state there have to be members of the party more or less addicted to Marxist doctrine which is certainly beyond the population at large. Such a role for the Church could be maintained – if at all – only by a disciplined body resembling the disciplined body of the Roman monarchy rather than the Church of England as it has been known in recent times. It is almost certain that it could not be so maintained, even if the adjustments of Christian doctrine to democratic theory which have been so in evidence in recent years were carried further. There have been older theories of democracy which might have allowed of such an accommodation, but that now current comports an equality of opinion against which no supernatural – and perhaps few natural – truths could hold out long.

However difficult it may be to determine what the national religion of England should be – and it has become increasingly difficult ever since the question was first admitted – there is an excellent case for there being such a thing as a national religion. It may even be asserted that there is such a thing, whether or not its existence is publicly admitted. No society ever held together for long without common presuppositions of a more·or less unarguable kind, matters which are thought of as belonging to the realm of fact rather than to that of theory, philosophy or optional belief. Successive formulations wear out – and in our world so full of talking they succeed one another faster than ever – but the fund of blind conviction from which they issue outlives them all. The formulations are more or less profound, more or less superficial, and the only test of their depth is the endurance of the formulae. It follows that what has endured for centuries should be treated with more respect than yesterday's invention which is already beginning to look a little tatty today. This goes for institutions as well as for verbal formulations. This is after all the primary claim of the Church itself – to have carried unchanging truth through the centuries, mixed admittedly with a more dubious and changing load of temporal matter. A national religion which claims to be Christian is a more or less local version of the same tradition. The truths which have their provenance from the Israel of King David and of the Roman Empire have been grafted, over centuries, on to the political – historical and geographical – facts of a particular nation. So far as truth is what is at stake, there is no question of one lot of truths – the Church's – superseding another. Facts – if it is facts that are at stake – illumine one another; they erase nothing but error. Of course the Christian religion is not merely a matter of fact, but if it is not in some sense that, it is nothing. The truths about political society – difficult in themselves to establish, but assuredly not more so than the truths about religion – are not hostile to it; they must, indeed, be merely part of the greater Truth which religion claims to hold. There is of course a reading of Christianity which splits the world, Manichaean-wise, into right-minded Christians, loving their individual neighbour – so they say – but reckless of the state and those evil-minded persons who see the service of the public entity, the *res publica*, as a duty not to be wished away on grounds of conscience. There was a mediaeval view – illustrated by Dante – which saw the Roman Empire as no less divinely appointed than the Papacy. It is certain that the existence of the Roman Empire facilitated the spread and secured the establishment of Christianity. These historical considerations apart, the common sense of the matter is that civil government is a necessity and that obedience to its laws is something no civilised person can excuse himself from. In practice this means for us loyalty to the constitution and government of the United Kingdom – which does not imply concurrence in the opinions or policies of the party in power at any particular moment. From this loyalty the Church is not excused. The temptation for the Church has always been to set itself up as an alternative society, an alternative political power, claiming special privileges, even a separate code of laws, for its own clergy if not for its rank-and-file

175

members, but the principle of equality before the law has long since been established throughout Europe. Churchmen and non-churchmen alike live within the structure of the state; without that love of country is either disingenuousness or mere sentimentality.

The system of relationship between church and state which is built into the Book of Common Prayer is at once simpler and more sophisticated than the vague notions which have in practice replaced it in recent years. It is entirely unideological, except in so far as it assumes that the state is in some sort Christian – a notion which now looks ideological because of the prevalence of democratic ideologies in the church itself. The current ecclesiastical attitude assumes that the church is a body of opinion to be set against the opinion prevailing in the government of the moment – that it is one of the clients trying to get the ear of the government. This is in fact to claim the status of a political party, willing to take over the reins of office, or at least to claim that a suitably right-minded party could take over the state and achieve the church's objectives. This is not only pure delusion; it is a denial of the reality of the church as of the state. Might one not say that the church can only be an infusion into civil society? It has to govern its own institutions – an operation at which it has not been a brilliant performer, of late – but can take no iota of responsibility from those who govern the state. The relationship of church and state, under the old Anglican system, was a matter of fact not of principle. The temporalities of the church were under the hand of the monarch, and it is still entirely within the power of the Queen in parliament to do what she will with them, nor would any alteration of the religion of the Crown alter that one way or another. If the spiritualities are not so subject, it is merely because neither church nor state conceives that they should be; the church, because the spiritualities are for her only what she says they are; the state, because it demands only a practical loyalty and is not a keeper of consciences. The only way in which the church should seek to influence the actions of the state is through the consciences of its members; the aberration of which we have seen so much of late is that she seeks as well – or even instead – to influence opinions, inciting political collectivities, initiating them, and in turn being used by political collectivities already in existence. An opinion is not a conscience, although it often passes for such. The manufacture of opinions is an altogether more facile and productive industry than the manufacture of men and women of patient and disciplined conscience; no wonder, perhaps, when their output of the latter has fallen heavily, that prominent church-men should be tempted to go into the easier trade. But that is a defection – the real defection, although more has been made, by the church's critics, of the possibly deleterious effect of some of the more widely trumpeted opinions.

The proper place for the formation and promotion of Christian judgements on public affairs is in those stations in the common-wealth to which members of the church have individually been called: for the Prime Minister, the question at all hours of the day is what the Prime Minister should do in each of the conjunctions of public business in which she finds herself; likewise with other ministers; likewise with Members of Parliament. So much is talked, in the necessarily deformed presentation of the public world given by the media, about those vague imaginations called policies, that it almost escapes notice that the real matter of public life as of private life is the ceaseless train of actions, the generally small, too easily negligible interventions in the passing business of the hour – so detailed and multifarious as inevitably to escape almost entirely from journalists' accounts of the happenings of the day and, by most of them, not understood in the most elementary way – for acting oneself and giving summary accounts of other people's actions are two very different occupations. For the ordinary citizen, not ordinarily burdened with a political role, there is the duty of trying to understand what he is doing and acting according to his conscience, whether he is one of those who go to meetings and join pressure groups or one who merely votes – or decides not to vote – when the constitutional opportunity is offered to him. The civic duty is equal for Christian and non-Christian; if the Christian conscience is superior, that may not be demonstrated in the activi-ties in which the former engages or, if it is, it is more likely to be to his neighbours in these activities than in any wider circle. In any case, if a 'demonstration' of the superiority of the Christian conscience means anything, it must be as an inkling of the truth of the Christian religion; and it is this truth, not a particular policy, that the churchman should be seeking to promote.

It may be too late now to stop the drift towards disestablishment. Those who look on this drift with complacency are often people charmed by that ideology of dissidence which has had a fashionable success for the last twenty years or so, and who see in it a new establishment in which they can take refuge now that the state no longer claims to be Christian. On this one may make two comments.

In the first place: acts of state in themselves are neither more or less Christian than they ever were. If anyone thinks otherwise, he should consult a history book as to the acts of governments in ages of faith. The second comment is: dissident groups seem to offer a hope of a stake in the *res publica* only in a certain recent, and no doubt fragile, phase of democracy, the product of peculiar conditions in some old, now industrialised, civilisations. Government, and the necessities of government, will last as long as the church militant itself, and it is only the state which can offer an enduring means of access to itself. There remains the alternative of trying to rebuild Christendom by fortifying the secular power of the Church on the mediaeval pattern, which could be done only by involving it in political corruptions far more pervasive than those resulting from a national establishment after the manner of the Prayer Book. The church as a political power is a political body, seeking to override or to subtract from the power of lawful governments. Lawful government is an absolute necessity of civilised life, and a church which set itself against this fact would have lost part of its truth. To bring the matter nearer home: the United Kingdom is all we have, in the way of government. Loyalty and obedience to it are the plainest of objective duties. That leaves no room for questioning its ultimate authority, including authority to bear the sword, or whatever weapon it may elect. It still leaves almost infinite room for discussion as to what should be done in our name, in any particular juncture. But there is no reason to suppose that a Christian enclave will show any special wisdom in these matters.

THIRTEEN

LOOK TO THE FOUNDATIONS

THE REVEREND FRANCIS D. MOSS

WE MAY, OR WE MAY NOT, be slaves to our conception of contemporary culture, believing that here lies the explanation even of our religious attitudes and of the forms in which they are expressed. 'The Times' Religious Affairs Correspondent, Clifford Longley, contrasting the views of Don Cupitt (Dean of Emmanuel) with those of Keith Ward (F. D. Maurice Prof at KCL) in his review of the latter's recent book,[1] says Cupitt 'stands for the *modern scientific culture*' in insisting that 'science has driven "God" religion to the fringe, where it is seen to be unable to stand its ground'. The contributors to *The Myth of God Incarnate* in 'shooting down in flames' the divinity of Christ (or in so claiming) 'were doing no more than stating . . . the general beliefs of ordinary people. Decade by decade, since the war, a large percentage of the population has shifted from professing "I believe in God" to "I believe in a Life Force or Spirit" ' . . . So, continues Longley, ' "Bad" religion is about dogma, fanaticism, communal strife – Iran and N. Ireland are the favourite cases cited – while "good" religion is the cultivation of an autonomous spiritual and moral sensitivity, full of tolerance, empty of propositions about facts in the "real" world.'[2]

In suggesting that the case for orthodox Christianity has been going by default, with few able defenders even from within the Churches, Longley goes to the heart of the matter. As a result, the market for such wares has almost disappeared. Whereas when I was ordained nearly thirty years ago there were some within the congregations which I served who had a genuine interest in Christian doctrine, in reading 'apologetics', today one might conclude that there were almost none at all. The number of worshippers asking for Bible Reading Fellowship notes has fallen heavily, and so has the number showing familiarity with the Scriptures themselves. Sensing, perhaps, the undermining of a rational basis for faith, competing interests have exploited their opportunity. Whereas formerly schools, clubs, and sporting interests tended at least to respect Sunday morning when organising group activities, this is no longer the case and young people who still worship are at least indirectly under pressure to desert their Church with increasing frequency.

The pastor who yet wishes to emphasise 'the sacred' is thus often desperate to find support for his concern, even regular church-goers tending to regard teaching and discipline as intellectualism and as 'bad' religion. In his extra-mural activities, e.g. in teaching in the local school, he will frequently discover that he cannot assume equation of the term 'God' with the God and Father of our Lord Jesus Christ, nor yet assume background acquiescence in the idea of Jesus as uniquely Son of God.

Taken in conjunction with the loss of mystique and the changes of emphasis in worship, the traditional Christian begins to find himself more and more isolated, rather as ethnic and religious minorities have often felt and do feel. But these latter are isolated groups rather than isolated individuals, and as such enjoy the social support proper to the group. In face of the threat of isolation as individuals, small groups and societies proliferate within the Churches, but nothing resembling a united and organised 'lobby' has eventuated. This may be due partly to a lack of common ground among traditionalists (e.g. as to the source(s) of authority in doctrine), partly to an unwillingness to risk 'schism' within the existing Churches (conceived primarily as organisations), and partly to fear of the 'ghetto' mentality. None of these points can be lightly taken, but if present trends, social and cultural pressures continue, it is very difficult not to conclude that the tide will sweep away those without adequate foundations and social solidarity in their maintenance and defence. We may agree with L. S. Thornton and Eric Mascall that divine revelation 'masters its environment by entering into it':[3] that this it has done, and can do. But it did so by uniting men and women in communal acceptance of, and submission to it; in other words it is evidenced in resilience by substantial corporate profession and by substantial corporate loyalty and commitment. Without these in actuality the case must fail.

References
1 *Holding Fast to God*, Keith Ward, SPCK, 1983.
2 *The Times* 12.1.83.
3 *Whatever Happened to the Human Mind?* E. L. Mascall, SPCK, 1980, p. 41.

FOURTEEN

WOMANHOOD, FEMINISM AND THE PRIESTHOOD

I. R. THOMPSON

I

WE MAY SAY that Christianity, as opposed to modern secularism, implies a profound reverence for womanhood. This point needs to be stressed because we are now in the throes of a powerful movement aimed at changing the whole basis of our sexual thinking. It is not just that reverence (for womanhood as for much else) is now out of fashion. Rather we are being conditioned – politically, educationally, socially – to accept a flat-earth philosophy which treats womanhood as a myth and which proclaims that there are *no* inherent differences between the sexes. In personal and psychological terms this means a dangerous swing towards masculinity since the new concept of 'unisex' is geared to the masculine lifestyle. What we have to face, therefore, is a fundamental attack on female personality.

Now the Christian view (traditionally, and as still represented by a majority of Christians) is that there are significant and God-given differences between the sexes. If we speak of *womanhood* or *womanliness* we use terms which derive from our Christian past and which have been enriched with Christian meaning. Also – and this is very important – we use words which imply a sense of *value*. Womanhood is not just a social or biological condition; it is a state of excellence, and the overtones of this word are of dignity, worth, virtue, etc. It is the same with *maidenhood* and *motherhood* (concepts which are likewise coloured by our Christian inheritance and which are now likewise threatened). Behind all these words lies a vision of woman as a being endowed with special grace (and graces); in whom qualities like devotion, modesty, purity, tenderness, find a particularly appropriate or excellent expression. They may also serve to remind us that a certain reverence is due to woman on account of her intimate connection with the processes of life. Since as virgin she is the temple and as mother she is nourisher of life, woman is, in a very special sense, the 'vessel of honour'.

We may also observe that those who, within a Christian context, have most emphasised the reverence which pertains to womanhood have been those (like Charles Lamb and John Ruskin) who have had most to say against female drudgery or supposed female inferiority – and they have rested their case on the inherent difference between the sexes. In an essay entitled 'Modern Gallantry' (*Essays of Elia*), Lamb mounts a searing attack on male boorishness and male hypocrisy but he concludes with an exhortation to woman 'to stand upon her female character as upon a foundation'. In order to fulfil her high destiny, woman, he implies, must be true to herself and to that which is uniquely hers. 'Let her first lesson be . . . to *reverence her sex*.' Likewise Ruskin, in his celebrated and influential essay on female education, states plainly:

> We are foolish, and without excuse foolish, in speaking of the 'superiority' of one sex to the other, as if they could be compared in similar things. Each has what the other has not; each completes the other, and is completed by the other: they are in nothing alike, and the happiness and perfection of both depends on each asking and receiving from the other what the other only can give.[1]

It is often said that the mind of a civilization is most clearly displayed in its literature. If we wish to know more about the qualities and excellences that have been attributed to womanhood we have only to consult the major European authors of any period from Dante to Dickens. According to Ruskin, and if we overlook the slight sketch of Henry V (exaggerated for political purposes), Shakespeare has no heroes, only heroines. And he represents those heroines as 'infallibly faithful and wise counsellors – incorruptibly just and pure examples – strong always to sanctify, even when they cannot save'. Likewise in the heroines of Scott we find 'a quite infallible and inevitable sense of dignity and justice; a fearless, instant, and untiring self-sacrifice to even the appearance of duty, much more to its real claims; and, finally, a patient wisdom of deeply restrained affection, which does infinitely more than protect its objects from a momentary error; it gradually forms, animates, and exalts the characters of the unworthy lovers, until, at the close of the tale, we are just able, and no more, to take patience in hearing of their unmerited success'.

The capacity of woman to save and ennoble man is a recurring theme in European literature and particularly in the works of the truly great: Dante, Spenser, Shakespeare, Goethe, Dickens, all return to it again and again. It is the capacity to become, as Beatrice was for Dante, 'the God-bearing image, the vehicle of the [divine] Glory and type of all other such communications of Grace' (Dorothy L. Sayers). As Ruskin pointedly asks: 'Are all these great men mistaken, or are we? Are Shakespeare and Aeschylus, Dante and Homer, merely dressing dolls for us?' Or is it rather that in womanhood, truly conceived and truly lived, there lies the sanctification of man's strength and the continuance of his purpose? To put the question another way: why is it, that in the mysterious attraction of the sexes at its most intense, there lies something discernibly religious, something which involves a quest, not just for personal gratification but for a *moral* excellence which only the other partner can offer? Is it by mere coincidence that when Christianity flourishes, romantic love flourishes; and that when Christianity declines, romantic love also declines? For Christianity is not a vision of undifferentiated unity, a belief that the All is the One and the One is the All. It is a vision of collaboration, of unity-in-diversity, in which personality and particularity achieve their highest expression. As the late Professor R. C. Zaehner observed, it is the denial of difference that creates the moral ambivalence and relativism in which evil thrives.[2] At the beginning of the Christian story is the relationship of a man and a woman, Jesus and Mary, who, like Adam and Eve, open a new chapter in the history of creation. To quote Fr John Saward:

> The divine Word assumed our human nature in its particularity; He became *a man* and was born of a woman. With that man and that woman begins the new history of the human race. In the words of S. Bernard: 'the first man and the first woman did us grievous harm, but, thanks be to God, by another man and another woman all that was lost has been restored to us.' At the heart of the new creation is the relationship of Jesus and Mary, of the God-man and His Mother, New Adam with New Eve. It is not simply the acts of God which

bring about salvation but the faith and obedience of God's handmaid, whose *fiat* reverses the disobedience of Eve.[3]

The glorification of Mary (as understood in Roman and Orthodox theology) prefigures the glorification of all mankind. As *theotokos* (God-bearer) and the special receptacle of the Holy Spirit Mary may be said to represent or particularize the Church, for all the attributes of the Church – i.e. all those attributes which will belong to the separate members of the Church on the glorious Eighth Day – already find their perfect embodiment in the Mother of God. According to this view of things Mary has an analogical relationship with all who believe, a relationship which is confirmed in another way. For as the Mother of Christ, Mary is also the mother of redeemed mankind, 'which, on the cross, is made hers by adoption in the person of St John' (Sergius Bulgakov).

We seem here to escape or transcend gender merely to return to it but in fact gender is a mystical consideration throughout. If Mary stands for the Church, and hence for everyone, still the Church is, as we know, feminine in its relationship with Christ (of which more below). Beyond this, there is the importance of Mary as a female human person – true womanhood in its response to God. Mary is 'blessed among women', maiden and mother: the comprehensive icon of the female sex. It is thus entirely appropriate that for Dante, as for innumerable other individuals, woman should become the 'God-bearing image', revealing through her *femininity* (as man, equally but differently reveals through his *masculinity*) the divine light and the divine goodness. For woman *embodies* – more literally and more directly than man; takes things more into herself; transforming thus personally what man transforms objectively or by the works of his hands. To woman, more intimately than to man, belongs the capacity to refine, to purify and thus to spiritualize. This, beyond question, is the experience of mankind. In the words of Goethe (the closing words of *Faust*):

Das Ewigweibliche
Zieht uns hinan.

(*That which is eternal in Woman lifts us above.*)

I would just add, in concluding this part of my essay, that denial of sexual difference (more properly, the belief that personality is not significantly affected by gender) would seem to raise at least one very serious philosophical difficulty. It is a difficulty inherent in the belief that outward or bodily form has no inward or spiritual significance, for this is to represent creation as fundamentally dis-harmonic. Now in *homo sapiens* the so-called secondary sexual char-acteristics – distribution of bodily hair, pitch of the voice, physical build, etc. – are particularly well-marked, and they do have the effect of suggesting not just reproductive function but masculinity and femininity. Man embodies strength, gravity, authority; woman embodies grace, beauty, and the physical equivalents of tenderness. That matter and spirit are somehow connected is a conviction that lies at the heart of all great art and poetry for it is the nature of the poetic vision to discern the spiritual in the material, and to realise this vision sympathetically through the material medium of the artist. As given by God, creation is organised towards its own apotheosis: it displays, we may say, the divine pattern and involves a profound correlation and free interplay between the material, the psychological and the spiritual. Sin and the Fall have a tragic power to disrupt this pattern and this correlation but, in our world at least, the pattern is never completely vitiated. Hence that which is ordained of God – as, for example, human sexuality – is potentially divine. Hence too the physical and psychological characteristics of sexuality are complementary and deeply harmonious; they enable us to say, with Ruskin, that *the body is the soul made visible*.[4] And both the physical and psychological characteristics of human sexuality hint at, and in some sort prefigure, the divine 'sexuality' of deified man.[5]

II

As Nicolas Berdyaev observed, 'every culture in the process of flowering and becoming more complex and refined exhausts its creative forces and spirit. Even its aims change.'[6] Among the more obvious aims of contemporary society are: the pursuit of pleasure and 'life' (as opposed to happiness and meaning); the worship of technology; and the substitution of political and economic for spiri-tual and aesthetic goals. It is within this social context that we have to view the growth of feminism, which is a complex phenomenon since it involves both a reaction against, and also an attempt to accelerate, the current direction of social change. Viewed simply as a protest movement feminism is a portent, for it witnesses to a growing sense of social unease. In a world which has abandoned not just Christianity but all Christian standards; in which permissiveness, violence and marital breakdown place woman in a particularly vulnerable position, it would be strange if feminism did *not* find its voice. Judged by the standards of the 1980s woman *is* the loser, at least some of the time.

Yet here we come to the crux of the matter: to the ultimate weakness of feminism and its own inner contradictions. For while feminism affects a concern for individuality and personal values it persists in denying to woman those gifts and charisms which are uniquely hers. Whilst aiming to criticise bitterly a world which has become far too 'masculine' it actually accepts this world and deifies it. A striking illustration of what feminism means in practice is afforded by current feminist agitation in the field of state education. Thus the fact that schoolboys are statistically more successful than schoolgirls in science subjects (though *less* successful in arts subjects) is explained as a consequence, not of sexual difference, but of what the architects of sex-equality like to call 'sex-stereotyping' in the home and in schools. Hence the recommendations (like those contained in a booklet for teachers published by the Equal Opportunities Commission[7]) that infant boys should be encouraged to play with dolls, and girls with mechanical devices; that male chivalry, differences in dress, and the voluntary segregation of the sexes should be discouraged; that girls' schools should de-emphasise the role of women as wives and mothers; that girls should be encouraged to develop a taste for rough and tumble, etc., etc. To those who reject the contorted reasonings of the new ideology such recommendations may seem bizarre, dangerous or even plain crazy; the fact remains that they are now taken seriously by an influential minority of the population. More to our present purpose is the implied equation of technology with power and hence with fulfilment. According to Jacques Ellul, an exaggerated respect for technology is the distinctive feature of modern society.[8] Thus girls are thought to be disadvantaged because they are less technologically-minded than boys. That this complaint involves a quite staggering value judgement seems to pass almost unnoticed. Yet the judgement is clear: the arts and the humanities are downgraded. The very things which (below virtue) used to be thought of as the hallmark and purpose of civilization (and to the greater enjoyment of which technology was supposed to be leading us) now lose their authenticity and significance. The relation between the ends and the means is reversed and perverted. The complaint ought to be that the humanities are already too much neglected and that woman (who is acknowledged to excel therein) is thus denied her proper contribution to society; a contribution which could help to reverse the dehumanizing tendencies of the modern world. But to this kind of reasoning feminism, or at any rate mainstream feminism, seems curiously immune.

Yet it is in the field of sexual relations that the failure of feminism is most apparent. Promiscuity (or if you prefer the modern euphemism, 'permissiveness') impels women into a world where men are the undisputed lords of creation and where the individual woman can become just one more female in the herd. Of the trauma of young girls trying to cope with life in a youth culture where sex is the customary password we hear nothing, or next to nothing, for there are some things that society prefers not to notice.[9] Yet as most schoolteachers know, the situation is serious – a fact amply confirmed by the available statistical evidence. Of the American teenage girls interviewed by Aaron Hass (*Teenage Sexuality*, 1979) 41% had had sexual intercourse by the age of sixteen, and in an earlier survey by Sorenson (*Adolescent Sexuality in Contemporary America*, 1973) the figure was 50% by the age of fifteen. It is possible to discount as unscientific the findings of the recent *Cosmo Report* (conducted by the magazine *Cosmopolitan* in January 1980) though here too the picture is of widespread (and increasing) sexual activity among younger teenagers. Moreover the *Cosmo* survey did try to investigate motivation, and here its findings may be accepted more readily. In the words of the commentary: 'Very few of the *Cosmo* women cited physical passion as the spur to their first experience' (p. 48). Often it was a form of pressure or stress, e.g. fear of losing a boyfriend or of being ostracized by the group. Thus (p. 45): 'Kinsey wrote in 1953 that there was "public condemnation" of youthful premarital sex. The *Cosmopolitan* survey-takers described the opposite. They felt publicly condemned when they postponed having sex' (*The Cosmo Report*, Linda Wolfe, Corgi 1982).

It might be thought that this state of affairs would appal leading feminists for it can hardly be said to conduce either to women's dignity or women's freedom of choice – contemporary youth culture stereotypes with a vengeance. In fact the prevailing emphasis of the sex-equality movement is in quite the other direction. Promiscuity is accepted and, in a manner, glorified. The demand is not that boys should be taught to respect girls (at any rate in *that* way) or that the commercial and sex-orientated pressures of the media should be

the subject of searching investigation (bearing in mind that teenagers are big business); it is for more, and more blatant, contracep-
tive advice. In the words of a teaching 'pack' designed to alert
teenage pupils to the need for more sex-equality:

> Just because there is a legal ban on sex before 16 doesn't mean
> that under-16s don't do it! The trouble is that the girl may
> have difficulty persuading her doctor to give her contraception.
> The doctor also has the right to inform the girl's parents if she
> is using contraception. So some girls are put off even going for
> advice, because they are frightened their parents will be told.
>
> It seems ridiculous that a doctor can refuse the Pill to a 15-
> year-old who is responsible enough to go and ask for it, yet will
> agree to give her an abortion when she comes back pregnant.

(*Taking Liberties, a teaching pack for boys and girls on equal rights*, pub.
Virago, revised edition 1979.)

III

I must apologise if I seem, thus far, to have ignored the Church of
England. In fact the challenge of feminism is now felt within the
Church as well as outside it, and in at least two ways this challenge
draws attention to the plight and human weakness of the Church
in today's world.

In the first place womanhood is a mystical concept and it may
be argued that the Church is now suffering from a failure of the
mystical vision. In the world generally, but also within Western
Christianity, one is conscious of a hardening process, a solidifying
of the surfaces; so that all things – physical as well as intellectual
– lose their resonance and translucence, their ability to transfigure.
The material is always and only the material: a closed world of
finite experience. We become 'practical'; 'realists'; to a degree,
cynics. Nothing has authentic value any longer; no moment in time
is a window to eternity. Contemporary Anglicanism shows a marked
trend away from the supernatural (as in doctrine reports) and from
the numinous (as in worship).

Secondly, and allied to this, is a certain measure of helplessness:
the almost despairing belief that secularism is winning or has won.
Thus the Bishop of Salisbury, in conversation with the journalist
Graham Turner (*Daily Telegraph*, 3rd January 1983), is reported as
saying: 'Anyone transported from the 1950s to 1982 by time-capsule

would think they were in Sodom. People said you could put the moral fences back but you couldn't.' It is an attitude which the bishop shares, perhaps, with most feminists, but it would have produced near-apoplexy among first- or second-century bishops who, after all, had to face something of the same problem. One could hardly imagine Polycarp or Ignatius talking like that.

It is within this kind of context that we have to view the Church's involvement with feminism. That the sex-equality movement is now exercising a considerable influence within Christian circles is illustrated by the recent decision of the British Council of Churches to embark on a 'comprehensive dialogue' with the women's movements (report, *Church Times*, 3rd December 1982). According to a statement issued by the newly-formed working party, 'the Church has traditionally reflected and endorsed society's treatment of women as inferior to men', and to counteract this the group will consider: 'non-sexist language in worship; the authority of scripture and tradition regarding the roles of women and men; the family and its alternatives [!]; sexuality; the clergy-laity split; feminist theology; and models of collective working'. One could be forgiven for thinking that the working party had already agreed its conclusions and that it merely remained to furnish the necessary evidence.

Which brings me, finally, to the question of women and the priesthood. For according to Dr E. W. T. Dicken: 'It isn't by mere coincidence that those who push hardest for a still more permissive society are those who put most weight behind Women's Lib and who most keenly urge the Church to accept women as priests. Not all who argue for the ordination of women, or for other radical ploys, fall under this condemnation but there is no doubt where the epicentre of the movement lies.'[10] As to the validity or otherwise of this argument we may note (1) that the BCC's reference to 'the clergy-laity split' (quoted above) is a clear comment on the women priests issue and on voting patterns within the General Synod; and (2) that in the USA, pressure to de-sex the Bible and the liturgy has become 'an integral part of the programme of many women priests and of those who support the movement' (*The Evangelical Catholic*, 15th January 1983). Even during the mid-seventies there were events in America (like the pre-emptive ordination of a self-professed lesbian) which made feminism an obvious issue in the campaign for women priests.

Which is not to say that it is the only issue. Feminism apart, it may be argued that there is a legitimate theological question here;

a question which sooner or later the churches were bound to consider. What needs to be recognised is that we are still a very long way from anything which could be properly described as a theological 'breakthrough'. The danger is that the Church of England, and other churches within the Anglican Communion, will proceed to ordain women unilaterally and in the not too distant future (a) because secular 'logic' seems to demand it, and (b) because of the continuing fierce agitation within the churches of those who favour women priests. We may or we may not be moving towards a fuller understanding of the priesthood but we do a disservice to the possibility of such an understanding if we fail to distinguish between Christian and secular thought. There is still too much of a tendency to view this whole matter in terms of rights and supposed disadvantages and to substitute, for the gospel of gladness, a petty and sometimes aggressive carping about 'unfairness' and 'injustice'. In this connection it may be appropriate to notice a part of the speech made by Bishop Graham Leonard (then Bishop of Truro) when the question of the ordination of women was last debated by the General Synod. I offer it, not as a conclusive argument against women priests, but as a reminder that Christianity is about grace and not privilege and that the way of the gospel is not the way of the world. The Bishop said:

I believe that the Scriptures speak of God as Father, that Christ was incarnate as a male, that he chose men to be his apostles, in spite of breaking with tradition in his dealings with women, not because of social conditioning, but because in the order of creation headship and authority is symbolically and fundamentally associated with maleness. For the same reason, I believe that the highest vocation of any created being was given to a woman, Mary, as representative of mankind in our response to God because symbolically and fundamentally the response of sacrificial giving is associated with femaleness. I do not believe it is merely the result of social conditioning that in the Scriptures, in the Jewish and Christian tradition, mankind and the Church is presented as feminine to God, to whom our response must be one of obedience in contrast to those religions in which the divine is regarded as contained within creation and is to be manipulated or cajoled in order to provide what man needs. In other words, for a woman to represent the headship of Christ and the divine initiative would, unless her

191

feminine gifts were obscured or minimised, evoke a different approach to God from those who worship. Instead of being reminded that we must respond in obedience to the divine initiative, a truth which I have learned in my evangelical upbringing and which I have never forgotten, we should be tempted to suppose that we can take the initiative in our dealings with him.[11]

Now the question of initiative has an obvious bearing on the matter under discussion. To put it bluntly we need to distinguish very carefully between human enthusiasm and divine illumination; between the imposition of change by the will of a political majority, and the gradual moving towards an overwhelming consensus (whether for change or continuity) under the guidance of the Holy Spirit. In this connection I would urge two final considerations, both of which would seem to counsel strongly against innovation in the short term.

In the first place, and as we now recognise, the separation of the churches is both tragic and a scandal: the consequence, on all sides, of human error and sin. We cannot simply abolish our divisions (that is for the Holy Spirit) but we have an absolute obligation to avoid anything which might make them worse. At the present juncture the ordination of women is clearly divisive, both ecumenically and within the Anglican setting. As the great apostle of development argued (apropos the Church of Rome but his words have a wider implication): 'the Church moves as a whole; it is not a mere philosophy, it is a communion; it not only discusses but it teaches; it is bound to consult for charity as well as for faith'.[12]

The second consideration I offer by way of recapitulation. For if, as I have tried to argue, we are currently confusing theology with feminism then an early decision to ordain women would be seen as, and would in fact represent, a victory for all those forces which seek to deny the metaphysical significance of gender. The Church of England needs to forget feminism and rediscover womanhood. It may be that in so doing she would rediscover herself.

References

1 'Of Queens' Gardens' (*Sesame and Lilies*), from which the ensuing quotations are also taken.
2 *Our Savage God*, London 1974, *passim*. Noted by Saward (*op. cit.* below).

3 *The Case Against the Ordination of Women*, John Saward, CLA, revised 1978, pp. 9–10.
4 *The Queen of the Air*, III; 168.
5 It may be thought that the Christian understanding of marriage also witnesses to the eternal implications of sexuality. This has always been the Eastern Orthodox position, as John Meyendorff explains (*Byzantine Theology*, Mowbrays, 1974, pp. 198–9):

> The Byzantines strongly emphasised the *unicity* of Christian marriage and the *eternity* of the marriage bond; they never considered that Christian marriage was a legal contract, automatically dissolved by the death of one of the partners. . . . Marriage, if it is a sacrament, has to be projected as an eternal bond into the Kingdom of God.

6 *The Meaning of History*, pub. Geoffrey Bles, 1936, p. 209.
7 *Ending Sex-Stereotyping in Schools*, revised edition 1981, pp. 6 & 8.
8 *The Technological Society*, Knopf, NY 1964.
9 See, however, *What About it Sharon?* by John Harvey, Penguin/Puffin, in which the problem is recognised very frankly.
10 'Priestesses: A Non-Negotiable Doctrine', *Faith and Worship*, Summer 1977.
11 *General Synod Report of Proceedings*, November 1978, pp. 1009–1010.
12 Wilfrid Ward, *The Life of John Henry Cardinal Newman*, London 1912, II, 296.

FIFTEEN

OPENING THE DOOR
THE LATE REVEREND
DOCTOR PERCY DEARMER

THERE WAS ONCE a man who wanted to escape from a certain prison: he tried to loosen the window-bars, he tried to work out the stones of the wall, he tried the chimney, and he tried the floor. Then suddenly a happy thought struck him. He opened the door and walked out.

I think the historian of the future will say: There was once a Church that wanted to escape from a great mess. Somehow or other this Church had failed to retain her hold upon her members: the people of the country had for centuries been drifting away from her; half the religious folk had formed themselves into other denominations; the great majority of the people somehow had given up going to church at all; those who remained faithful were, in spite of a great Revival, still in singular ignorance as to the principles of their own religion: as a consequence, many of these were so sluggish as to be a source of weakness rather than strength; others were zealous, but their zeal was a source of division rather than of the unity which maketh force. So her enemies raged against her; her own children rushed hither and thither and were not satisfied . . . .

This Church was, in fact, in a mess. She had tried so many ways of escape! She had tried Geneva; she had tried Rome; she had essayed a mixture of the two in varying proportions, which was called Moderate; she had tried *laissez faire*, by which each man did what he found easy and thought nice. . . . The one thing that she had never tried to do was to carry out her own laws, and to apply her own principles.

Then one day she had a happy thought. She would be true to her own self, to her own laws. She opened the door, and walked out.

NOTES ON CONTRIBUTORS

Anthony Kilmister is Executive Director of a registered charity financing medical research and providing welfare facilities for patients. His book *The Good Church Guide* was published in 1982 simultaneously by Blond & Briggs and by Penguin Books. Born in Swansea in 1931 where his father was a physician in general practice he became a communicating Anglican while at Shrewsbury School. A founder member of the Prayer Book Society he is its current national Vice-Chairman and is an Executive Committee member of the Anglican Association. A regular contributor to journals and newspapers he has also broadcast on numerous occasions.

Stephen Neill was Prize Fellow of Trinity College, Cambridge, before becoming a missionary in South India (1924–44). He was Assistant Bishop to the Archbishop of Canterbury (1945–8) and served on the World Council of Churches (1946–54). Among his academic posts were Professor of Missions and Ecumenical Theology, Hamburg (1962–9) and Professor of Philosophy and Religious Studies, University of Nairobi (1969–73). Since 1978 he has been Assistant Bishop in the diocese of Oxford. He is the author of many books including *Christian Faith and Other Faiths* (1961), *A History of Christian Missions* (1964), *The Interpretation of the New Testament* (1964), *The Church and Christian Union* (1968), *Jesus through Many Eyes* (1976) and *Salvation Tomorrow* (1976). In preparation is a three-volume *History of Christianity in India*.

John Jacques was born in 1912. He read Philosophy, Politics and Economics at Oxford and obtained a B.Litt in Philosophy at Trinity College, Dublin. He was ordained in 1937 and was a parish priest from then until he retired in 1979. He has written two books on ethics, innumerable articles and is preparing a book on Richard Hooker. He lives in retirement in his beloved Lincolnshire Wold and his hobbies are walking and reading detective novels.

Eric Lionel Mascall is Emeritus Professor of Historical Theology at the University of London. Among the foremost theological writers of our time, his literary output includes countless books which have become classics. Early in 1983 an essay of his in *Tracts for our Times* marked his golden jubilee in the sacred ministry. Priest of the Oratory of the Good Shepherd, he has been associated for many years with St Mary's, Bourne Street.

Francis D. Moss is Rector of Mobberley, Cheshire, to which he moved from Kemerton in Gloucestershire. Founder and for many years President of the Anglican Association he is now its Patron. Francis Moss has written extensively on Anglican affairs and is currently editor of the half-yearly review *Faith & Worship*.

George Bernard Austin (born 1931) is Vicar of St Peter's, Bushey Heath in Hertfordshire, and is a Church Commissioner. A member of the General Synod of the Church of England, he also serves on the Central Board of Finance of whose staff committee he is Chairman. Canon Austin is a member of the Assembly of the British Council of Churches and has been a delegate to the World Council of Churches, Vancouver, in 1983.

Peter Mullen is Vicar of Tockwith and Bilton with Bickerton in Yorkshire. He was educated at Liverpool University and St Aidan's College, Birkenhead. He was ordained in 1970 and has worked in parishes in Leeds, Manchester and Oldham. From 1974 and until 1977 he was Head of Religious Studies at Whitecroft High School, Bolton. Books include *Beginning Philosophy*, *Thinking about Religion* and *No Alternative* (jt. ed.). He is a regular contributor to national newspapers and to radio and television. His dramatic chorus *St Mark* was produced on Radio 4 in 1979 and he writes and presents programmes for Yorkshire Television and Tyne Tees Television. He is editor of *Faith & Heritage*.

O. R. Johnston read Modern Languages at Queen's College, Oxford, subsequently taking further qualifications in theology and education at London University. After some years of teaching he became in 1974 the first full-time Director of the Nationwide Festival of Light, an interdenominational Christian charity supporting Christian values in society. A life-long Anglican his writings have been widely published, his most recent book being *Who Needs the Family?* (Hodder & Stoughton, 1979). He is a Lay representative of the Oxford Diocese in the Church of England's General Synod and is married with two daughters.

Roger Homan is Director of the Centre for the Study of Religion and Society at Canterbury and a Senior Lecturer in Education at Brighton Polytechnic. His first degree was in religion and his doctorate was in sociology. He is the author of many articles in books and learned journals on education, sociology, religious history and international affairs. His latest book, *The Victorian Churches of Kent*, is published by Phillimore. He married in 1982.

David Alfred Martin (born 1929) is University Professor of Sociology at the London School of Economics and Political Science. A leading activist in the Prayer Book cause, he is a Vice-President of the Prayer Book Society. In 1975 he became President of the International Conference of the Sociology of Religion. Among his recent books are *A General Theory of Secularisation* (1978), *Contemporary Dilemmas of Religion* (1979), *Crisis for Cranmer and King James* (ed.) (1979), *The Breaking of the Image* (1980), *Theology and Sociology* (jt. ed.) (1980), *No Alternative* (jt. ed.) (1981).

C. H. Sisson, born in Bristol in 1914 and educated at Bristol University and in France and Germany, is known primarily as poet, translator and critic, but he has also had wide experience of practical affairs as a senior official of the old Ministry of Labour. He is one of the editors of *PN Review* which in 1979 published the immensely impressive Petition to the General Synod on the Prayer Book collected by David Martin. He is the author of *Anglican Essays* (1983) which discusses the political stance of the Church of England.

T. E. Utley who is 62, is joint Chief Assistant Editor of the *Daily Telegraph* and, having graduated in history from Cambridge, formerly served on the editorial staffs of *The Times*, the *Sunday Times*, *The Observer* and the *Spectator*. He is the author of a number of books on contemporary politics, including *Enoch Powell: The Man and his Thinking* and *Lessons of Ulster*.

I. R. Thompson (born 1936) is Head of the English Department at Frederick Gough School, Scunthorpe, and is a former member of the General Synod of the Church of England. He has written and lectured extensively on contemporary Church affairs and Anglican liturgy. He founded and was the first editor of *Faith & Worship*. He is married with four daughters.

Percy Dearmer (1867–1936) became a priest in 1892 and served as curate at four successive churches until 1901 when he was made Vicar of St Mary's, Primrose Hill, London, where he remained until 1915. In 1919 he was Professor of Ecclesiastical Art in King's College, London, and in 1931 was made Canon of Westminster. As well as novels he wrote extensively on many ecclesiastical subjects and by his death in 1936 he had greatly influenced contemporary English hymnody.